G000039340

Peter Jones	**Sarah Beeny**	**Mike Clare**	
Theo Paphitis	**Doug Richard**	**Julie Meyer**	
Deborah Meaden	**Michael Birch**	**Simon Woodroffe**	**...ugh**
Duncan Bannatyne	**Sahar Hashemi**		**Caprice**

Tim Ferris	Andy McLoughlin	Rebecca McKinlay	Kemi Laniyan	Antony Chesworth
Lynne Franks	Brad Burton	Gavin Wheeldon	Ashley Friedlein	Simon Swan
Matt Kingdon	John Paleomylites	Salma Shah	Chey Garland	Tremayne Carew Pole
Ian Walker	Glenn Shoosmith	Simon Duffy	Naomi Andersson	Harriet Vine
Trevor Baylis	Sara Murray	Richard Needham	Laura Tenison	Barry Hearn
Eileen Gittens	Claire Novis	Patrick Caiger-Smith	Neil and	Karen Hanton
Seán Brickell	Lisa Langmead	Imran Hakim	Laura Westwood	Sean McPheat
Nick Wheeler	Alexandra Finlay	Sam Conniff	Mat Clayton	Jonathan Simmons
Lindsay Drabwell	Tristram Mayhew	Kanya King	James Lohan	Scott Robert-Shaw
Dave Wallwork	Mark Turrell	Richard Moross	Daniel Sheridan	Vivianne Jaeger
Jamie Murray Wells	Christian Arno	Charlie Mullins	Matt McNeill	Will Wynne
Alistair Mitchell	Nikhil Shah,	Millie Kendall	Rosie Wolfenden	Rhodri Ferrier
Gordon Mac	Nico Perez	Fraser Doherty	Errol Damelin	Heather Jenkinson
Divinia Knowles	Alastair Lukies	Jennifer Irvine	Ed Baker	Jack Lenox
Simon Nixon	Alan Gleeson	Sokratis Papafloratos	John Mortimer	Alex Cheatle
Giorgio Burlini	Gavin Dein	Walid Al Saqqaf	Sarah Watson	Glenn Watson
Peter Ibbetson	Emma-Jayne Parkes	Will de Lucy	Alexia Leachman	Sophie Cornish
Graham Lucas	Al Gosling	Steve France	Gregory Bockenstette	Jim and Geoff Riley
Kerry Swinton	Ben Keene	Darryn Lyons	Ryan Carson	
Bradley McLoughlin	Michael Smith	Mark Soanes	Richard Grigsby	

Dyson	**Bebo**	**MOBO Organisation**	**?WhatIf!**
MoneySupermarket	**Coffee Republic**	**Glasses Direct**	**Mr & Mrs Smith**
YO! Sushi	**BeatThatQuote.com**	**Go Ape**	**SuperJam**
Lastminute.com	**Kiss FM**	**King of Shaves**	**TopTable**

4Networking	*Baylis Brands*	*Garland Call Centres*	*iTeddy*	*Public Zone*
BalineumBeyond	*Carsonified*	*Imaginatik*	*Matchroom Sport*	*SquidLondon*
Booking Bug	*Cyclescheme*	*Magic Whiteboard*	*MTD Sales Training*	*TrustedPlaces*
Bulldog Natural Grooming	*Dreams*	*Moo*	*PlayMade Engergy*	*Green Hands*
Corporate Homes	*Huddle*	*Pimlico Plumbers*	*Ruby & Millie*	*Call of the Wild*
Ryman	*Livity*	*Reward*	*Spectrum Office*	*By Caprice*
Fin's	*Monitise*	*Red Letter Days*	*Solutions*	*Trading4U*
Hg2	*Palo Alto*	*SnoozeShade*	*The Pure Package*	*Heather Jenkinson Design*
Lingo24	*Dragons' Den*	*The 4-Hour Workweek*	*TribeWanted*	*The Founder*
Mixcloud	*Skip-Hop*	*School for Startups*	*ekmPowershop.com*	*Ten UK*
Oxford Learning Lab	*Teeny Beanies*	*MySingleFriend.com*	*Feel Good Drinks*	*5M Coffee Company*
RBS and NatWest	*Amplify Trading*	*Angela Mortimer*	*Antares Supplies*	*Not On The High Street*
Sign-up.to and eTickets.to	*ArenaFlowers.com*	*Ariadne Capital*	*Wonga*	*The National Enterprise*
Tatty Devine	*Big Pictures*	*Blossoming Brands*	*Wordia*	*Academy*
The Extreme Sports Company	*Bright Ideas Trust*	*Broad Grin*	*Blurb*	*B.Hive*
The Bannatyne Group	*Charles Tyrwhitt*	*Claire Dances*	*Buddi*	*Tutor2U.net*
Ambition Communications	*DaisychainBaby*	*Econsultancy*	*JoJo Maman Bébé*	
Applied Language Solutions	*Dust and Vac*	*Gatszu.com*	*Mind Candy*	

THE SMARTA WAY TO DO BUSINESS

Matt Thomas and Sháá Wasmund

CAPSTONE

This edition first published 2011 by Capstone Publishing Limited (a Wiley Company)
© 2011 Smarta Enterprises Ltd

With Contributions from Ian Cooper, Business Development Consultant www.iancooper.co.uk

Registered office
Capstone Publishing Ltd. (A Wiley Company), The Atrium, Southern Gate, Chichester, West Sussex, PO19 8SQ, United Kingdom

For details of our global editorial offices, for customer services and for information about how to apply for permission to reuse the copyright material in this book please see our website at www.wiley.com.

Library of Congress Cataloguing-in-Publication Data

ISBN 978-1-907-31252-6 (paperback), ISBN 978-0-857-08092-9 (ebk),
ISBN 978-0-857-08109-4 (eMobi), ISBN 978-0-857-08110-0 (ePub)

A catalogue record for this book is available from the British Library.

Set in 10 on 12pt Arial MT by Toppan Best-set Premedia Limited
Printed in Great Britain by TJ International, Padstow, Cornwall

Contents

Foreword
Theo Paphitis

There are a few really simple reasons why I wanted to get involved with Smarta.com and this book.

Without any doubt this is a very exciting time to be in business. You can now start a business and take it to market quicker and with less money than ever before. Technology and social media mean you can tell the world about it with the click of a button. As such, starting a business is a viable option for more people than ever before.

The business world has changed beyond recognition and continues to change at a fast pace – but some things never change. In business, you never know what's around the corner and the only certainty is uncertainty. What does that mean? It means you're going to make a few mistakes along the way which, for all the advances in technology, will slow you down. For some people, unfortunately, those mistakes will be business critical.

Time and time again on *Dragons' Den* I see the same problems holding back very promising businesses that will never fulfil their potential because the owner hasn't the experience or know-how to avoid common pitfalls or look at the bigger picture to make necessary changes before they lose too much money.

That's why I passionately believe the practical, real-world business advice Smarta provides is worth its weight in gold – both to those small business owners accessing it and to the UK economy which should benefit from seeing more businesses survive and ultimately prosper.

To be able to instantly access help and the insights of some of the best business brains in Britain is incredibly valuable – and would have saved me both time and money if Smarta had been around when I was first starting out.

You can't underestimate the value of real business insight from real business people, either. If I want to bounce an idea around, who do I contact? Not a 'business expert' or 'coach' who's never run a business themselves, that's for sure. I go to people who've been there and know what they're talking about.

Of course, I know many of you don't have established entrepreneurial contacts or even people who are self-employed or running their own small businesses to turn to. That's why I'm so proud to be involved in Smarta and this book in bringing together the thoughts, experiences and knowledge of more than 100 brilliant business people for you all to access.

I'm not unfamiliar with the world of business books, either. I've read hundreds of them as well as writing my own and featuring in several *Dragons' Den* books. When I heard what Shaa and Matt had planned for *The Smarta Way to Do Business*, it was a relief to hear they weren't about to write another book of business theory and rhetoric promising much and delivering little to actually act on, to sit alongside all the others gathering dust on the shelves of your local book store.

My advice to them was to keep it real and practical; pack it with entrepreneurs who know their stuff and businesses enjoying success right now; and to make it modern, relevant and something readers can act on.

I'm delighted they've delivered just that – and that's why 'I'm in'. **Enjoy!**

Introduction
Been there, done that,
DOING IT NOW

O K, let's great straight into this. We like you already. We're excited you've picked up this book. We're delighted you want to start your own business and learn some exclusive insider tips on how to make your existing business really smart.

Why? Because we're 100% convinced that *now* is the most opportunity-rich time there's ever been to be in business. We think business has changed and is continuing to change fast – and that it's changing in your favour.

A new set of business rules has emerged favouring a generation of switched-on, networked and hungry individuals who are empowering both themselves and the consumer with a new type of business that's altering the business landscape beyond recognition.

Individuals like you. People who are smart enough to realize that working for yourself is not just preferable to working for someone else, it's increasingly viable. We call you the 'do-ers'. People who don't just talk about starting a business, or moan about how much they hate their jobs, they do something about it.

If you've always thought about starting a business and haven't quite summoned up the courage to do so, it's time to stop procrastinating over a decision that inside you've already taken – just get on with it. Ask yourself whether you're happy doing what you do. Like really, really happy, not merely quite happy or happy as in you like the people but not the job. Do you start Monday mornings buzzing about the week ahead, or have you already got an eye on Friday?

> ❝ *Time for some tough love* ❞

Time for some tough love: you really need to stop dreaming about what you *might* do and start doing what you *should* do. There's love in the toughness though, because we know there's never been such an opportunity for you to achieve the life you long for if your heart's really in it. More and more smart people are following their hearts and making their dreams of working for themselves come true and they're no different to you. Whatever your excuse, it's time to stop making it.

At Smarta we've interviewed hundreds of big-name entrepreneurs and we speak to thousands of business people every week. That's why this book is for you. It's written, by people like you, and it's full of stories and advice from people like you.

People who once felt the same cocktail of excitement and trepidation as you inevitably do at this moment. People who also had jobs that were a means to an end, families to support and debts to pay. People who didn't necessarily have the experience, skills or qualifications, but who, when they realized the potential positive impact of running their own business, embraced those opportunities and made them happen.

> **" The business people in this book have been there and done that – or are selling the t-shirt "**

The business people featured in this book have been there and done that – or are doing it now. If they don't already have the t-shirt, it's because they're busy redesigning it ready to sell on at a profit.

At Smarta we believe there are only two ways to learn: by your own mistakes and from other people. That's why this book isn't full of business school textbook theory and management strategy, it's crammed with real-life, practical advice straight from the people who know best: smart business people who've build smart businesses.

We've mined the best brains in business for your consumption because we believe business advice in the UK has not yet capitalized on its most valuable business resource: the knowledge of its entrepreneurs.

None of the entrepreneurs and business people featured in this book were paid for their advice. They agreed to take part for one simple reason: they share Smarta's ambition to bring together in one place the collective wisdom of the UK's best entrepreneurs and make it accessible to all.

As a result, you'll find vastly contrasting views on the same subjects – and that's the point. There's no one way to do anything in business and we won't pretend there is. Instead we'll collate all the different ways we see small businesses working at the moment and frame them in the context of how we think the business and economic climate is evolving.

This book has been a collaborative project with more than 120 contributors offering their insight over an 18-month period. In a way that couldn't be more representative of how we think the smart businesses of tomorrow will work and how we, at Smarta, see our role in the business community.

We hope you enjoy the book. Join us online at Smarta.com to access more free business advice and entrepreneur interviews like you find here – but also to contribute your own experiences to Smarta and meet and connect with like-minded business people.

The smartest business owners realize that while individually they're good, collectively they can move more quickly and achieve more. That thought process underpins this, the first Smarta book.

Read it, tell us what you think about it and how it can be improved, then tell us your story – and you never know, you might well feature in the next edition.

Part 1
The smartest businesses will start this decade

1.1
New world order: All the rules have changed

"We're going through a revolution again. There is another transformation happening. The costs of starting a business are being decimated again, the speed at which you can bring something to the world is increasing in speed again. Thus if we can do the whole thing much faster and cheaper we're going to be able to do different businesses in different ways. There's a new way to start a business coming – it takes very little time, very few people, very little capital and can be profitable quite quickly. Thus the rules are about to change again."
—Doug Richard, School for Startups and *Dragons' Den*

"This is a great time to start a business. Everyone is looking at things differently, seeking fresh answers or a new approach. Consumers want great value or originality and investors are looking to back great passion, commitment and ingenuity – plus there are some great deals to be done out there as suppliers compete to service your new business. If your idea is strong, and your determination levels are high, the future is very exciting."
—Sophie Cornish, Not On The High Street

If there's one thing all the entrepreneurs Smarta speaks to have in common, it's that they're all thoroughly energized and excited about being in business right *now*. Oh, and they're impatient. They can't sit still because they want to get moving. They don't have enough hours in the day or days in the week for the ideas in their head because they realize what opportunity-rich times we find ourselves in.

Smarta's excited too and our belief that we've entered a new, exciting time for business was our main reason for writing this book. Reject, ignore and banish any notion from the national press, politicians or even business lobby groups of doom and gloom, economic hardship and credit crunch. We're not denying any of those things, we're just not – like all the smartest business people right now – distracting ourselves with them either. The truth is, for the people starting exceptional businesses, the economy is irrelevant. Yes, we said it – and yes, we stand by it.

Make no mistake: this is a phenomenally exciting time to be starting or running a really smart business. If you're thinking of starting a mediocre business we might be more cautious. But if you want success badly enough then you genuinely have never had so many opportunities to make that happen. And it's never a bad time to start a great business.

The world has changed. The rules have changed – and we promise you, they've changed in your favour. Whatever the state of the economy and the national debt and whether or not we've got stealth taxes, deficits and cost-cutting coming out of our ears, business is open for trade like never before.

What do we mean when we say everything has changed? We mean everything. Again, forget the 'business world' for a moment – that's rarely where the best businesses are dreamt up, after all.

Instead, focus on the world around you. In the past few years it's changed immeasurably. Compared to ten or even five years ago, the way we work, play, communicate, consume, earn, spend, borrow, save and take in our news – these have all changed unrecognizably.

Every raw function of our everyday lives has been touched by the emergence, convergence and development of technology and the internet. These innovations have changed not just our functions but how we form opinions, express opinions, our expectations and our desires.

The hurtling pace of change shows no sign of slowing – and yet this is only the start. The internet has only been in most of our lives for 13 years or so. It's barely a teenager with spots, for heaven's sake. Imagine its potential when it's fully grown up and graduated.

The smart businesses out there are already busy keeping up with this new world, adapting and tailoring their products and services to its ever-evolving demands, while the even savvier are constantly looking to push, lead and help influence the future by pre-empting consumer patterns. These businesses aren't pushing products at consumers, they're using social media to hear what products consumers want and then providing them. Welcome to the new world order.

As the consumer demands more and more choice, we're seeing more and more flexible, small businesses serving the niche markets that cumbersome big businesses are too languid to service and too archaic to identify. Next time you see a household brand collapse, as sad as it is for the employees, ask yourself how many were actually catering for their former customers' changing needs. Not many.

And for every monolith that crashes into the wasteland there are opportunities aplenty for small businesses waiting to pick up the crumbs and do a superior job. Technology isn't just fuelling the crash of big businesses, it's powering the rise of small businesses as well. And here's where the rules have changed in your favour.

All the costs of starting a business – which for years have been prohibitive to those without money and given the power to those with money – have all but been eroded. The fundamental and crucial components you need to start and establish a business are, by the day, becoming almost free.

Serious barriers to entry such as the cost of building a website or hiring a developer and a marketing executive, which even three years ago might have cost £50,000–£100,000 – have now almost disappeared.

Brilliant ideas which could have become billion-dollar businesses but never got past a failed bank loan application now don't need that bank loan. Their founders can start growing that business regardless and then prove they're worth investing in once they've established a customer base.

You can turn yourself into an expert and a respected brand on Twitter, build yourself a website on WordPress, start trading globally on eBay and hire your first employees without spending any real money or even thinking about an office – and all before you've even quit your day job. Do you know what? You might never quit your day job!

There isn't one path any more. The options aren't few and constrictive, they're many and empowering. There's no one way to start or run a business any longer. Instead there are many ways and you're free to choose the one that's right for you.

> **" You'll always have multi-nationals, but there'll be fewer of them. For every 200-employee business there will be ten 20-person companies working more flexibly and creatively "**

Business has been democratised. You don't need to be skilled, you just need to put the time in – and you no longer require vast sums of money either. In the new world order of business, skills are cheap and passion, knowledge and time are the important currencies.

Collaboration has replaced obsessive and defensive competition. We no longer see ourselves as one person or one small business fiercely competing against all the thousands of other businesses. Instead we're starting – or at least the smartest businesses are starting – to work collaboratively with other small businesses.

More businesses will form alliances, if not full joint ventures, with other small businesses, whereby you can work together for the shared, greater good rather than competing with each other. The successful entrepreneurs of this decade won't be hard-nosed sales tycoons or, contrary to popular belief, social media gurus, but simply people who understand people.

Those leaders who stay close to their customers, their staff and their partners and build powerful relationships with all three will prosper and be those most able to capitalize on change.

The business landscape will change still further. There will be more small businesses and fewer big businesses. Obviously you'll always have the multinationals, your BPs, your Tescos, your BTs, but there will be fewer of them. For every 200-employee business there will be ten 20-person companies working more flexibly and creatively, in terms of both how they do business and how they do their work.

> ❝ **Being exceptional will be the benchmark for business success in the 2010s. To be exceptional you have to go over and above what other people are prepared to do** ❞

Of course, not everyone who starts up a business will survive. Opportunity ensures nothing. With the explosion in opportunity and the number of small businesses, the need to be exceptional at what you do only intensifies. Being exceptional will be the benchmark for business success in the 2010s, whether you're big or small, well established or a day old. Be exceptional and people will want to work with you and spend their money with you.

To be exceptional you have to go over and above what other people are prepared to do. So success depends on whether you're prepared to go the extra mile in customer service or put in the another hour on a Sunday night, on how you treat your employees, partners and customers, on whether you're able to think innovatively and embrace change.

> ❝ **You have to work with uncertainty and embrace it as an opportunity to get ahead** ❞

The only certainty in business now is uncertainty – but you have to work with that uncertainty and respond to it as an opportunity to get ahead.

The truth is, what we know today could be completely outdated in a year's time. There are people who still cling to the belief that what worked in the 1980s and 1990s and made them successful will carry on working now. In some way they might be right, but as a whole what's working now won't work in two years' time and you've got to keep adapting.

WWW
Read the predictions of 30 top entrepreneurs:
www.smarta.com/business-brains

If there's one thing you won't find from the entrepreneurs and business leaders offering advice in this book, it's predictions about how the business landscape will look in 10 years' time. Why? Because they don't know. But what they do know is you can't look to the past either. You can only chase the future by embracing the present.

Smarta in five

1 All the rules have changed in your favour

2 The barriers to entry have been shot to pieces

3 This is only the start: the web is still a teenager

4 Social media has changed the face of business

5 Nobody knows the future, but are you operating in the present?

1.2
It's never been easier to get ahead

"What we've got to get away from is this idea that entrepreneurs are better than or different to business people. An entrepreneur is that person who goes out and risks their own money and their own time and energy in a private endeavour, and anybody can do that."

—Tim Campbell, Bright Ideas Trust

I believe every single one of us have entrepreneur qualities within us, it is just the entrepreneur within can remain dormant all your life. Entrepreneurs just happen to activate what everyone has already got."

—Sahar Hashemi, Coffee Republic

> "Anyone starting a business today can take advantage of all sorts of technology at a reasonable cost. It's much easier to work on the move and communication channels are very cost effective."
> **—Peter Jones, National Enterprise Academy and *Dragons' Den***

> "In America being an entrepreneur is encouraged. It happens less in the UK. So I think we just want to say you can do this: you can have an idea, you can launch it, especially if it's web-based. It's never been a better time to do that because it's affordable and somewhat recession-proof because your costs are very low."
> **—Ryan Carson, Carsonified**

Let's get one thing clear: *you* can start a business and *you* have as much chance as succeeding as the next person. Even if you don't have an idea yet, take confidence that the playing field has never been more level.

Encouraging though it is, this isn't news. Two of the bestselling business books in recent years, by our friends Sahar Hashemi and Duncan Bannatyne, have taken the title *Anyone Can Do It* and demonstrated how anyone, from any background and without any formal business training, qualifications or training, can apply themselves and achieve astonishing levels of success.

We know this and the business world, as highlighted by Smarta.com, is increasingly full of brilliant, inspirational stories of people who've battled against the odds to achieve business success. Not everyone will succeed in business, of course. But for the first time, the opportunity to work for yourself and monetise your talent is open and accessible to all.

> **"Everyone can start a business or monetize their life outside a traditional salaried job"**

While technology has completely reconfigured key business functions, it has also led a cultural and ideological shift. More people now believe they can start a business and more people want to. In the past they might have wanted to do, and in practice actually been capable of doing so, but for whatever reasons felt it was beyond them.

For decades, one of the chief psychological barriers preventing many more people starting their own business has been the perceived level of risk involved. While embraced by true entrepreneurs, risk is something generally associated with danger for most people and so best avoided. And let's face it, most of us aren't risk-takers. Happily, many business people aren't either. Fortunately then the costs of starting and marketing a business have become so low, what might once have felt like an almighty gamble is now much more of a calculated risk.

Ten years ago when the *Tomorrow's World* notion of starting a business for next to nothing in a matter of minutes with just a laptop and a mobile started to emerge, it was at best fanciful and worked better as iconography than in reality. You couldn't make a decent e-commerce website for under £20,000 and while you might be able to work from home and on your own, you were in trouble the minute you left your phone. It simply wasn't real life.

Now the financial cost of starting a business and the skills needed have also transformed. Now the notion of making your own website is an acceptable one without the caveat 'but only if you've got pretty damn impressive HMTL skills'. It's a given anyone can have a go at doing it. We're beyond early adopter stage. Setting up a website now isn't only for techies who understand the potential and know how to use the technology. We are at the next stage where the tools are legitimately useable for those who try.

It's also too simplistic to say that anyone on the demographic fringes previously restricted by cost and time, such as those with children, those with low earnings and students, are now more likely to start businesses. While it's true that they undoubtedly benefit from the advancements and shifts we're seeing, the benefits are empowering for everyone.

> **"Whoever you are, you can harness the power of social media to make you more productive, become more competitive and help you secure more customers"**

More than anything, technology has created a belief: an entrepreneurial or enterprise mindset, shared by more people than ever before. Whether you're 21 or 51 and running any type of business, you can take advantage of the new tools and opportunities open to you and harness the power of social media and its various gadgets and widgets to make you more productive, become more competitive and help you secure more customers.

What you need is a mindset that embraces the opportunity and doesn't stand still, ignore the potential or be scared off by any obstacles. The real shift is the drawing of a new starting line in the sand, the levelling of the playing field. While in the past anyone who had the right skills to get ahead in business was not stopped from doing so, undoubtedly it remained harder for some than others. But now skills are cheap and ideas and knowledge are valuable. With many of the traditional obstacles removed, anyone with the intellectual property and entrepreneurial mindset can succeed.

In addition, whether it's been statistically proven or not, it's now widely perceived to be safer to start a business than it was in the past. 'Starting your own business' is the number one career choice of young people under the age of 23. Given that we institutionalize people through education, and more often than not parental guidance, to pick a safe and earnest career, that's a quite a compelling fact.

Jobs for life certainly don't exist any longer. So if there isn't a safe job, what's the next safest thing you can do? When you work for yourself you're in control of your own destiny. You are responsible for whether something succeeds or not. As the costs of starting up fall and the need to borrow diminishes, so does the level of risk. People of all ages are seeing starting a business as an equal career choice to becoming an accountant or a lawyer or any other career where ultimately your performance doesn't necessarily dictate how secure your income is.

Starting a business has growing appeal for all ages. Those towards the end of their traditional careers are beginning to see it as an opportunity to utilize all the skills and experiences they've picked up to earn money for themselves and take on a new challenge. Young people tend to have fewer responsibilities and see running their own business as a viable career option that's just as valid as becoming a teacher or a lawyer. Given that the average student debt now tops £23,500, there's certainly a case for it being a cheaper option.

Welcome to the enterprise nation.

Smarta in five

1 No obstacle to starting a business is now insurmountable for anyone

2 Technology is democratizing business and you don't need to be a techie to benefit

3 Starting a business is now a calculated risk, not a shot in the dark

4 Starting a business is now a viable career option

5 It's cheaper to become an entrepreneur than to go to university

1.3
Age of the individual

"We're entering a land-grab of expertise. Each individual has the opportunity to be the brand or nexus around something."
—Doug Richard, School for Startups and *Dragons' Den*

"It's about doing everything you can to illustrate that you're the expert and you really know what you're doing – show people why they should be doing business with you."
—Matt McNeill, Sign-up.to and eTickets.to

This is the age of the individual. It's now perfectly possible to take your passions, expertise or expensively earned qualifications, whatever you know a lot about and can inform or entertain other people with, and build a financial world around them. We're not claiming you'll make yourself a millionaire by doing that – we think that will happen to a handful at the most – but we do think if you're good enough and work hard enough you might make a decent living; or, crucially, you'll do it by working for yourself than you work taking someone else's orders. That's quite exciting, don't you agree?

How do we propose you do this? You take whatever the niche is that you know most about and build a personal brand around it. You become known. You become the place to hear, find out, trust and buy. You become the person people think of first when they think about that subject. You're who people recommend.

You make content around your passion and knowledge – blogs, video blogs, photographs, webchats; you use social media networks to engage in conversations around your chosen subject; and you work non-stop to make your content the de facto destination for the latest advice, comment, news, gossip and anything else.

Let's be clear, we're not talking about churning out a couple of blogs here. The idea is that you work harder than anyone on the internet in your niche. Really. Harder than magazines, newspapers and television do in the same area. That's why you need a niche: focus on something that the mainstream don't do justice to and you can, for all the people who, like you, wish there was more great content for them to consume.

> **" Work harder than anyone on the internet in your niche "**

Your content has to be exceptional – not necessarily in terms of production quality, but in the value it delivers to people who really care about the subject you share a connection with. The more passionate your content is, the more stripped down and in depth it is, the better. For this to work you have to be producing something original and authentic. Faking it just won't wash: people will see through you and you just won't be able to create content that's good enough.

You also need to know how to push your content. You'll need to drive all the social networks and media spots hard. That's not just about sending out your content, either. It's about engaging in conversations, debates and arguments that are happening in your niche, whoever is having them and wherever they're going on. You need to be proactive in finding them and then play an influential role. Likewise, you need to be on call as close to 24/7 as you can to be helping people out and answering any questions they have that they expect you to know the answers to.

Sounds like hard work, right? Well, it will be. But at least it'll be your own hard work, for you. And depending on how well you do it, fairly quickly you'll start to gather a very healthy brand and a set of followers who see you as a 'super editor' or 'knowledge centre' for your subject.

This following – your tribe, as it's been dubbed – is how you'll eventually make some money for all your hard work. There's a school of thought that you should grow your tribe first and look to monetize it later by building product around it and working with affiliate marketers to draw revenues from the audience you attract. The jury appears to be out about how realistic that is and for how many people.

However, it's more than conceivable that should you hustle your way to the top and genuinely become the main authority on the web for your chosen subject, there would be numerous ways to make that a lucrative accolade. But, how many niches are there up for the taking and what are your chances of usurping the incumbents?

> **In an economy where skills are cheap and knowledge is priceless, those with the knowledge have exciting opportunities**

Well, never say never, but we suspect the rewards won't be so great for being the 72nd UK authority on stamp collecting. That said, if stamp collecting was your passion and you started a company selling stamps, doing all of the above – even if you only rose as high as 72nd in the ranks – wouldn't be a bad idea. It would certainly be a lot more productive and better value than taking out advertisements in stamp magazines, local newspapers, office windows, with Yell or buying pay-per-click advertising as your other options to attract customers.

Plus your tribe, no matter how modest, would also have a longer-term, recurring value in terms of repeat sales and personal recommendations.

Just because you're building a world around you and for almost zero cost, you shouldn't stop looking to grow with the help of others. Indeed, you absolutely should seek others to help you get ahead quicker. This doesn't mean employing people, but looking to swap skills and resources with other individuals and, if there is any resource available, outsourcing work.

The small business world is fast becoming a vibrant hub of individuals exchanging and trading to help each other get ahead without the need to burden themselves with the cost of employees. Businesses will never stop needing people, but increasingly many can now cope without employees.

Don't just think about how you can broadcast your expertise, but how you can trade it and use as a bartering tool to get ahead. It doesn't mean you spend your time slogging away for other people – that would defeat the purpose of working for

Landgrab A race to secure market share. Especially relevant to a new market.
Tribe A brand or individual's passionate band of customers, fans or supporters, usually online and through social media websites.

yourself. Instead it means getting connecting and networking hard with other small businesses so you can share skills, make bulk orders together, collaborate on marketing campaigns.

Building a personal brand should be the most public thing you ever do. And the more people you can feed off, the wider known and more powerful your specialist knowledge will be.

The principal shift in business rules would be the same as well: instead of deploying your skills or knowledge for someone else's benefit, you'll be working for yourself.

In an economy where skills are cheap and knowledge is priceless, those with the knowledge have exciting opportunities ahead. The landgrab to become the expert in your niche might already be well under way, but unlike the battle for market share in the past, it'll be your expertise and ability to communicate through social media that will mark out your chances of success in the new world order of business.

Smarta in five

1 Look to your passions and expertise for business inspiration

2 Find your niche and make great, authentic content

3 Assess your ability to monetize your tribe

4 Become the 72nd most important person in your niche

5 Use knowledge not money as your marketing currency

1.4
Social media = business

"I am a social media evangelist. I think it's a wonderful way to communicate. I blog, I tweet, I have my Facebook page, my BlackBerry is at the end of my fingers all the time. In the old days I had a secretary and 50 people in the office and I didn't even know how to turn a computer on. Now, I'm always checking in. I'm lost if I don't have ... In fact, where is my BlackBerry?"

—Lynne Franks, B.Hive

"You need to understand social media. You still need good content, you still need to have a clear message, but the context has changed – and that's all. People can get very confused and place too much importance and significance on it. You need to understand that a lot of the principles remain the same. The marketing mix is what's changing."

—Sam Conniff, Livity

> "Social media has allowed me as a business person to be honest and bring some sort of new-found honesty to business. Businesses can't hide any more. If you choose to hide, someone who's not hiding will elbow themselves to the front."
> **—Brad Burton, 4Networking**

> "The way to think about it is that if you have a website, what are the different ways I can get people to my website? So how do you use things like Facebook or LinkedIn or Twitter to market your products and services?"
> **—Ashley Friedlein, Econsultancy**

Note the lack of the word 'marketing' in the title of this chapter. It's no mistake. Social media is business – not marketing. We're passionate believers that social media is the single biggest driver of the way business has changed over the last two years and that it will continue to catalyse change in the future.

Social media is business, unequivocally. There's not a business that shouldn't be using it in one way or another, certainly not a business owner that shouldn't be – indeed, the smartest business owners and business people are already putting social media at the heart of their businesses.

Before you write us off as raving social media evangelists, let us explain why. We actually think social media is a bad name. Social media would be far better understood if it were called 'collaborative business' – because that's what it is. If it were called that, people would immediately think of it as a business tool and shed all connotations of it not being serious or even not for business.

> **" 'Social media' would be far better understood if it were called 'collaborative business' "**

Social media is serious and it's also here to stay. Social media is the next generation of business communication and is powering the next phase of business collaboration. We progressed from riding a horse to travelling by cart to a car to a plane. In the same way, social media is a natural development of our ability to communicate. It has many far-reaching powers, but it's no more complicated than that. It's just a newer, faster, easier way of communicating that lets us interact with more people simultaneously, build relationships more quickly and amplify all the good things that we're doing.

Every business can find a way of using social media better, whether it's finding, understanding, keeping tabs on or interacting with its customer base and competitors, doing research and development, a bit of marketing, developing powerful business relationships or being proactive in dealing with a crisis.

Whether you're Nestlé in the middle of a PR disaster and using social media effectively as part of your response or a hairdresser using it to tweet when the snow means you'll have to cancel half your appointments or putting out a special offer for your customers, social media has quickly evolved as the No. 1 business communication tool. It's real time, it reaches more people than anything else on the planet and, bar the time you put in, it's free.

> **"social media has quickly evolved as the No. 1 business communication tool – it's real time and it reaches more people than anything else on the planet"**

When we look at the changing face of business, social media is arguably the key driver in lowering the barriers to entry and levelling the playing field between large and small companies. We believe it should play such an integral role in the way you shape your business that social media is woven into many of the chapters of this book. However, there are also specific chapters examining how smart companies are using it well and how best to use, what in our opinion is the daddy of all business social networks, Twitter. It's also worth checking out the chapters on collaboration and networking, which have a strong social media slant.

For now though, let's focus on just why social media is so important, for any cynics out there still convinced it's not really for them. How can we say that with such self-assurance? Easy. We just keep coming back to the same old argument: because your customers use it.

Yes, even yours. Unless, that is, you honestly think your customers aren't one of the 500 million Facebook users or 165 million Twitter users or 75 million LinkedIn users or responsible for any of the 200 billion videos viewed on YouTube every single day.

It's hard to believe you couldn't be convinced by these stats, but just in case you aren't, how about getting your head around this: 71% of the global online community used social media during March 2010 alone. It's estimated a mind blowing 859 million people are using social media. Quite simply, your customers are among them – and we guarantee by the time you read this, the figures will be out of date and larger again.

Social media has changed the way we behave as customers, clients and consumers – and so it has to change the way we behave as businesses. Fortunately all of this change is to your advantage and empowering you to build products and deliver

WWW
Read more about social media at www.smarta.com/social-media.

Collaboration Working together with one or more other like-minded companies or individuals to achieve shared goals.

services your customers really want, and to find new customers far easier than ever before.

There's no disputing it, even if you're only listening to Twitter and Facebook you're better informed as a business owner about your customers' behaviour. In turn, there's a strong case that almost every business should have a blog and be on at least one (and almost certainly more) of Twitter, Facebook, LinkedIn, FourSquare, Flickr or more trade-specific sites such as Trip Advisor.

The case looks even stronger when you consider the disadvantage of not being on there, not having profile in front of your customers, not listening and being aware of what your customers and competitors are saying in your market place – as well as missing out on the personal profiling and networking opportunity social media offers.

In truth, you can't afford to ignore social media. Your entire business reputation is likely to be made and judged on it. Only 14% of consumers trust ads, yet 70% trust bloggers. 78% value personal recommendation above anything else and are willing to pay more for products rated highly by others. Social media is fundamental to business success in the modern world and will only become more so. That is why it's not 'marketing' it's just 'business'

Smarta in five

1 Social media is business – there's no hiding from it!

2 Your customers use social media, but what are they saying?

3 Social media has democratized marketing

4 Traditional advertising is redundant

5 Social media isn't a fad – if you're not on board already, buy a ticket now

1.5
Why big really isn't always better

"The best companies think big, start small and move fast."

—Julie Meyer, Ariadne Capital

"In a big company, you get to do one thing – in a small company you get to do absolutely everything. You learn an enormous amount, and you have responsibility for everything. You also don't have to go to any one else for decisions, so you can move really fast, do your own thing, have a bit of fun, make a few mistakes, and learn a lot along the way. It's been a good ride."

—Dave Wallwork, Feel Good Drinks

On the rare occasion you see a story about small businesses in the media, you can guarantee it'll be the same doom and gloom about how hard it is running a private business, how difficult it is to access funding and how the government is taxing the life out of profits and investors alike.

We're not denying any of that (and we'd like more breaks for small business owners), but what you're not seeing publicized is how this is also a fabulous, opportunity-rich time to be running a small business. While the economy has nose dived, the technological and cultural shifts of recent years have been to the advantage of small business owners savvy enough to take advantage.

As we covered in the last chapter, the emergence of social media has levelled the playing field, giving small businesses access to marketing opportunities they could previously only dream about.

This means that, along with lower production costs to launch websites and make content, it's not just cheaper to start a small business, but more viable to stay small, nimble and extra flexible for longer. There are now alternative ways to take on employees, which means you no longer require offices to seat them in and can deploy your resources instead on building better products and services and chasing bigger deals.

What is more, the growing appetite among small companies for collaborating formally and informally to catalyse

> **It's not just cheaper to start a small business, but more viable to stay small, nimble and extra flexible for longer**

their reach, buying and bidding power, access to skills and specialist resources is eating every day into the competitive advantage that money traditionally brought big business.

We've also seen a strange dichotomy that as fast as we move forward technologically, we're also reverting to the past in our desire for the local, authentic and real. We've grown tired of faceless organizations, call centre robots answering our specific questions with generic answers from a script which translates into 19 different languages and the dubious ethics behind corporate brands that answer to no one.

More than ever, consumers want to be treated as the individuals they are, to be listened to, to be made to feel special and to perceive they're receiving value for their spend. What is more, for many purchases they're prepared to pay a fair price for value as well – even if they're on a budget, price alone does not dictate many people's buying decisions. Consumers are increasingly demanding trust: they want to know about the people behind the companies they buy from, how their products are sourced or manufactured and about the business's ethics. They want to be able to ask questions and to get responses.

It's not only consumers who feel this way, either. It's employees as well. More top earners are leaving corporate roles and, if they're not starting their own business, are taking jobs in small companies where they're treated like individuals not numbers, feel they're listened to, and where they're making a compelling contribution and are rewarded not with a bonus but with a slice of the profits they've directly helped earn or shares in a company they're helping to grow. Alternatively they're opting for careers in social enterprises, where their work benefits not them or any individual but a cause.

Somewhere in the pursuit for ultimate efficiency and scalability, big business – with very rare exceptions (stand up John Lewis Partnership, we applaud you) – forgot all this. Once you're that cumbersome, languid, tied up in bureaucracy and indebted to shareholders, it's pretty damn difficult to change.

Small businesses have no such excuse. Provided that they're listening to consumers and even more carefully to the specific needs of their customers, they could be capitalizing on all of big business's failings.

The rush to get big is overrated. A loyal and engaged customer base which repeat buys, and can be gradually convinced to make larger transactions, is almost always more valuable than a large number of one-off sales. And it's always more economical. Attracting new customers costs money and takes time – two things you won't have as a small business.

> **" If you're small, flexible and taking advantage of the emerging technologies at your disposal, this is a truly great time to be a small business "**

Smart small businesses flaunt their size. They lure customers by being personal or local or specialists. These are your killer advantages as a small business and where your larger counterparts can't compete, so accentuate at every opportunity. Build relationships with customers and, as you would in any other relationship, keep it fresh and exciting by acts of kindness and spontaneity. Give customers more than they expect when they don't expect it. Over deliver. Don't saddle yourself with excessive costs in doing so, just anticipate what will turn a satisfactory transaction into an enjoyable and memorable one. It could be as simple as remembering a client's birthday or putting a packet of sweets in with an order.

Move quickly where others can't. It takes big businesses months to launch a marketing campaign, from the signing off of funds to the recruitment of an agency, conception of a plan, booking of media and execution of concept. When campaigns cost

Scalability The measure of a small business's potential to expand based on its current model.

millions, you take the time to get them right. You might not be able to afford million pound media, but in turn you can react to breaking incidents.

You're agile so use it to your advantage. During a tube strike in London in 2010, savvy independent restaurants had mailouts hitting their travel weary customers' inboxes offering one-off lunch discounts to cheer them up. The smallest of gestures can get you recognised and remembered. The smartest small businesses are always on the look-out for opportunities to impress. They're quick, nimble and always ready.

If you're small, flexible and taking advantage of the emerging technologies at your disposal, this is not a bad time, as the press would have you believe, but a truly great time to be a small business.

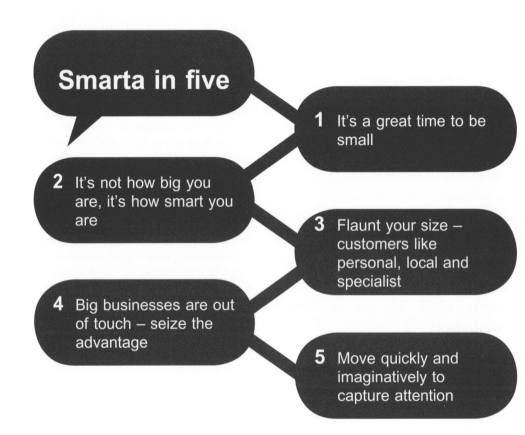

Smarta in five

1 It's a great time to be small

2 It's not how big you are, it's how smart you are

3 Flaunt your size – customers like personal, local and specialist

4 Big businesses are out of touch – seize the advantage

5 Move quickly and imaginatively to capture attention

Part 2
What smart
businesses do

2.1
Become the exception by being exceptional

"With every new business we start, we have to make sure there's a point of differentiation – if there isn't, then we don't do it. For us, it's about four things: vision, passion, irreverence and freedom."

—Al Gosling, The Extreme Sports Company

"We made sure we were unique. No other business in the world is offering natural male grooming products."

—Simon Duffy, Bulldog Natural Grooming

"The first thing I look for in a business is something that excites me. Will it make we bounce out of bed in the morning because I'm excited or make me bounce back into bed because I'm bored?"

—Theo Paphitis, Ryman and *Dragons' Den*

S mart businesses are exceptional. They exceed expectations. They go beyond the standard, they surpass the norm; they're loved, they're respected and they're copied. But most important, they're remembered and they're talked added.

The smart businesses right now are those that people are telling their friends about. They're the companies that have a product or service so exceptional that their customers want to recommend it and want to identify themselves with it. Or they're smart companies that offer superior customer service, provide a local service so useful that the community wants to embrace it, or produce marketing campaigns and content so powerful that they go viral within seconds of release because people think they're cool and want a share.

" Never has it been so important to be noticed and talked about "

Never has it been so important to be noticed and talked about. Never has word of mouth, the oldest marketing tool in business, been so powerful and rich with opportunity. Or, in truth, so critical in differentiating your business from all the others out there.

If you're genuinely about to launch a product or service that's so revolutionary it's solving a problem that no business has ever solved before, then congratulations, because you have an excellent chance of making your business stand out. Imagine how easy it was launching and marketing the first toothpaste for sensitive teeth or the first no-effort tin-opener or the first frozen chip. You had something people genuinely wanted and you simply had to find a way to reach them.

If you're honest, though, you're probably not launching something entirely new or if you are, it's into a marketplace that already exists – and that's where the challenge begins. Don't worry, because almost all the smart businesses out there weren't launching anything that fundamentally new either, but they realized they still had to find a way to be spotted and talked about.

In the past if you had a business idea, say a new shampoo, and wanted to take it to the masses, what did you do? If you had the money you advertised to as many targeted people across as many relevant media formats as you could. Again, if you were first to market, super. But now, even money isn't going to guarantee that you don't get lost in the sea of adverts that all look the same – and that's assuming anyone is looking at them anyway.

Advertising is dying and we've moved full circle back to the power of recommendation – except that word of mouth in the 2010s is amplified via the networks we're all growing. Instead of the trickle effect of customer telling customer, if you've got something people want to shout about then your shout can echo to thousands within seconds.

> **"Word of mouth in the 2010s is amplified via our networks"**

You can't buy attention any more, you have to earn it. It's up to you, not your wallet, to stand out and grab people's attention. Increasingly, in this new entrepreneurial landscape, the most effective business ideas are those that spread. Smart businesses are embracing that and making themselves exceptional in ways that people want to talk about.

Smart businesses differentiate themselves by thinking, looking and acting differently from the businesses around them. Different doesn't have to mean weird, though. Sometimes when people talk about the need to be 'different' and 'standing out from the crowd', the average person running an average business thinks 'that's not me' or even

> **"You can't buy attention any more, you have to earn it. It's up to you, not your wallet, to stand out"**

'that can't be me'. They think 'I don't want to be the weird or wacky one', 'I don't want to stand out'.

But that's not what we're talking about and neither is it how the smartest businesses get talked about. The difference can be very simple and it can be about getting the small things right (see Chapter 2.9).

Smart businesses make themselves exceptional in many ways. It might be that they provide customer service above and beyond anyone else in their space; it might be focusing on the design and look, not just the pure functionality, of their products; it could be speed, efficiency, even price. It could be that they're particularly web savvy, building online communities around their physical proposition that offer extra value to their customers and make people feel part of something exciting.

Smart companies build exceptional brands because they come to stand for more than the mere product they sell. When people think about Innocent Drinks they don't think of a drink, they instantly remember the exceptionally memorable bottles and branding, the funny ditties on the labels; they think about a company that is fun, ethical, connected with its customers; and they possibly remember some of the stories it's had in the press and maybe even about its owners.

WWW

View the 100 small businesses we think are exceptional: www.smarta.com/smarta100

Innocent is a smart, exceptional company because it has worked hard to be memorable and talked about for all the right reasons – chiefly that it looks to engage with its customers and go the extra mile to make them feel included in the story.

This book is full of examples of how you can make your business exceptional and first-person accounts from the people running smart companies.

> **If you strive to be exceptional, then it's twice as easy to succeed – you will have a customer base who will promote your product**

Smart companies realize that if you strive to be exceptional, then it's twice as easy to succeed. Instead of the dual challenge of having a product to promote and a customer to find you, you will have a customer base who will promote your product – and that's smart business.

Smarta in Action: Call of the Wild

Name: Mark Soanes
Company: Call of the Wild
Company profile: Multi-award-winning Welsh company that provides all-inclusive adventure experiences in the wilderness, in an environmentally sensitive manner.
Founded: 1998

Overview
Call of the Wild has won loads of business awards, including a Smarta 100 award and the Welsh Small Business of the Year Award. How has it achieved so much? By being exceptional, of course.

How they do it
Call of the Wild has gone over and above the call of duty to differentiate itself from other adventure-tourism destinations.

The business was set up by three friends who wanted to run a business with its roots firmly planted in its local community. They started by setting up their eco-friendly adventure training centre in a former mining area that was one of the most socially and economically deprived parts of Wales. They've since renewed a real sense of pride in the area by recruiting only local staff and making it a tourist destination. They're intent on providing employment opportunities to local youngsters. And they do things like sponsor local sports teams too, which doesn't cost them much, but means loads to their community.

The team are also committed to teaching clients about the countryside and culture of the Brecon Beacons National Park. Staff explain Welsh heritage and customs to customers.

Call of the Wild has taken too many measures to make the business environmentally friendly than we have room for here. But as a few examples, electricity is sourced from green energy sources, water is from a natural spring rather than the mains, and all rubbish and food waste are recycled. It has stopped 3,320 plastic bottles from being used per year and has so far planted 2,000 trees at the centre to offset its carbon emissions. It was one of the first companies in the region to achieve Green Dragon Level 2 Environmental Award.

Smarta in five

1 Good enough isn't good enough

2 People talk about exceptional businesses

3 Word of mouth is the most powerful sales tool in business

4 Different doesn't have to mean wacky or weird

5 The small things make a big difference

2.2
Stay ultra-lightweight and flexible

"I'm a disciple of the ultra-light startup – as many costs as possible should be variable, and you should have as few costs as possible, thus making it much easier to succeed."

—Doug Richard, School for Startups and *Dragons' Den*

"We retain 100% of the control of our company. We haven't given away any equity. It means we can make all the decisions as we wish. It's a bit more free, a bit more fun and a bit more independent."

—Nikhil Shah, Mixcloud

Bigger is no longer better (if it ever really was). The smartest businesses out there at the moment are priding themselves on staying small for as long as they can. They realize that just because the costs of starting and even marketing a business have tumbled, it's still way too easy to strangle it with other unnecessary overheads.

Instead, the smartest businesses are keeping themselves flexible and efficient by resisting taking on many of the traditional fixed assets companies saddle themselves with and finding alternative ways to resource.

Fixed assets Essential permanent items of your business meant for continual use that you can't easily to turn into cash, such as property, equipment, staff.

Smart companies reject the notion that size is a measure of success or status as a business. They don't measure their progress as a business on how many people they employ or the square footage of their new offices – yet how often do you hear these figures quoted when you ask how big someone is?

You know the response: 'We've been going for 18 months, are up to 12 people now and have just moved to a 5,000 sq. ft. office right in the centre of town. We're doing really well.'

Even the government defines and groups businesses by the number of people they employ. But what exactly does this prove?

Smart businesses are more concerned about the limitations of such burdensome overheads and more aware of their inflexibility and (more often than not) their lack of efficiency. Instead, they talk about sales, secured business, mapped-out routes to growth and, crucially, profit.

Smart businesses start life as lean as possible, resist gaining excess weight and understand the health risks of becoming bloated. The smart people starting them begin with the bare essentials and only add costs when they're justified and are going to pay for themselves by the money they're going to bring into the business.

> **Smart businesses start life as lean as possible, resist gaining excess weight and understand the health risks of becoming bloated**

And when we mean basics we mean basics – an office isn't a basic and staff aren't basics. If you don't need either of these to start with, then don't take them on.

The point to all this isn't to save every penny at any cost, however. It's not about being cheap or denying your business the resources it needs to prosper. It's not even about being frugal (although that's not a bad attitude to have). It's about being smart with your money and spending it when and where it'll have maximum effect, both in terms of determining your success and also limiting your risk should the economy turn or trade become less favourable.

It's about not burning your cash before you need it, it's about doing what's best for the business. Smart businesses aren't anti-cash, they're just clued up about the advantages of being small and flexible.

They appreciate that new businesses rarely get things right first time and that increasingly small businesses (and indeed larger ones) of any age need to be able to react and adapt to changing consumer trends and market conditions. They realize that those who move quickest have a distinct advantage.

They stay lightweight so they can try things out and move on quickly if they don't work. They're able to perfect, test and change a model before scaling it up and so lower their exposure to risk and enhance their chances of success.

Smart businesses also look to collaborate with like-minded partners and bring in skills on a freelance basis as and when needed, instead of rushing to recruit. They don't look to solve issues of productivity by adding bodies; often this just adds to the cost of the problem.

> ❝ **Think big, start small, grow fast** ❞

What can you learn from them? Think big, start small, grow fast. Smart companies that deliberately stay lightweight don't lack ambition. In fact, it's usually the complete opposite: they're focused on the bigger picture and end goal for the business and they don't lose sight of that.

Starting small and being financially cautious is a sensible measure for any type of business. It's fairly obvious advice for those with little money to start with and modest growth aspirations (although not blowing what cash you do have will give you more time to get it right), but it's also wise for those with big plans.

Fortunately, technology is making it easier and cheaper for us to operate with fewer overheads and smart businesses are collaborating wherever possible to get ahead more quickly by collectively pooling resources and skills. (See how smart companies are collaborating in Chapter 2.5.)

WWW

Free guides, features and tips on managing your finances: www.smarta.com/manage-your-finances

Of course, you'll need to spend money eventually, but it's a way safer bet to do so once you've got revenue coming in, can afford to pay yourself and have proved and tested your model with a growing nexus of customers.

Growth almost always requires financing and for most people and most businesses that's external finance. However, it does pay to make sure you're ready for it before going after extra money. If you take finance having already proved that your business can be profitable and that your cashflow is under control, the investor or the bank is far more likely to lend you money and on better terms.

Embrace being small and question all costs, but don't delay growth unnecessarily either. The point of starting small is being able to expand quickly when you're ready and the opportunity is ripe. Save your money until you've a proven business model, clearly defined route to market and a fully formed plan ready to execute. That way you'll see a lot better return on any investment. And if you don't have funds, you'll be in a far better position to raise them. Until you're at this point, don't burden yourself with unnecessary overheads or investors who are keen on a quick return.

Smarta in Action: Mixcloud

Founders: Nikhil Shah, Nico Perez and Mat Clayton
Company: Mixcloud
Company profile: Mixcloud is rethinking radio. Listen to great radio shows, podcasts and DJ mix sets on demand. Upload and promote your own Cloudcast for free.
Founded: 2009

Overview
Nikhil Shah and Nico Perez came up with the idea for online radio website Mixcloud in 2008 while they were studying at Cambridge University. They knew they wanted to retain control of the company, so instead of going down the traditional route of getting a loan, they 'bootstrapped' instead and paid for it themselves.

How they did it
They keep things as cheap as possible. 'We retain 100% of the control of the company,' explains Shah. 'We can make our decisions as we wish. It's more free, it's more fun – and we're independent!'

To start, the pair decided to do a skill swap with a friend. Perez did some design work on his project and the friend, Mat Clayton, did some technical work for Mixcloud. In fact, the boys were so impressed with their friend's work, they brought him on board as a co-founder.

Mixcloud has also saved money by opting to base itself in a 65,000 sq. ft. warehouse in north-west London. The warehouse is owned by housing project Camelot, which leases out vacant properties to 'guardians' who look after them at bargain-basement rents. Shah, Perez and Clayton lived and worked in the warehouse for the first year.

'It's just good training for actually running your business like a business, rather than getting in bucketloads of investment and cash and spending it on things that potentially aren't important,' says Shah.

Smarta in five

1 Staying small buys you time and lowers risk

2 Offices and employees are not representative of success

3 The more overheads you take on, the less flexibility you have

4 Proving your model before borrowing is favourable to investors

5 Start small, think big, move quick

2.3
Put social media at the heart of everything

"When people say Twitter doesn't work or Facebook doesn't work, it's a bit like saying talking to people doesn't work. It's exactly the same. Social media has brought honesty. You can't hide any more."

—Brad Burton, 4Networking

"The more you can invest in participating wherever your community is, the better. That's where people are and that's where they're open to hear from you. What would be the alternative? Spending money on advertising? No – the power of the interactions between people on social media is very personal."

—Ryan Carson, Carsonified

Believe the hype. Social media is changing the way all smart businesses are operating. It's every bit as powerful as its evangelists are promising, and more.

The really smart businesses already have social media at the heart of everything they do. That's everything. Smart businesses already realize that social media is so much more than a mere marketing tool and are using social media in a number of ways to gain competitive advantage.

While everyone else is standing around scratching their heads, developing a 'social media strategy', hiring any number of gurus and experts or still procrastinating over how something that Jonathan Ross and Britney Spears use could possibly be relevant to the very real challenges of running a business, the smartest companies are already using social media to grow powerful networks of admirers, contacts and potential customers and clients.

Smart companies realized a while back that, among other things, social media is the world's biggest living room, pub, playground, bus-stop, consumer testing panel, market research hotbed – and that it's not just that everyone is there, but anyone is allowed in.

Before they'd even considered using it to 'market' a single message, smart companies were and still are using social media to observe and listen to the 'buzz of the crowd' – the hundreds of millions of people using social networks – to ensure their products and services are in line with the fast-changing appetites of today's consumer.

Speed is the new currency of business: blink and you'll miss a fad, react and you could make a killing from it. Close your eyes and you might not recognize the business climate around you. Smart businesses saw this happening, watched for a while and then dived in to be part of the debate, to help shape conversations taking place in their sectors and to establish reputations as the companies that listen and understand what customers in their space want.

> *Speed is the new currency of business: blink and you'll miss a fad, react and you could make a killing from it*

Smart companies don't see or treat social media as a just a direct marketing tool – or as a sales tool either. Sure, they get new business from it, possibly more than they do any other form of true marketing or sales, but they don't go into it with a return on investment (ROI) mentality from day one. Not because they don't expect a return or measure what they do, but because they appreciate that their social media activity feeds into many other aspects of their business.

Smart businesses use social media to build tribes of customers around their personality, identity, expertise, knowledge, their commitment to go the extra mile and their willingness to connect and interact on a personal level.

What does that mean? It means they put themselves where their customers spend their time and where their customers have conversations, because they want to join in. Then they join in.

If a smart company sells bicycles, it makes sure it's part of the conversation on Twitter on the best cycle routes, tracks, equipment, cyclists, tournaments – basically anything in the world of bicycles. It uses http://search.twitter.com to search for people looking for cycling help on Twitter and offers it, even if it's never spoken to that customer before and there's absolutely no chance of a sale there. Where people watch cycle videos – on YouTube essentially, as that's where 90% of videos are watched – someone from the company's there commenting on cool videos or commissioning and uploading videos its customers might like.

> " *Smart companies don't treat social media as a marketing tool – or as a sales tool* "

If its customers are uploading cycle photos on Flickr, it does the same or comments on them or runs a competition for the best Flickr cycling photo every month. It joins and sets up cycle groups on Facebook. On LinkedIn it sets up and contributes to groups and discussions on cycling issues and rights.

The company starts a blog, posting pics and reviews of new cycle releases. It comments on developments in the cycle industry and campaigns by cyclists, it starts petitions lobbying government for more stringent road protection for cyclists. It posts pictures submitted by customers and readers of its cycles, interesting rides, tips for others. It makes great content that cyclists want to read.

But crucially – and you really have to listen to this bit – in all of this activity, the company's not trying to sell. It's not even trying to force people through to its website. It offers links at every point where it makes sense, of course – but not when it doesn't.

A company that does this is using social media to build a tribe – a tribe of people who see it as a destination and an authority on anything to do with bicycles. Why? Because that breeds respect, trust, brand love, word of mouth – something way more powerful, targeted and far-reaching than any advertising campaign our smart cycling company would otherwise have been able to afford.

And all of this activity breeds a tribe of potentially life-long customers. The smartest companies realize that by getting social media right, they're building a tribe of loyal customers who won't just yield one-off transactions, but long-term sales and personal recommendations – and that's where the real value lies for any business.

Smart companies realize that the power of social media has reached only a fraction of its potential. It's very much in its infancy, but all the signs suggest it will continue to shape how both consumers forms their buying decisions and businesses develop their whole strategy. If it isn't already, in the future social media will be impossible for businesses to ignore. Anything that forms the most powerful source of research, communication, networking, marketing, customer service and interaction and sales generation isn't a fad and won't disappear. Social media will only play a more active role in both our consumer and business lives.

The real power of social media is its reach. It's catapulted the reach of a small business from its local vicinity or limited web presence and gifted it the potential to reach millions of people within minutes. This signifies a democratization of business, as your reach is no longer representative of your size or resources, but something much fairer: your reputation and the quality of service you deliver. Going the extra mile for one customer now isn't about the individual act alone, it's about how many people that person will tell, and how many more the people they tell will tell.

> ❝ *It won't be social media or social networks but social business or social commerce* ❞

Everything good you do can spread virally to build your reputation, while anything truly exceptional you do that would engage not just your tribe but anyone outside your space has huge potential to make a landgrab that's the equivalent of months and months of multimillion-pound marketing.

Of course, this works both ways. Social media can also amplify all the bad things you do as a company – and even smart companies make mistakes. The difference is, smart companies react quickly to turn their mistakes into something positive.

They're continually monitoring social media for any negativity associated with their brand and for disgruntled customers – and they move quickly and positively to address any problems. If they mess up, they fess up and they look to put it right. Never underestimate a customer's satisfaction at having a problem dealt with quickly and satisfactorily. We don't expect companies to be perfect 100% of the time, it's how they deal with mistakes when they happen that affects our assessment of them. Generally we appreciate it when they then treat us as individuals and resolve the situation promptly and positively.

The smartest businesses are also forging partnerships every day through social media, meeting like-minded companies with shared aims and striking deals that are mutually advantageous.

Smart companies are encouraging not preventing their employees from representing their companies on social media, being brave enough to embrace their desire to be brand ambassadors and realize that customers enjoy dealing with people and real talk, not logos and scripted mission statements.

Don't ignore social media, don't pay it lip service, don't palm it off to your marketing agency or intern: put it at the heart of everything you do and you'll be staggered at its potential and power.

The smartest businesses realize this, but they also realize that their biggest opportunities from social media are the ones they don't actually know about yet. The next big opportunity in social media will be the next social media destination or trend. As we go to print in November 2010 or when you buy this book, who knows if that will still be Twitter, as it is now?

The smart companies *will* know though and they'll be ahead of the curve because, quite simply, they listen. Their customers will tell them how and where they want to interact with them and provided that they're listening, they'll be there and building relationships while the big companies are still spending big trying to hit last year's hot space.

Smarta in Action: Tutor2u.net

Founders: Jim Riley and Geoff Riley
Company: Tutor2u.net
Company profile: publisher of e-learning resources for various academic subjects, used by more than 3,500 schools and colleges in the UK and in more than 85 other countries..
Founded: 2002

Overview
Tutor2u has blogs for each of the academic subjects it covers, producing on average 30 blogs a day. These drive an estimated 25% of total revenues from people who register on the site having read them. Blogs are distributed via Facebook, email marketing, Twitter and RSS feeds (a lot of schools put the RSS feeds onto their own networks).

How they did it
"We try to think about the way that our customers want to be updated," explains co-founder Jim Riley. "Our social media strategy has to be informed by what customers want and need.".

Having a joined-up strategy is key: "In every part of our digital communications, whether that's a blog entry or email or even printed media we send out to teachers and schools, we always refer to the new Facebook page and encourage people to visit it – and most importantly click that Like button." As a result, the Tutor2u Facebook page has nearly 2,500 fans.

Tutor2u experiments to fine-tune its strategy. We're doing some specialised Twitter accounts and feeds – so there might be a feed on the latest politics news, populated by politics blogs.

"We're also running personalised Twitter accounts," Jim explains. "I run one and my twin brother Geoff does, so teachers and users can very much see the personal brand that's part of the site as well just our pure teaching content. People buy from people they feel they know and trust – so if you can make it personal it's much more effective than just a corporate Twitter account or Facebook page."

Tips
Integrate your social media efforts so they drive traffic to each other, and tailor your offering according to what works best for your customer. Experiment to fine-tune your strategy. Have a personal face on social media as well as a business one.

Smarta in five

1 Your customers use social media – not necessarily

2 It's about more than marketing messages and selling

3 Build a tribe of people who trust you

4 Social media breeds long-term customers

5 If you mess up, then fess up and turn it to your advantage

2.4
Tell stories people want to hear

"Brand values don't just happen. If you determine what sort of company you want to be and, equally important, what sort of company you don't want to be and write that down and communicate it clearly, frequently and often, then actually you've a pretty good chance of attracting those people who respond well"
—Tristram Mayhew, Go Ape

"I was offered a book deal before the project started and I was like, 'Hang on a second guys', but they said it was a good story and I was sitting on all this debt, so I was like, 'Okay, fine – I'll write a book about something that hasn't happened yet'. It obviously gave us a lot of credibility and it was something that would guarantee more publicity in the future."
—Ben Keene, TribeWanted

"We had to battle against the brand awareness of the biggest players in the men's grooming industry to reach new customers, so we approached [comedian] David Mitchell. We couldn't pay him anything like as much as other people he's working with, like Apple or the government, but I think he liked the fact we gave him a lot of creative licence. The result was our Soap Box content, a series of videos with David Mitchell talking about everything and anything. It's had 2.9 million views so far and been picked up by press including the Guardian and FHM."
—Simon Duffy, Bulldog Natural Grooming

> "We went off air for a year so we could get a legal licence, but to maintain brand awareness we created a magazine called *Touch* magazine, and we made sure we had a mailing list. We kept in touch with them via that – it was given out at all the clubs, and it was all about Kiss FM – it was written by the DJs, but we couldn't mention it. It was better to build the brand subtly."
> ## —Gordon Mac, Kiss FM

> "I remember in the early days of snooker, having eight snooker guys in the room. I said, 'OK, Jimmy White you're the ducker and diver, you're the artful dodger character. Steve Davis, you're a bit boring, very reliable, you wear black suits, white shirts, and drink water. Willie Thorne you're a maniac gambler, you're going to be the tipster, the Jack Roulette. Tony Meo, you're Italian. You're going to cry a lot. Today's sports consumer wants to know much more than stats on performance."
> ## —Barry Hearn, Matchroom Sport

Every picture tells a story and so should every business. The sooner you establish your story – and it is very much *your* story – the better. And don't for one minute think you don't have one. Every single business has a story: you've just got to find it, crystallize it and learn how to work it.

Truly great businesses have a story that perfectly encapsulates their brand, tells their target audience what they're about, differentiates them from the competition and that, crucially, their customers buy into and want to become part of.

Will King, founder of shaving products company King of Shaves, has been talking about the story behind his company's growth to date to anyone who would listen for many years. Anyone who's ever heard the story won't fail to have been enamoured by his mission to establish what he passionately believes is a superior product – initially a shaving oil to replace foams or gels – going up against shaving giants such as Gillette with a tiny fraction of the marketing budget.

Not only does he have a good story that he tells well, it's one his customers can join in with. Will is a huge advocate of customer testimonials and promotes them wherever possible. Anyone who uses Twitter and tweets a complimentary message about King of Shaves gets retweeted by Will. What does that mean? It means lots of people send such messages every single day, because they know someone is listening and they know they'll get heard by not just the man behind the company but other people with the same opinion. How often does that happen when you write a letter or email or telephone a company?

Like the supporters of an underdog non-league football club on a cup run or the fans of an up-and-coming band who hope one day the rest of the world will cotton on to what they've already discovered, Will now has a band of loyal followers, his tribe if you like, sharing and actively contributing to his mission – and that's massively powerful.

It's really simple. If you tell someone a story and it's interesting enough, they will listen and want to come back for more. If it's really good, they'll tell their friends. If it's exceptional they'll become emotionally attached to it and want to become part of it.

What you're telling isn't just the story of your business, though. In fact, it shouldn't be. Not everyone can peddle the David v Goliath story effectively and it would lose impact if we all tried. Plus, it's true that not all businesses or even the people behind them make fascinating stories. Instead, the smart businesses that don't have a story ready-made are making great, relevant content about the world around them – which, if they're in business for the right reasons, they're massively passionate and knowledgeable about.

Passion and knowledge are infectious: people are attracted to them, they trust them and they buy into them – especially if they share that passion, which it's fairly safe to assume your customers do.

You need to be continually telling stories about everything you do *and* what everyone else is doing in your space. Will's not just an expert on King of Shaves, he's an expert on shaving, on male grooming, on entrepreneurship, wherever people relate to him and his business. And he's frequently talking, writing, giving interviews and tweeting on these subjects.

> **"You need to be continually telling stories about everything you do and what everyone else is doing in your space"**

If you run a caravan park in Cornwall, then of course you should be telling us all about the stories coming out of the park and how you started it, but you should also talk about why Cornwall is such an exciting place to visit at the moment. Or even tell us about caravans.

Your passion shouldn't only be your caravan park in Cornwall, it should be caravans and Cornwall. Why? Because that's where your customers' passions and interests lie. It's a connection you share. You have to show people you care as much as they do and the easiest way to do that is to tell them all the stories you come across running a business that's so engrained in a sector and place they care so much about.

The best way to tell your story and to get people engaging with it is to create content they'll want to engage with. It's that simple. What is more, you don't have to be a novelist, journalist, cinematographer or photographer to make great content. Smart businesses realize that great content is two things: it's real – it's you not someone else – and it's made by someone who's knowledgeable and passionate. Obviously, there's a degree to which presentation and professionalism are important, but people care more about great, passionate, knowledgeable and authentic content than they do about flowing prose and HD-quality footage.

Another thing smart companies get right is that they work out what they're good at. Don't go making videos if you're a total nervous gibbering wreck in front of a camera or your subject doesn't lend itself to the format. Likewise, don't write a blog if you know your words aren't doing a service to what's in your head or your grammar is a serious issue (although you could always get someone to proofread your work and it hasn't stopped the dyslexic Jamie Oliver capturing a huge audience on Twitter). Richard Branson hates public speaking and you rarely catch him doing it.

> **" Pick what you're best at – but pick something "**

Pick what you're best at – but pick something. The obvious place to start is a blog. Despite the arrival and our unapologetic promotion of Twitter and microblogging (140 characters or less), blogs are very much alive and kicking.

WWW
How to write a blog: www.smarta.com/blogging

The key is, whether you're video, writing a blog or just using Twitter as your content outlet, it has to be something people want – and it has to come natural to you. You have to find it easy. If you don't find it easy it's either the wrong format or you're not running a business that you're passionate about. Because that's what your content needs to be – an articulation of your passions.

> **" If you're truly passionate about something you should have no problem thinking of 50, or even 500, things to say about it "**

If you're truly passionate about something you should have no problem thinking of 50, or even 500, things to say about it, and each of these is a story. You just need to find a format for communicating them.

And if you really put time and effort and maybe even a little bit of money into producing exceptional content, you really will see exceptional returns.

Go Ape founder Tristram Mayhew produces a quarterly magazine free of charge for everyone on his mailing list about all the upcoming activities at the various tree-swinging activity centres. But he focuses on the magazine being as good a read as any you might buy, not just an ad-filled brochure. As such his customers actually read it, engage with it and contribute to it. As a result, the magazine has become a must-read for all rope-swinging enthusiasts, not only Go Ape customers.

Likewise, Mayhew decided to set up and film a staff member riding the UK's biggest ever zip rope and he put the video on YouTube. To date it's had 500,000 views and Go Ape now regularly releases video of its rides and activities to a captive YouTube audience who all, of course, have the option to click through to the Go Ape website to become customers.

Go Ape's website also has a vibrant community commenting on and interacting with its blog. It showcases customers in action and the company organizes a series of charity events which the website then profiles.

Smart companies produce content people want not because they've got time and money to waste, but because they see the intrinsic value it returns in word-of-mouth promotion, social media currency and building a loyal, engaged, passionate, long-term customer base.

Smarta in Action: Bulldog Natural Grooming

Founders: Simon Duffy and Rhodri Ferrier
Company: Bulldog Natural Grooming
Company profile: Bulldog makes all-natural men's grooming products. Natural grooming is about caring as much about what you put on your skin as what you eat. The company launched with Sainsbury's in 2007 and its products are now available nationwide.
Founded: 2006

Overview
Having launched in 2007, Bulldog founders Simon Duffy and Rhodri Ferrier found themselves pitted against some of the biggest players in the men's grooming industry in the battle for brand awareness. While their research had showed that their customers were very loyal, it was letting prospective customers know about the brand that posed a problem. And without a marketing budget to rival L'Oréal's, the Bulldog boys had to think creatively.

How they did it
Because they had a limited marketing budget they decided to turn to the internet, which gave them the most scope to do something innovative at a low cost.

Looking at their customer profile, comedy seemed a natural fit. When the boys discovered that someone in their building knew *Peep Show*'s David Mitchell, they got in touch with him immediately.

The result was 'Soap Box', a series of videos with David Mitchell talking about 'everything and anything'. While Bulldog couldn't pay Mitchell 'anything like as much as other people', he was attracted by the fact the business gave him plenty of flexibility, allowing him to talk about anything he wanted.

The ploy worked: with more than 3 million views, Bulldog saw its name mentioned in the likes of the *Guardian* and *FHM*, increasing brand awareness enormously.

Tips
'Big brands are faceless and feel distant,' says Duffy. That's where the small companies have an advantage, because they feel more personal and have the freedom to be more innovative. By going that extra distance to bring in customers, the Bulldog boys increased brand awareness and boosted their credibility. 'You don't have to follow big companies' tried-and-tested methods,' explains Duffy. 'Don't be afraid to think there's a better way of doing things.'

Smarta in five

1 Storytelling generates interest and engagement

2 Every company has stories to tell

3 Great content is built on knowledge and passion

4 Authenticity and passion are more important than production quality

5 Make content that's true to what you do and who you are

2.5
Collaborate with other smart companies

"We went from being a small company that uses LinkedIn, to being a company anyone who uses LinkedIn might have heard of."

—Andy McLoughlin, Huddle

"I had to make us appear bigger than we were, so we went down the corporate venturing route and we were subsumed into a company called Morse, a big technology reseller. They had a £350m turnover, with 200 staff – and I believe being a small percentage of a big number is much better than being a large percentage of nothing."

—Alastair Lukies, Monitise

> "We saw an opportunity to white label our content, putting it under the brand of a partner. Websites like MSN or ITV have a very, very large volume of visitors and they might be interested in financial products. That gives our partner a relatively cheap form of income where they don't incur any marketing cost to generate revenue. So we effectively monetize traffic they already have."

—John Paleomylites, BeatThatQuote.com

One of the most powerful movements being embraced by the smartest of small businesses is collaboration: the simple yet previously alien concept that rather than continually looking over your shoulder for competitors, you openly look for ways to help each other grow.

As businesses become smaller and look to shed as many fixed assets as possible, it makes total sense to share resources, skills and means where that's beneficial for both companies. Increasingly, the skills or resources you once needed to invest in heavily in order to grow can now be accessed by working with other companies or individuals – and that's an exciting proposition if it means you can free up that money to spend elsewhere.

Smart companies are collaborating in many different ways: joining forces to pitch for government contracts they'd otherwise be too small to tender for; using their combined buying power to reduce their costs; sharing collective wisdom, skills, resource and expertise to crack new markets and territories.

They're forging partnerships with strategic aims, either as ongoing collaborations or for set projects or periods of time. Smart companies aren't just looking at how they can sell to their target market, they're looking at how they can sell to other people's target markets as well; not in a competitive sense, but as a collaboration that could benefit both companies.

In today's economic climate there isn't a company that wouldn't welcome the opportunity to add a revenue stream, bolster an existing one or provide an additional service that adds extra value to their overall proposition. Teaming up with a company that's complementary to your offering is an ideal way of doing that.

For once this is something the big companies have been adept at for a while. Ever wondered why when you open your bank statement you get marketing information from other companies? These mass marketing exchanges might not be particularly creative or compelling to the consumer, but they allow companies to multiply their reach quickly and with little effort.

WWW

Start making contacts now on the Smarta network: www.smarta.com/network
or ask a question and get it answered in real time: www.smarta.com/q+a

Teaming up with innovative small companies can provide an efficient way for large companies to break into a new sector or market. Incubating a new company and providing it with the resources, reputation and contacts it needs to grow fast can be more affordable than putting together a whole new arm of the business. Often you simply can't replicate the skills and creativity of a start-up. These 'corporate venturing' agreements can be hugely powerful opportunities for small businesses with disruptive ideas in established markets where penetration is tough. If that's you, it's an option that's definitely worth thinking about.

Collaboration is providing the smartest companies with two powerful advantages: speed and flexibility. It's a simple equation that by pooling resources and skills they can get ahead more quickly than in the past – and with lower overheads, the growth is less risky. Independently you are strong, but collectively you are stronger. By expanding your network, you expand your possibilities and opportunities – and it's about where those opportunities take you.

Every smart business needs to collaborate. As a small business there's only so much you can do. You are hindered by the finite resource of you. Even if you have three or four people working for you, you are still a small team. Equally, every small business owner only has 24 hours in a given day – but by collaborating with other small businesses, you're able to leverage your combined skills and resources to your mutual benefit.

Partnerships and joint ventures aren't anything new, of course, but in the past they've been steeped in legality. Today's move to collaborative working is less structured, more informal and embraces the individual as well as the company.

Collaborative businesses don't just have one or two strategic partners with whom they look to dominate single markets at a half or a third of the cost (although this can work and can be wiser than trying to crack it on your own), they build networks of powerful relationships in different spaces that they can work with to achieve a wider reach and at a fraction of the cost.

Again, embracing social media is key here. Smart businesses are not only using it to leverage their brand and communicate with their customers, but also to build powerful relationships with like-minded businesses whom they can work with to get ahead. Like the most powerful networkers (they're usually the same people, by the way), collaborative business owners aren't merely thinking how others can help them, but what they can offer. In doing so, they're meeting people with an interest in helping them back and forging relationships on the basis of not what one can do for the other, but what they can achieve together.

This is far from mere social networking, though. The most powerful business relationships are happening both offline and online. Relationships are built over time and based on trust. It shouldn't be a surprise, then, that despite several well-populated small business networks such as Smarta, physical face-to-face networking is also a massive growth area.

The growth of the 4Networking community and its more relaxed, open breakfast events at the expense of traditional stuffy networks and their archaic, complicated, restrictive and off-putting referral systems is testament to the growing desire among smart business people to be frequently meeting

" Smart companies are increasingly thinking 'Who can I work with to make that happen?' "

and exchanging views with other business people and building safety nets around their businesses.

Smarta exists, remember, for us to bring together the hugely valuable experience and the advice of a host of small businesses in one place for everybody to access. And while we edit the content, it's you, the business owners, who shape what's on there and are contributing your views and opinions, bonding with people who either you can help or who might be able to help you, and usually both.

There's a school of thought that in the future smart companies won't have employees, instead they'll work collaboratively with individuals whose skills they need as and when they need them. It's an interesting concept and one which highlights the growing necessity to make fixed assets flexible and the expectation that the individual will monetize their skills.

Smart companies are increasingly thinking 'Who can I work with to make that happen?' before they think 'In order to make that happen who should I hire?'. The same logic applies to any serious expansion and, to a degree, collaboration will keep some companies smaller (in terms of people and offices) than they previously were. But as we've said, since when did it make sense to measure success by the number of people you employ and the size of your offices?

There might be fewer companies jumping up in size using these traditional yardsticks, but by working collaboratively, there should also be more competing with bigger companies tied down by exactly that type of overhead. If you want to get ahead, embrace the power of the crowd.

Corporate venturing Where a typically innovative small company is invested in and fostered by a larger corporate for mutual benefit.

Smarta in Action: Spectrum Office Solutions

Founder: Graham Lucas
Company: Spectrum Office Solutions
Company profile: Spectrum started off as a business which offered general office support. It provided IT, web pages and bookkeeping. However, following the trend of what people want and need, 98% of the business is now bookkeeping.
Founded: 2006

Overview
Having launched his bookkeeping business in 2006, Graham Lucas found that traditional marketing techniques weren't having the desired effect. With stiff competition from other local businesses, approaches such as sending out emails or flyers to locals weren't working as well as he had hoped. He needed a new way to get the word out about his business.

How he did it

After a couple of years of business, Lucas decided to try something new to spread the word to local businesses. Instead of paying for ineffective advertising, he decided to look for a partner. Having spoken to local accountancy firms, he found one and made an agreement that they would begin recommending one another to clients.

For Lucas it was like having free advertising – and Spectrum comes with a stamp of approval from a trusted accountant.

'It's a win–win relationship for both of us,' explains Lucas. 'We both get more work from it and our clients like the fact we can recommend someone they can trust to do another service they need.'

Tips

When you're looking for a partner, look for someone in the same or a similar field to you. Find out what sort of recommendations they're willing to provide, and don't forget to let them know when a client recommended by them comes to you.

Smarta in five

1 Look for collaborators not competitors

2 Smart businesses build networks and safety nets

3 By pooling resources and skills you grow more quickly and take on less risk

4 Use social media and physical networking to build collaborative relationships

5 Think what you can do to help other people, not how they can help you

2.6
Worship the ground customers walk on

"Recognise your customer and that's by saying hello to them and recognising they were there last week. Make them feel special. Build a rapport and a relationship – it's very difficult to leave somebody you believe you've got a relationship with."

—Deborah Meaden, *Dragons' Den*

"If we have a couple of thousand pounds spare, instead of spending it on a glitzy PR launch, we spend it on our members. Our clients are the ones who will tell other people about us. They are our marketing. And that's where we should be investing."

—Alex Cheatle, Ten UK

> "We send an automatic response after customers' visits, saying we'd like to hear from you if you didn't have a good time. I personally ring them if they've had a bad time. We had 435,000 people going through our courses last year. If the chief gorilla rings you up, I think either you can assume he spends a lot of time on the phone, or it doesn't happen very often."
> **—Tristram Mayhew, Go Ape**

> "My Next customers want an entirely new product every season. Littlewoods, on the other hand, find a new product, love it, and want it back season after season. You just pay attention to what really works for each customer, and understand who is your target market – who are you facilitating for?"
> **—Caprice, By Caprice**

> "You do it quickly and you get it right – think, if I was a customer, what would I like? What would I expect?"
> **—Nick Wheeler, Charles Tyrwhitt**

This is simple. Customer has to be king. Always. No exceptions. None. Why? Because without customers you don't have a company. Customers aren't just the people who buy what you sell, they're the ones who should decide what you sell, how you source it, manufacture, package or deliver it, how you grow and develop.

The smartest companies are customer focused and put customer service at the very heart of everything they do. It's not rocket science, yet if you look at some of the largest companies in the world you can make the case for customer service having become a bygone art. In the chase for efficiency and scale, too many of them have lost sight of their customer. Instead, product and marketing took over and the customer has been left lost in the system of automated answering machines and management levels who defer responsibility to each other.

Small, agile, smart companies realize that the desire for customer satisfaction and face-to-face interaction never went away and are busy putting it at the core of their operations. Remember that people buy people first and no matter how big it may make you appear, resist the urge to automate anything. If you want to know how you can differentiate yourself from high-street heritage brands with multimillion marketing campaigns, look at what they don't do: it might be as simple as picking the phone up when it rings.

> **People buy people first – don't automate anything**

As a small business you deal with your customers on a daily, personal basis, you're not ten levels removed from them from shopfloor to HQ boardroom. You're on the front line. You see their emails, you hear what they have to say, you understand their problems and frustrations. The smart companies embrace that and turn it to their competitive advantage.

They realize the one golden rule about customers. One rule and one word encapsulates the single most important thing a business needs to do to ensure it understands its customer base, delivers products and services they want at the price they want and with the level of customer service they expect. What's that one-word rule?

Simple: just *listen*.

'Listening' has been woven into endless marketing campaigns over the years, but how many companies are actually doing it? The smart companies don't tell people they're listening, they prove it. They get out on the shopfloor, on the streets and on social networks interacting and speaking to their customers, asking them how they can improve on what they do already – and the results shape what they do as a company and how they behave.

Smart companies don't lose sight of what their customers want and are continually exploring how they can focus on their customers even more: how they can deliver the services they want before they even know they want them, and providing a flawless journey when making a purchase or using services.

Smart companies also understand that not all customers want the same things. This is where small, flexible companies can really score. Avoid putting your customers into boxes and appreciate that while it might be easier for you (and usually is a good idea) to segment your offering, doing so might not work for everyone. Be flexible wherever possible and that will be appreciated and returned by loyalty and repeat sales. Let the big companies be rigid and tell people for no logical reason that 'the computer says no'. You shouldn't have computers and systems making your decisions, you should have people saying, 'Yes, we'd love to help you do that'.

> **Don't have computers and systems making your decisions, have people saying, 'Yes, we'd love to help you do that'**

WWW

More free advice on customer service: www.smarta.com/customer-service

And when there is an issue or problem – and small businesses can do this more easily – address it quickly, personally, proactively and with honesty and integrity.

The smartest businesses have always had the customer at their heart. They've listened from before day one. Smart companies segment their customer base and speak to them about their individual needs. Then they grow their business by rolling out targeted products and services their customers actually want and will consequently pay a premium price for. Contrast this to a blanket, one-size-fits-all solution that actually doesn't fit anyone particularly well and so isn't worth a premium price and requires more effort to market and sell.

We said at the top: it's simple. And it is: the better you know your customers, the more you listen, the more closely you analyse who they are and what they need, the easier everything will be.

The smartest companies totally get this and that's why you don't see them buying mass media advertising. They don't need to scattergun advertise with the hope of hitting the target once for every 50 bullets fired, because they already understand what their customers really want and where they are.

Smarta in Action: Glasses Direct

Founders: James Murray Wells
Company: Glasses Direct
Company profile: Online glasses retailer, selling glasses, contact lenses and hearing aids at a fraction of high street prices
Founded: 2004

Overview
James Murray Wells began looking for lucrative business opportunities while he was still at university. When he had to fork out £150 for a new pair of glasses, he found his niche: "I looked at them and I thought, 'It's just a bit of wire and glass, why does it need to cost so much?'," he says. He decided to create a business that could offer £15 pairs of glasses over the internet. Since inception, Glasses Direct has saved UK consumers some £30m, and has an impeccable customer service record.

How he did it
Buying products online can be risky: the colours may be slightly different, the sizing might be off, or the style might just not fit you in the flesh. To help give his customers peace of mind, Murray Wells has developed an online 'aug-reality' widget that allows visitors to the site to 'virtually' try on any set of frames simply by staring into a webcam. The glasses are superimposed onto your face, almost by magic and, when you move your head, the glasses move too so that you can examine your new specs from all angles. If you buy them and decide they're not for you, you can return them, no quibbles, within seven days. And, if you're still unhappy, Murray Wells lists his personal email address on the Glasses Direct site to deal with complaints directly.

The website is bursting with positive testimonials from happy customers – and Murray Wells is always looking to improve customer service further, requesting feedback and suggestions from Glasses Direct customers.

Tips
Technology is your friend when it comes to honing your customer service offering. If you run an online business, use video, blogs and social media to engage with consumers. Murray Wells may be using cutting edge augmented reality for his business, but a simple photo upload device would have worked too. Make sure you adopt the technologies that are right for your business – and your budget. A no-quibble returns policy is also a great way to build trust with your customers. They won't feel like you are out to fleece them, and are more likely to buy from you again if they're not stung for postage on returns.

Smarta in five

1 Your customers should be integral to every business decision

2 People buy people first – stay personal

3 Treat people as individuals

4 Make sure you're always listening

5 Deliver tailored solutions

2.7
Keep bottom-line a top priority

"Stocks go up and down. Someone might say to me, 'You're £20m richer today than yesterday' and I'd say, 'Yes, but I'm going to be £20m poorer tomorrow'. As long as the profit is going in the right direction, the share price will take care of itself."

—Simon Nixon, MoneySupermarket

"Profit is sanity. That's all there is to it."

—Theo Paphitis, *Dragons' Den* and Ryman

"You have to know, when all hell breaks loose, who pays the PAYE bill. Who's the banker of last resort? You've got to constantly be planning. Be paranoid."

—Julie Meyer, Ariadne Capital

For all the rapid change we've seen the economy and business landscape undergo in recent years, in tandem there's been a somewhat comforting reconfirmation of some of the more traditional business values. If the renewed call for face-to-face customer service acts as a reminder that technology and efficiency of scale don't provide all the answers, a return to focusing on bottom-line profit is perhaps a lesson more from the businesses swallowed up and spat out by this recession.

The smartest companies setting up and growing now are profit focused from day one. That doesn't mean they're profitable from day one, but from the onset they have a clear vision of how they'll make a profit and have plotted out when they'll break even.

You can't afford not to think this way. The big exits based on web stats only and no sign of a revenue stream let alone a break even disappeared when the venture capitalists packed their money away and decided to batten down the hatchets for the foreseeable future.

Focus on profit shouldn't be seen as a sign of the times, though – it's a fundamental rule of business that every company and its founder should be addressing right from the moment an idea pops into their head. If you don't have a clear map or plan to follow and no measure of how productive or successful you've been, you'll be hugely ramping up the risk involved in your venture and limiting your control over the future of your business.

Smart businesses realize that while they're not making profit they'll always be beholden to someone else. If you're not making a profit, you're relying on your bank, your family, your investors, your VCs, your equity. You have to make a profit in order to be free and truly in control of your destiny. And, even more obvious, you have to make a profit to make money – which should be the goal of every business and something we're assuming you're going to need in order to pay yourself.

> **" Decisions shouldn't be governed by profit, but profit should always play a role in the decision-making process "**

Smart businesses accept that it's almost impossible to predict how long it'll take to break even, but they're focused on one answer: as soon as possible. What is more, they have a clear, plotted, charted route to profitability – even if it's three years down the road, there's a clear roadmap of how they'll get there based on what business they'll be doing. It might not be 100% fireproof, but it's realistic and viable.

It's not always as simple as chasing any and all revenues. That can't drive you to profit – and smart businesses realize that. You have to balance all spending decisions by assessing how much money something can bring into the business against potentially how much it can hold back growth and more lucrative or rewarding future incomes – and there's a fine balance between the two. Smart businesses strike that balance. Often it's about effective timing, for example at which point the business's cashflow can take on moving to the new offices it needs to expand without lumbering it with an overhead it can't yet sustain.

Decisions shouldn't be governed by profit, but profit should always play a role in the decision-making process.

Smart businesses look at ways to reduce and control their fixed overheads to stay profitable and keep their cashflow positive. A smart business will look at how many of its key functions and fixed overheads can be outsourced and freelanced. That's not just about people, it's about the offices, space, hosting. Doing this allows a smart business to scale as it grows, as opposed to the past when you had to invest heavily up front to undergo a period of growth.

www

Get your accounts in shape with an online accounting software package: www.smarta. com/business-builder

The key to profit is looking after cashflow – and the key to that is attention to detail, organization and putting in place a big, loud warning system when action is needed (and acting when the alarm goes off). For more on managing your cashflow, go to Chapter 5.2.

Growth can be a challenge as much as an opportunity, and smart businesses know to keep just as close an eye on the bottom line when the work is flowing in as when it's not. Smart businesses turn down work. It might be one of the big no-nos of working for yourself, but really, there is a time when you should turn down work. If you don't have the resources to complete the job, then not only do you stand a fairly good chance of disappointing the client, you also run the serious risk of overtrading, one of the stupidest yet incredibly common ways good businesses end up going bust. Overtrading is just as big a killer as undertrading.

> ❝ *Overtrading is just as big a killer as undertrading* ❞

Overstretch yourself and then find that fulfilment of an order takes longer or costs more than you expect, and it doesn't take much for your cashflow to become strained as a small company. Either limit the risk by working for part-advance payment or look to secure credit off the order with suppliers and possibly try to share the workload with another company if you're adamant you can't turn away the business. However you choose to manage it, secure yourself by keeping some working capital alive for unexpected delays in payment or costs you haven't foreseen.

Overtrading Taking on more work than you have the resources to fulfil. Often a result of unforeseen (or unprepared-for circumstances) such as late payment or the need for new machinery.

Smart companies are honest with clients. Let them know immediately if you can't take on a piece of work; they'll appreciate you'd rather not take their money than do a job badly or late. Plus they'll see you're in demand and leave with a positive impression for future deals, where you might even have the ability to negotiate a higher price for them to secure your time.

> **Smart businesses are fiercely protective of their margins and don't sacrifice them no matter how big the apparent opportunity**

It's all too easy to focus on growing revenues when you're establishing a business, but it really does stand for nothing if you never see a clear margin on all your hard work. Whether they're run by money people or not, smart businesses are fiercely protective of their margins and don't sacrifice them no matter how big the apparent opportunity. If an opportunity is one where you lose money not make it, then it's not a business opportunity – simple as that.

Bottom line The decisive last line of your accounts sheet which reveals a business's real state of profit or loss. The true success or failure of a sale is only known when you see the difference it makes to the company's bottom line.

Smarta in Action: The Pure Package

Founder: Jennifer Irvine
Company: The Pure Package
Company profile: Based on the principles of the 'perfectly balanced diet' and portion control, The Pure Package is the leading UK Company of its type to offer freshly prepared, ethically sourced and convenient meals direct to your door.
Founded: 2003

Overview
When Jennifer Irvine came up with the concept for a service that would deliver freshly prepared, ethically sourced, nutritionally balanced meals straight to your door, she knew she was on to a winner – but the idea of standing up in front of a bank or a panel of investors made her nervous. 'I knew that they would ask really reasonable questions like "What do you expect your sales to be?" and I'd have to make up the answers,' she explains. Instead, Irvine knew she'd have to make a profit and reinvest it – fast.

How she did it

Irvine realized the best way to make a profit was to get the money up front, so that's what she did, asking her clients to pay in advance for 10 days' worth of food, which was about £300 a go – and she put this money straight into the business.

Using this method of cashflow management, Irvine was able to expand the business to the point where she could move it out of her house. The only problem was, she wasn't yet at the stage where she could afford premises. To resolve this, Irvine gave her clients an offer they couldn't refuse: 90 days' worth of food at a slightly discounted price, netting her £3,000 per customer. 'Not only did I get premises, but I also bought a huge oven you could fit five men into,' she says.

Tips

Managing cashflow can be challenging, but it is possible. Don't be afraid to ask your customers to pay up front. If you're struggling with cashflow, or you'd like a profit to reinvest into the business, it's one of the easiest ways to do it. Equally, though, always make sure you can deliver – or you could end up owing money you can't pay back.

Smarta in five

1 It's a cliché for a reason: 'Turnover is vanity, profit is sanity'

2 Focus on how you'll make profit from day one

3 Plot your break even and measure your progress

4 Avoid overtrading

5 Get organized and protect your margins

2.8
Open in the right place, at the right time

"We run a system where we can get to customers' houses within an hour and sometimes within 10 minutes. That's really where we specialize. I think one of the danger points of businesses is, you know, they want to be all over the place, but there's enough people in the areas you live in."

—Charlie Mullins, Pimlico Plumbers

"Wonga is in some ways like a black cab in London: it's a hugely convenient service, it's really fast, and it serves a short-term need for people from time to time. We're not trying to make this a lifetime habit for people. This isn't the tube in the transport analogy. This is a different kind of product. It's not about being inexpensive, it's about providing a great service that customers really like and feel like it's good value for money."

—Errol Damelin, Wonga

Surely just being open or available to deal with your customers in a place and at a time that's preferable to them doesn't make a business that smart, right? Wrong. It might be the simplest of principles, but being in the right place at the right time is one of the key differences between those truly smart businesses making serious money with the most basic of propositions, and often really dumb companies who have brilliant concepts but don't put them in front of customers' noses when and where they need them.

Let's start with retail. The vast majority of small, independent retailers in the UK open from roughly 9.30 a.m. to 5.30 p.m., yet most people work during these hours. As a nation we're working longer hours and have less time to shop, yet most small shops aren't staying open longer or at different times to accommodate us. Is it any wonder we shop online in the evening instead?

It's not just shops, either. Try getting a haircut after 7 p.m. or on a Sunday and it's more difficult than it should be. Butchers have been hit hard by the expansion of supermarkets, yet how many open on Sundays on the very day the majority of people in the UK are most likely to cook a meal?

When we pop out to buy our lunch in most city or town centres, we are presented with an array of wholesome and healthy food to take back to the office, yet come the evening and what can I get to take away? Not much beyond fast food, fish 'n' chips, Chinese or Indian. On days when we have our cars at a local garage or need the services of a tradesperson or something delivered, why do we have to arrange to arrive to work late, leave early, work at home or pay extra to have it delivered at the weekend?

The smart businesses sniff out such problems as opportunities to gain competitive advantage over their competitors with less vision. They see that it makes sense to be open when their customers need them to be. They analyse their hours of activity, experiment with opening later or earlier and trade between their optimum hours.

> **"Smart businesses see that it makes sense to be open when their customers need them to be"**

For some that's where the problem lies. Either the business's optimum hours lie outside what the owner is comfortable working or the answer to maximizing income is actually just to be open longer.

Clearly it's not possible for one person or a micro-business with just one or two staff to operate a physical business 24/7. And closer to the truth, working a 15- or 18-hour day, seven days a week isn't why most people decide to start their own business.

> **"The easier and savvier approach is to think creatively about how you can stay open longer"**

The smart businesses realize there are ways around flogging yourself for the extra income or working the hours you want to break even – the easier and savvier approach is to think creatively about how you can stay open longer. Perhaps open only during peak hours and shut up shop in the dead time between 10–12 and 2–5? The more obvious answer is to employ people to manage the shop at different times. It takes trust, the willingness to delegate and let go of being in constant control and also some serious financial management to ensure the reward warrants the investment, but perhaps being open longer could generate the extra revenues you'd only anticipated hitting by opening a second store – and it would be at far less risk.

The other way involves taking even less financial risk and that's to collaborate with someone complementary who could use the space when you're not. Perhaps a hairdresser could collaborate with a freelance stylist, who they think is good and has been tried and tested, to rent the salon out for a day on Sundays.

It's not just about when you're open, it's also where. There's a company we can learn from here that Smarta would never usually herald: the kebab shop. Kebab shops succeed in selling a product to people who wouldn't normally, in their right mind, desire or purchase their product. Yet by positioning themselves next to pubs, clubs, train stations, bus stops and taxi ranks, they succeed in selling what people don't want. Of course, the human propensity for fat and salt after alcohol contributes significantly here, but you see the logic.

Smart businesses realize that making life easy for their customers is a compelling USP (unique selling point). Victoria Jackson left a career in recruitment to set up her own firm, but how was she going to differentiate herself in a massively crowded marketplace? Easy: she's turning her inability to afford an office to her advantage by providing a highly personalized service, visiting candidates at locations and times that suit them, even if that's at their homes in the evening or at cafés near their current workplace during their lunchtimes. Why? Because nobody else is doing it and already people are telling her they wouldn't have bothered getting in touch if her hours were the standard 9 to 5.

Online businesses aren't excluded from this chapter, either. Even if your customers can buy from you 24/7, can they contact you 24/7? Do you do anything to combat their frustration if they can't? Do you send them a message saying 'Sorry, we only answer calls between 7 a.m. and 7 p.m. but let us know when is good and we'll call you back'? Do you direct them somewhere they can get help in the meantime?

Smart businesses have accepted that 9 to 5 is dead, that people don't work it any more and they don't run their businesses around it. If you want people's money you have to be open when and where they want to spend it, not just when you want to take it.

Smarta in Action: 5M Coffee Company

Founder: Glenn Watson
Company: 5M Coffee Company
Company profile: A coffee consultancy company that helps people improve their coffee knowledge and produce café-style coffee at home, and also provides training for cafés.
Founded: 2008

Overview

5M has two clear markets. The first, self-styled baristas for whom haute coffee is an interest pursued strictly in their free time, all tend to be hard-working individuals working 9 to 5, if not later. Those in the second, actual cafés, are always frantically busy during the day. That means Watson has to work outside 9 to 5 to win their custom.

How he does it

Watson visits the people pursuing coffee making as an interest in their own homes at weekends and in the evenings, providing training using their own coffee machines. This has a double advantage for the client: 'If they need follow-up help on the phone, we know what kind of machine they have so can tailor advice for them.' Watson says that if he operated in normal working hours, 'the home user market just wouldn't be accessible'.

He visits his second group of customers, actual cafés, early morning or late evening when they'd usually be closed. Again, he visits them. 'This means they get much better quality of training because they're not constantly focused on the next customers about to come in.'

The out-of-hours service and home/on-premises visits work to Watson's favour too – and not just because they earn him more sales. He doesn't need to rent premises or buy coffee machines, keeping overheads to a bare minimum. And he loves the fact he can try new coffees his customers have discovered.

Watson also gets to massively increase his income by doing a full-time job during the hours his business doesn't operate. If a client wants a daytime appointment he simply refers them to a competitor – 'it's a very sharing and friendly industry'.

Tips

Operating outside normal hours and locations doesn't have to cost you extra. Structure your business cleverly and it could actually make you massive savings.

Smarta in five

1 Most people work during normal opening hours

2 Analyse when your optimum hours are and be open then

3 Collaborate to be open longer without working harder

4 Be where your customers won't be able to resist you

5 Make life easy for people

2.9
Make a big deal of the small things

> "I set up SuperJam Tea Parties about a year ago. We run tea parties for elderly people in community centres, schools, workplaces and even just people's homes, with free tea and scones. In the past year, we've had about 120 parties, the biggest ones we had up to 500 guests."
>
> **—Fraser Doherty, SuperJam**

> "Rather than trying to reduce the price, we have increased the quality of service. We now employ better engineers, we make sure their training is more up to date, and we make sure they can get to their jobs quicker, with a tracking system fitted to the vans. What we've done is improve this service, giving more value for money."
>
> **—Charlie Mullins, Pimlico Plumbers**

> "Our stores have feeding areas, they have customer toilets, some have fresh flowers and they all have a white shop fit which has to be kept clean. I'm afraid I do walk around stores and check for dust, because if they're not kept clean, a customer with a new-born baby won't want to spend time in our stores. Attention to detail is part of our brand."
>
> **—Laura Tenison, JoJo Maman Bébé**

Smart businesses make a big impact by doing the small things other businesses don't bother with. They go that little bit further to exceed their customers' expectations and leave a lasting memory.

> *Every decent company takes care of the big things – but only the smart ones take care of the big things and the small things*

Every decent company takes care of the big things – but only the smart ones take care of the big things *and* the small things. You have to do all the big things just to be as good as everyone else, and there's little room and fewer ways to prove you're better. But if you take care of the small details as well, people will sit up and take notice.

What do we mean by small things? It can be any number of things: from extra special customer service, say a post-sale call just to check everything is OK, or maybe a thank-you card for your clients' business.

Ideally it'll be something that adds extra value or shows appreciation or makes that customer feel special; something that makes them feel like an individual who's really appreciated and not just any old punter prepared to pay up. Think of how often you are made to feel that way by large, faceless corporations who communicate through the most efficient, bare minimal and least-human forms of communication. Does it leave you glad that you've given them your business or keen to repeat the experience? Probably not.

Getting the small things right is about making people feel like people and not just customers. Here Smarta founder Shaa Wasmund – and co-author of this book, of course – insists we give a big shout out to her local café Windy Stores, in sunny Whitstable. Why? Because owner Tony goes the extra mile for Shaa by remembering her name, taking the time to chat to her and her son Jett and ensuring he's always got goat's milk in the fridge, even though she's the only person who ever drinks it and she might not be in for over a week if she's up in London.

Would a big business do that? Of course not. Would an accountant or bank manager question that decision when looking at the accounts and stock control of a small business? Possibly, yes, but a smart owner of that business, like Tony, would override them because they'd see the bigger picture.

The bigger picture is that Shaa bores the hind legs off anyone who's visiting within a 100-square-mile radius of Whitstable (and now the whole of the UK) that

Tony is the nicest man in the town and runs the amazing Windy Stores, which is the must-visit destination when you're hungry or hankering after a coffee over the papers or a chat with the locals. Or all three.

The small details don't work in your accounts all the time or immediately, but smart business owners realize the value of looking after customers – especially those most likely to keep coming back and telling the world about your generosity – and make them feel loved.

It's not just micro-businesses and one-on-one relationships that can make their customers feel special with something extra. Think of the small things as the 'would likes' or 'nice to haves', not the 'must haves'. When we buy a television the 'must-haves' are that it arrives in one piece, it works and there's nothing missing. Really, that's how little we've come to expect, isn't it?

Imagine then if, for a small or even no extra charge, the delivery person also made sure the television was all set up, working, linked to your DVD and satellite box, asked you if there was anything else he or she could help with or if you needed to dispose of your old set, and gave you a copy of the *TV Times* as a gesture of appreciation for shopping with the company.

That's getting the small things right, and what would the cost be to the business? Not a lot. Indeed, *TV Times* would probably appreciate the extra circulation and exposure and give you copies for free in exchange for a shout out in the PR you do around your amazing customer service.

Smart companies understand the value in return sales and focus on building customer loyalty, not merely securing the one-off transaction.

> **WWW**
> See a video interview with the Firebox founders: www.smarta.com/firebox

Firebox, the gadget and toys website set up by Michael Smith and Tom Boardman, is a prime example of a company continually looking for cool ways to engage with their customers above and beyond simply making a sale.

They've always put sweets in with orders and a couple of Christmases ago they offered free 'bloke wrapping' (you know, cheap paper, whole rolls of sellotape), which proved a novel way of giving people something extra, getting some nice PR at their busiest time of the year and ensuring plenty of people were telling their friends about the funny 'extra' service they got at Firebox.

At Dreams beds, started by Mike Clare, he made sure that all the delivery people took slippers with them so they didn't walk dirt into people's houses, and offered old bed disposal as standard, free of charge. As a result, Dreams became known for its customer service and won numerous awards (and, it's worth noting, sold for a reported £400 million).

Think what extra you can give your customers that will help them feel appreciated and valued, put a smile on their face and make them want not only to tell other people about how great you are but to come back to shop or do business with you again.

> **WWW**
> Watch a video on how Mike Clare grew the Dreams empire: www.smarta.com/dreams

In one respect the extra can be as simple as remembering people's names, recording their dates of birth so you can send them birthday cards, gifts or special discounts, or contacting all your clients to check they're happy and if there's anything else you could be doing for them to make the service you provide even better. Ask yourself how many other providers will bother to do that? How will it look that you're the one who does?

At the other end of the scale, look at your processes and see what you can do as standard which will mark you out from the crowd enough to justify the financial outlay. Smart businesses always overdeliver and you should be looking for ways to get your customers talking positively about you.

Get the big things right as the norm and you compete; get the small things right that others don't even bother with and you start to win.

Smarta in Action: Tatty Devine

Founders: Rosie Wolfenden and Harriet Vine
Company name: Tatty Devine
Company profile: Tatty Devine is a jeweller with a difference. Famous for its bright, inventive jewellery, each piece is proudly made by hand in London under business principles of fairness and fun. Stocked in boutiques around the world, adored by celebrities from Kanye West to Jodie Harsh and regularly featured in the fashion press, Tatty Devine has even been named one of the world's 50 coolest brands by *Dazed & Confused.*
Founded: 1999

Overview
Art students Rosie Wolfenden and Harriet Vine's partnership began the day they found some bags of leather on the ground and decided to make wrist cuffs to sell on Portobello and Spitalfields markets. They later successfully opened the Tatty Devine shop, with a bright, quirky interior which showcased the brand's playful style. When they launched a website in 2006, the pair needed to find a way to make receiving a Tatty Devine product purchased online as exciting as walking into the shop.

How they did it
'We like to make customers smile,' explain Wolfenden and Vine. So they started thinking of ways to do that, and came up with the idea of making their packages experiential.

Instead of a dull, brown envelope, Tatty Devine customers receive a specially designed bubble envelope that looks like a pink sweetie bag. Customers have their order placed in a branded box, wrapped in branded tissue paper, sealed with a branded sticker – and they always get something special, such as a badge, a sticker, a lollipop or a pencil. The company even makes a special ring at Christmas which comes free with orders over £50.

If the customer seems pleasant – if they write a friendly note with their order, for example, or they've gone an extra mile to make an order – they'll get something extra. 'We pack things nicely and include those extras so people are really excited about the whole package, not just the jewellery inside.'

Smarta in five

1 Every business will do the big things right, so it's the small things that matter

2 Make people feel appreciated as an individual, not just another customer

3 Give people something 'extra' they weren't expecting

4 Continually improve your service and not your costs

5 Focus on long-term customers, not one-off transactions

2.10
Keep it real and honest

"At 11:00 at night, if you're privy to it, you will see me getting drunk – and it doesn't make me any more ineffective as a businessperson. It makes me more real."

—Brad Burton, 4Networking

"We always make sure our prices are given before we attend any job, which I think is very important. Yes, we're going to be a profitable company – but what it does mean is that we can send quality engineers. We're not scraping the barrel to get the rubbish that's out there. We pay a good rate and we expect a good engineer. And you'll find that in the plumbing industry, the cheapest is the dearest."

—Charlie Mullins, Pimlico Plumbers

'Real' is one of the most powerful words in business right now and our guess is it's only going to become more important in the mindset of both the consumer and the entrepreneur. Again, social media is partly behind this. Because we now have lines of communication with even the biggest companies and communication systems not just to amplify the good things in business but also to expose the bad, companies are way more accountable than they ever were before.

In the past, big businesses have been able to hide behind the mechanisms of size: the layers of management, a single nameless spokesperson, multimillion-pound advertising campaigns, automated telephone systems and overseas call centres.

Some companies are still hiding behind all that – but they're crazy to do so. The smart companies realize that the consumers' expectations have changed. They now expect not just to receive a product or service in exchange for their money, but they want to know how that company operates ethically and environmentally, they have increasingly high customer service demands and if something goes wrong they expect immediate explanations and action.

And why shouldn't they? The fortunate truth is that small businesses have little choice but to embrace honesty. They don't have the large-company paraphernalia to hide behind and should instead be embracing transparency and making it part of their brand, message and identity.

> **Small businesses should be embracing transparency and making it part of their brand, message and identity**

Smart businesses don't hide from their customers, they put them at the centre of everything they do and build their companies around them. They're true to what they do. They ask people what they want and, just as crucially, what they don't want and the company isn't doing well, and they deliver the solutions.

Smart businesses don't fake it. They don't tell clients they can deliver results 100% better than they really can and deal with the consequences once the paperwork is signed. They offer value because they know that if they do that

> **Smart businesses don't fake it**

that customer will return with more business and recommend them to others.

Smart businesses don't fake who they are and what their products are. If they market and price themselves as a premium proposition, then that's what they seek to provide. Likewise, if a smart business's model is to sell high units at low costs, then that's what they charge. If they claim to be organic, ethical or green, they're authentic in their claims.

They also market themselves authentically. And when they're using social media and claiming it's the MD speaking, they make sure it's the MD not an intern, a PR agency or a so-called social media expert on a conversion rate.

Why do they do this? Because smart businesses realize that they're accountable and that if they try to fake it, sooner or later they'll be found out and any trust they had with their customer base – and trust is everything – will be eroded.

Innocent Drinks is possibly the most celebrated company of recent years for its transparency from top to bottom of the business, from the branding and messaging in its bottles to detailed accounts of the production of its products, to the way it makes itself accessible to its customers by offering them the possibility of popping in and saying hello or ringing the 'banana phone' at any point to speak to a real person.

Now majority owned by Coca-Cola, the Innocent brand appears to have made the transfer from independent company to being part of a multinational corporation by being honest at all times with its customers.

Even in a business where there's not a natural emotional attachment or the product isn't essentially 'good' and PR friendly, it still pays to be honest and real – especially as a small business. It's a well-used maxim and we make no apology for repeating it, because 'people do buy people first'. And that's never been more true. Put your people at the forefront of your business and, provided that they share your passion and vision, they'll be able to pass that enthusiasm on to your customers better than any marketing message.

> **"If you mess up, then fess up"**

The other time smart companies score by being honest is at times of adversity and difficulty. Again, if you mess up, then fess up. As we said earlier, everybody makes mistakes and so everyone appreciates that companies will mess up. So apologize and put right the wrongs quickly and appropriately. Never try to hide, gloss over or shift responsibility. The minute anyone finds out the truth, which they will, the initial mistake will pale into insignificance compared to the reputational damage you'll then have on your hands.

The smartest businesses are also honest with all their investors, suppliers and customers, no matter how desperate the situation. Honesty leverages understanding, trust, belief in the founders and the business and a willingness to help out when times

> **"Honesty leverages understanding, trust, belief in the founders and the business and a willingness to help out when times are hard"**

are hard or you're in need of special favours. Dishonesty leads to suspicion and, at times, overreaction when you least need it.

Smart businesses thrive by harbouring trust in all their business relationships. You'll never be trusted unless you're being honest.

Smarta in Action: Go Ape

Founder: Tristram Mayhew
Company: Go Ape
Company profile: Grab some friends for an exhilarating day out swinging through the trees and flying along zip wires.
Founded: 2002

Overview

When Tristram Mayhew started Go Ape in 2002, he knew he wanted his business to exceed customers' expectations. 'I wanted them to come out with a "wow" experience, because word of mouth is by far and away the best marketing tool,' says Mayhew. To implement the best possible customer service, he needed to find a way to measure the level of service his staff were providing and ensure customers' experiences were as good as they could possibly be.

How he did it

Mayhew realized that being transparent with his customers was the best way to gain their trust. To find out what his customers thought of their experiences, he sent them a customer feedback form. 'Whenever anyone comes, we send an automatic response the next working day saying, "Thanks for coming, we really hope you had a great time – but if you didn't, we'd really like to hear from you."'

When a customer gives a bad review, Mayhew says he phones the customer himself to find why they gave that review, and apologizes if it's the company's fault. 'I think it's quite powerful when it comes to building the brand. I take it personally if something goes wrong. If you have a problem and the Chief Gorilla rings you up, I think you can assume either he spends a lot of time on the phone or it doesn't happen very often.' With more than 550,000 customers a year, it's probably safe to assume the latter.

Tips

While building an interactive, branded customer feedback survey did cost Mayhew around £7,500, you can build a feedback survey relatively cheaply using a tool such as SurveyMonkey.com. For Mayhew, whose business is heavily reliant on customer recommendations, getting the best possible level of customer service was crucial.

Smarta in five

1 If you're not real, social media will expose you

2 Embrace authenticity and make it part of your identity

3 Treat customers with intelligence and respect

4 Be transparent when you mess up

5 Being honest with investors, suppliers and partners buys you trust and flexibility when you need it

Part 3
What smart
people do

3.1
Realise there's only one Theo Paphitis

"When we set the business up, I was pregnant with our first child. We registered the company the day our first daughter was born. It was absolutely chaotic."
—Laura Westwood, Magic Whiteboard

"I was given a sabbatical for six months, but I wanted to start a business. I bought some designer briefcases and sold them on eBay for a bit of a profit. I was quite impressed with the huge audience eBay generates – so I started composing a business plan."
—Bradley McLoughlin, Trading4U

"It is a risk – but I'm passionate about it. If I wasn't, I wouldn't put as much energy into it or be as dedicated. The end result wouldn't be the same."
—Lindsay Drabwell, DaisychainBaby

There is, indeed, only one Theo Paphitis, celebrated serial entrepreneur, star and biggest investor of BBC's *Dragons' Den* and, of course, Smarta board member. Theo's turned around and grown numerous businesses such as La Senza, Ryman the Stationer, Contessa and more recently Red Letter Days. Today these firms are market-leading successes.

Born in Cyprus, he emigrated to the UK aged 6 and by the time he was 16 was working as a tea boy and filing accounts at a Lloyd's of London insurance broker. While Theo rejects the 'rags-to-riches' tag in preference of 'boy-done-good', his story is every bit that of the self-made millionaire, serial entrepreneur.

He lives the lifestyle too, with a three-acre gated Surrey estate complete with indoor swimming pool and private gym. He's owned the football club he supports, has a £1-million collection of cars including a £300,000 Maybach and a chauffeur to drive them, and a yacht in the Med. Theo is a fixture in *The Sunday Times* Rich List and with a burning passion to keep on succeeding, he's a true entrepreneurial heavyweight. Theo's an inspiration to anyone starting out in business. He joined the Smarta board primarily because he shared our vision of mining the wealth of experience he and other big-name entrepreneurs have garnered and making it freely available for others to learn from.

However, while they don't come smarter than the likes of Theo Paphitis and some of the other high-profile entrepreneurs featured on the Smarta website and in this book, it would be wrong for us to pretend that to start and run a really smart business you have in some way to emulate Theo and Co.'s spectacular achievements.

It's easy to look at the successful entrepreneurs and, while being inspired, develop an insecurity complex about whether you've really got what it takes and end up less, not more, likely to take the plunge and start a business.

The truth is that there are thousands of really smart business people you've never heard of who are happily living fulfilled and energized lives controlling their own destinies by making their business dreams a reality.

Whether or not you end up enjoying similar trappings of wealth to Theo and the top table of entrepreneurs is actually immaterial; it's highly unlikely that's what motivated them or will motivate you now. Ask him and, while rightly unapologetic about enjoying the trappings of his wealth, Theo will tell you it was a desire to succeed in business which drove and continues to drive him and that the luxuries are merely welcome by-products of his work.

He might enjoy a celebrity status and lifestyle now, but 30 years ago Theo Paphitis was just like you: someone looking to better themselves by starting a business. He had no magical powers and, equally, he was certainly a successful business person before he hit our television screens.

So if a smart business person doesn't necessarily look like Theo Paphitis, what do they look like? If that question can be answered – which is doubtful – it's simply that smart business people don't have to look like anything or anyone. So there's a chance they look like *you*.

Forget any notion that you need to be born an entrepreneur. The idea that there's some kind of gene you're born with has been exhaustively addressed by some of the world's greatest thinkers. Bar the future scientific discovery of entrepreneurial DNA, it's likely to continue to rumble on with the same dissatisfaction and lack of a conclusion.

Far more scientific seems to be the proof that absolutely anyone of any demographic can build a successful business. That's not to say they will, of course, and it would be naive to assume that those in business don't face the same socio-economic and class constraints that govern any other career. But if you want it badly enough, you can have it.

Smart business people don't look any particular way. They don't have a minimum amount of money in their bank accounts, they don't necessarily have big cars let alone yachts, they probably don't even travel first class on the train. They're not necessarily ladies who lunch, members of the local golf club or pin-striped fat cats.

They don't run a particular type of business either. They're not necessarily the leaders of industry or web wizards blazing a trail. None of these are prerequisites to being a smart business person. Indeed, the entrepreneurs contributing to this book disprove more than they prove in terms of demographic groupings.

Instead, successful business people are best judged by the way they live their lives and how they run their businesses. The smartest business people are those who are doing something they love that improves the quality of their lives – not just the quality of their bank balances – and offers similar satisfaction to both their customers and the people who work for them.

> **Smart business people are best judged by the way they live their lives and how they run their businesses**

The adage 'If you can get paid to do something you love doing, then you'll never work again' was made for running your own business and is something all smart business people subscribe to. Of course it's hard work and painful at times and smart business people are notorious adrenalin junkies who thrive on never resting, but that's because if you're genuinely doing something you love and are passionate about, it will always seem worth the effort. The minute it doesn't, you need to consider how worthwhile what you're doing really is.

> **The adage 'If you can get paid to do something you love doing, then you'll never work again' was made for running your own business**

Smart business people follow their heart and their passion, create working worlds around them and can't wait to get up really early every morning with a smile on their face to get to work.

And it's almost always people who are this enthused about what they're doing who produce brands, products and services that customers love, because it naturally follows that you will do something better if you're passionate and motivated.

It also usually follows that savvy business people only do business in things they love, enjoy or are passionate about and will only work with people they love, enjoy and respect.

If you're looking for smart business people, look for people who were where you are a few years ago. Those who through blood, sweat and tears and no shortage of smart decisions have made the dream happen. You're just as likely to find these people on your high street, at your local networking event or on Smarta as you are by looking to replicate Theo Paphitis – because, much as we love him, he's just one, high-performing example of the many, many smart business people out there whose achievements you're very capable of mirroring.

Smarta in Action: SuperJam

Founder: Fraser Doherty
Company name: SuperJam
Company profile: A range of 100% pure fruit jams sweetened with grape juice and made using super fruits, such as blueberries and cranberries.
Founded: 2002

Overview
Fraser Doherty was no ordinary teenager. When all his friends were sitting in their bedrooms playing video games or worrying over their GCSE subject choices, Doherty decided he wanted to start his own business – at the tender age of just 14.

How he did it
Inspired by his grandmother's jam making, Doherty asked her to teach him the recipe. 'I got really excited about it, so I ran to the supermarket and bought some fruits and sugar and made a few jars of my own,' he says. He began selling jam door to door to neighbours, and at 16 decided to make a go of it as his own business.

Approaching a buyer for a major supermarket may sound daunting, but for 16-year-old Doherty it made perfect sense. During a Waitrose 'Meet the Buyer' day, he had a chance to pitch his idea to one of the supermarket's senior buyers before he had even had a chance to find a manufacturer or build a solid brand for his product. "He thought it was refreshing to see a teenager trying to reinvent something that has been around for hundreds of years," says Doherty. With encouragement from the buyer, Doherty found a manufacturer and worked with an advertising agency on a brand. A year later, and SuperJam was stocked in Waitrose stores across the UK.

Smarta in five

1 Every big-name entrepreneur was once where you are now

2 Absolutely anyone can build a successful business

3 Smart business people don't measure success by the standards of big-name entrepreneurs

4 Only a small percentage of people start businesses to get rich

5 Follow your heart and the career path that will make you happy

3.2
Temper optimism with realism

> "Good innovators have that blind faith in an idea, but at the same time they're realists. This is the difference between an inventor and an innovator. Innovation is not just about the fantastic moment of conception of a great idea, it's seeing that idea through."
>
> **—Matt Kingdon, ?WhatIf!**

> "We were probably a little bit too optimistic in the beginning. At the start, we had a month-by-month cashflow, then it got down to week-by-week. Then there was a coup d'état in Fiji, so I had to sit down with Tui Mali, the chief. He's not a businessman, but he said, 'Look, I know you have to go and find the money otherwise this thing is over.'"
>
> **—Ben Keene, TribeWanted**

Anyone who starts their own business is optimistic by nature. To believe you can make enough people part with enough of their hard-earned cash to support your own living and create a business that survives among 4.3 million others is proof enough. There isn't a business owner out there who doesn't believe in what they're doing. Indeed, it's that enthusiasm and optimism that encourages them to take the risks (see Chapter 3.6) that others don't.

Where statistics and advisers suggest they'll fail, business people believe they'll succeed. That's what drives them on and encourages them to search for opportunity where others dare not look. They seek sales where others don't bother pitching, form part-

> **"Mistakes make us a little more cautious and hone our decision-making skills"**

nerships with individuals others dismiss, and get the discounts, deals and freebies others don't bother asking for.

While they're few and far between now, the happy-go-lucky, Del Boy wheeler-dealer market trader who could sell ice to Eskimos does exist. Those traits of optimism, while represented differently, are alive in plenty more business people busy hustling opportunities every day.

It's fair to say that entrepreneurs tend to begin their business lives top heavy with enthusiasm and optimism. The very act of starting a business breeds confidence, whether through the natural hope of achieving a better standard of living or through a forced determination to prove wrong the people who doubt you've got what it takes or that your business will work.

In a working environment when you have to lead people and make all the decisions – a new experience for many – business people are forced to learn confidence, and so optimism. If you don't feel like that, the need to conform to the alpha duties often sees the owner act boldly anyway.

Optimism can be misplaced, however. You only have to look at shows such as *Dragons' Den* to see the misplaced belief of the many who fiercely believe they've got the next Dyson or Google on their hands and are happy to pump any amount of their precious savings (as well as anyone else's) into their grand plan. You know, the ones who have remortgaged their properties and borrowed to the hilt and will continue to do so despite all rational evidence and five esteemed business people pointing out they don't have a viable business, let alone an investable one.

For those not exposing their zealousness on national television, misplaced optimism usually manifests itself in a series of costly, early mistakes caused by over-stretching themselves trying to do too much too soon, overambitious forecasting, overspending or overtrading. Either that or it leads to a lack of any focused growth because the company's resources are always stretched trying to do too many things instead of one thing really well. Even the best people can naively wander into business opportunities that seem more promising than they actually are and get stung. It happens to everyone and always will; such is life.

It's learning from these mistakes that gradually makes us a little more cautious, hones our decision-making skills and makes us thinking twice next time an opportunity which seems too good to resist comes along. Learn to resist in order to exist. Caution and cynicism are the children of experience and it's only natural we become increasingly risk averse the longer we're in business. As such we take fewer risks, are less creative and become less innovative the more advanced our business gets.

However, canny business people make sure they don't lose that raw entrepreneurial enthusiasm and optimism, because that's the zest that drives them to do whatever it takes to succeed. When realism overrides optimism the business can be left with an unhealthy culture of fear, become too structured, lack adventure or dexterity and be reluctant to do 'whatever it takes'.

This is often seen in entrepreneurs' second businesses which, while not making the same mistakes as their first, also lack vibrancy and originality because the founder no longer has the gumption to experiment and try things out.

Smart business owners understand the value of maintaining healthy doses of both optimism and caution in their decision making. They're neither hopelessly naive in the pursuit of their dreams on day one nor reticent to try out new things and experiment. Indeed, they fight to keep creativity and innovation at the heart of the business.

> **Smart business people keep their impulsive tendencies in check**

These entrepreneurs keep their impulsive tendencies in check, know when to say 'no' and focus on the core business because the risk outweighs the potential reward. Smart business owners also have no qualms about making changes if something isn't working and won't pursue something that's clearly not working simply to protect their egos.

To really succeed, small business owners need to maintain their creative flair and move quickly to take advantage of opportunities that come their way. Optimism is crucial to that – while it needs to be countered by a healthy dose of realism, let it be extinguished completely and you'll lose your edge.

Smarta in Action: Heather Jenkinson Design

Founder: Heather Jenkinson
Company: Heather Jenkinson Design
Company profile: A small interior design business and colour consultancy working with architects and private clients for both commercial and residential projects.
Founded: 2007

Overview

When Heather Jenkinson had been in business for four years, she decided to bring a partner on board to share out the responsibilities.

Having spoken to an experienced business woman who had been in the same situation, Jenkinson realized you can't just go out and find a business partner – they usually find you. So when a young, newly qualified interior designer approached her with a business idea she couldn't believe others weren't exploiting, Jenkinson jumped at the chance without thinking her decision through.

What happened next

After five months of planning, the new designer moved into Jenkinson's studio, but there were immediate warning signs the partnership wasn't going to work. A deal the new partner had secured with her last place of work, a large company, fell through, and her timekeeping was 'embarrassing', says Jenkinson, turning up more than half an hour late every day.

Jenkinson continued to ignore the signs of trouble. 'If I'm honest, I was desperate to have a business partner, so I overlooked the obvious red flags,' she confesses.

The pair planned to redevelop Jenkinson's website, but on the morning of a photo shoot, Jenkinson received a text message from her new partner saying she was pulling out. 'I had spent quite a lot of money on flowers for the shoot, but of course, I immediately saw it would never have worked. I had allowed her access to my supplier and financial files – and in return, she had ripped holes through everything I had worked for over the last four years.'

Tips

'I was so angry with myself for being naive and exposing the bones of my business,' says Jenkinson, but it's easy to get caught up in the optimism of it all, particularly if it's something you've wanted for a while. To prevent this from happening, be cautious: look at the numbers and, if in doubt, get advice from someone with more experience.

Smarta in five

1 If you encourage creativity and positivity you'll see opportunities others aren't looking for

2 Counter your natural optimism with a healthy dose of reality

3 Don't expect others to share or understand your positivity

4 Make sure your optimistic outlook doesn't cloud your judgement

5 Have a positive approach to opportunities but make business decisions

3.3
Stop making excuses and DO IT!

"Everyone, absolutely everyone, doubted we could do it. One guy we talked to from a prospective partner openly belly-laughed in what was the rudest meeting I've ever had. I looked about 12 and we were told we just had no chance."

—Alastair Lukies, Monitise

"The one thing you need as an entrepreneur is drive: why would you want to give up a nice job where you can go home on time and have a nice life? Most of us are products of our own experiences and there's usually something somewhere that gives you the drive to do it."

—Simon Woodroffe, YO! Sushi and YO! Group

"On the plains of hesitation lie the blackened bones of countless millions who at the dawn of victory lay down to rest, and in resting died."

—Mike Clare, Dreams quoting Adlai E Stevenson

> "One thing I learned at a very early stage in my business career was that if you tell me I can't do something, that's like a red rag to a bull, and I'll do what I can to prove you wrong."
>
> **—Imran Hakim, iTeddy**

Smart business people know what they want and they make it happen. They don't talk about it, they do it. If they're unhappy with the life they have, they change it. If they want to become someone else, they become it. They really believe the world is theirs if they want it. This isn't arrogance, it's just belief and recognition that if they want something bad enough and are prepared to work hard enough for it, it'll happen. They might not even know how to make it happen but, as we discussed in the last chapter, they have the optimism and courage to dive in and make a start.

And they're right. After all, every single one of the business people you see featured in this book and on the Smarta website are testaments to that: they've made it happen. Not one of them decided not to bother because the risk was too great or the timing wasn't right. They had the self-belief and the gumption to take the plunge.

If you really want to succeed in business, you've got to stand up and make it happen. If you really want to go into business, why haven't you done it yet? Why do you keep putting it off?

Smart business people don't sit trapped in an unfulfilled career desperate to take control of their own destiny and do nothing about it. They're not the ones who continually tell you they'll start their amazing business. They don't talk about 'one day'; they did it yesterday. They're the ones people point at and say: 'If they can do it, so can I!'

Before you start making excuses about other people not having the same challenges and risks as you, stop. Stop right where you are. You're wrong. Sure, some people have more money than others, some people have more responsibilities than others, and of course, starting a business is a huge,

> **"Before you start making excuses about other people not having the same considerations and risks as you, stop"**

landmark career choice that warrants more than a little consideration, but – and you've really got to accept this if you're going to get ahead – the obstacles you face are no different to anyone else who's taken the plunge.

At some point, if you really do want it, the excuses have to stop. Enough procrastination and time for some doing. Smart business people accept that if they want it bad enough, the reasons holding them back are actually quite lame. Instead, smart business people tackle the obstacles holding them back and turn them to their advantage.

Here are the 10 most common reasons cited for putting off starting up – and why, in the eyes of a smart business person who wants to succeed more than anything, they're actually just lame excuses.

1   I don't have much money

This is the most common reason holding people back from starting businesses, but also possibly the weakest and the one smart business people solve very easily.

Look at it this way: millionaires start businesses all the time and fail; but savvy business people with nothing start businesses all the time and succeed. If you had loads of money you'd only blow it anyway, like most cash-rich start-ups do. Stop complaining and do what increasing numbers of smart business people are doing: start at home, start small and work with what you've got. It might take you longer, but you'll have a stronger business in the end.

2   The bank won't give me any money

Even lamer and not something holding back the smartest business owners right now. Accept it and move on. Start small, prove the bank wrong by generating some sales and watch how it changes its mind in a year's time when you've proved you're a viable business.

3   I literally have *no* money

OK, look, some of the smartest business people running some of the most successful businesses started with nothing. From small acorns they grow great oaks – and the good news is the entrepreneurial earth has never been so fertile. Don't let a lack of money delay you. Start something, start the process in some small way. Inaction will get you nowhere.

If you want to knit and sell jumpers but can't even afford the wool, then start a blog for free and start telling people about these amazing jumpers you're going to make and sell and why they'll be the best jumpers they'll ever have seen. Generate interest and an audience, make yourself an expert on knitting. Do that and you'll become an attractive proposition to someone with money who'll see the business sense in helping you monetize your passion.

4   I don't have time

Smart business people always have time. How? Because they want this more than they want whatever else they're spending their time on. The choice is yours. You can't buy time, so make some. What do you think everyone else running their own business does? They make sacrifices. They give up television. They stop going to the football. They stop socializing so much. If you really want it really, really, really bad, you'll find the time.

Focus on your downtime hours. What do you do between 5 a.m. and 8 a.m. and 9 p.m. and 2 a.m.? Sleep? Read the paper? Watch television? Pick the sacrifice that will make your dream a reality and make it.

5   I'm waiting for a killer idea

Smart business people don't get hung up on the idea myth, they're busy differentiating, improving and executing better ideas that already exist. Don't sit around waiting too long for that killer idea or it might never arrive. You don't need to have invented a sector to be the best business in it –

and the pioneers of new ideas are rarely those that capitalize on them. They know what they're good at, what they're passionate about, what they could do better than anyone else – and they start building it. If it's better, people will buy it.

> **" Pick the sacrifice that will make your dream a reality and make it "**

6   I'm waiting for the economy to improve

Why? Smart business people plan to start great, not mediocre, businesses and there's never a bad time to start a great business. Only average businesses are dependent on outside factors. Smart business people are busy proving and establishing their businesses in challenging economic climates safe in the knowledge that if they can do that, they'll prosper come more affluent times. Microsoft started in a recession, what more reassurance can you want?

7   It's risky giving up my job. What if I fail?

Smart business people pursue what is going to make them most happy, but they look to minimize the risks. Of course quitting your job to start a business is risky: you could fail. There are no assurances you won't. Now we've established that, what are you going to do? Pursue your dream or sit wondering for the rest of your life what might have been?

Take Canadian hockey legend Wayne Gretzky's words as inspiration: 'You'll miss 100% of the shots you never take.' Learn to accept the risk and focus on limiting it with effective planning and by starting small – or better still, as a lot of smart people are doing, by carrying on working for as long as you can until the business has regular income to support you.

8   I don't have the skills or experience

Know what? You're right, you probably don't. But most of the smart business people growing successful companies didn't either – they've had to learn as they've gone along. The truth is that in business you don't know what you don't know until it's too late. Smart business people generally don't worry about what they don't know, they find ways of getting around the situation. If they're not numbers people, they get someone in who is. Smart business people work collaboratively to cover each other's skills gaps.

9   People say it won't work/I'm too old/I'm too young

Smart business people defy their critics because they believe nobody in the world is more passionate about making their business work than them. Of course, they're not

WWW
Start *doing* now, take the first step by visiting www.smarta.com/starting-up

always right and for every business that works, several won't. But if billionaire business angels and VCs struggle to pick out the next big businesses, why waste your time listening to anyone else or even your own self-doubt? Smart business people believe in themselves and prove everyone else wrong.

10   I don't know how where to start

Smart business people don't worry about where to start, they just start. The smartest of the smartest are continually seeking help and taking advantage of the growing amount of free advice and number of tools available to them. They also focus on knowing their business and being the most passionate people in their space – that alone has an intrinsic value.

If you're serious about starting a business and want to take lessons from those who have been there and done it, take just that one idea: they went there and did it. Nike coined the phrase, it's Smarta's mantra, it's more than a little cheesy, but it's nonetheless as relevant as any more carefully phrased business maxim: *just do it*. Smart business people do.

Smarta in Action: The Founder

Founder: Jack Lenox
Company: The Founder
Company profile: The Founder is the independent student newspaper of Royal Holloway, University of London. It was established as an uncensored voice on campus to provide students with news relating to Royal Holloway, hold the powers that be to account and allow the free exchange of ideas and opinions.
Founded: 2006

Overview
When Jack Lenox arrived at Royal Holloway in 2006, he decided he wanted to get involved with the Students' Union magazine, but was disappointed with what was being produced. Having suggested a number of changes to the editorial team, he found he was ignored. Not to be deterred, he decided to set up his own student magazine.

How he did it
Jack says he found setting up the newspaper itself surprisingly simple. Having spent time on the internet, he got quotes from printers and headed into the university's local town, Egham, to scope out the advertising potential of a new student newspaper.

Lenox found a key ally in a local estate agent – who agreed to pay almost £1,000 to advertise in the paper – persuaded some friends to write for him and started laying out the first edition.

When it came to subsequent issues, though, Lenox realized that keeping up the momentum of a weekly newspaper would be challenging. 'I was missing most of my lectures and simply didn't have enough hours in the week,' he says.

Instead of giving up, Lenox restructured his business, moving it to fortnightly and coming up with package deals for advertisers. 'Now The Founder, which is in many ways more of a social enterprise, makes a small profit each year which is reinvested into equipment for the following year's board,' says Lenox.

Tips

Don't be too stubborn about trying to do exactly what you set out to do. Be realistic – if the circumstances don't pan out quite as you expected them to, adapt to fit them. But don't be afraid of being persistent. 'Theo Paphitis himself told me he couldn't see how it makes any money – but I took it as a compliment,' smiles Lenox.

Smarta in five

1 Abandon the notion that a billion-dollar idea will fall from the sky

2 Set the start-up wheels in motion as early as possible

3 Quit your job as late as possible

4 Start small, start part-time, start with a blog, just start!

5 Don't make lame excuses – everyone has obstacles

3.4
Build meaningful relationships

"Meeting people, exchanging stories is great. Creating relationships is what holds businesses together."

—Richard Moross, Moo

"No business is built in isolation. You need a support network of other entrepreneurs who are going through the same kinds of things to pick you up and give you advice."

—Michael Smith, Mind Candy

"When you work for yourself and you're in a box room, you've got no one to talk to, no one to bounce off. Nothing happens in business without people and appointments."

—Brad Burton, 4Networking

Smart business people in today's business world don't network in the old-fashioned sense of shaking hands and swapping business cards, they actively build meaningful relationships. They're obsessed with people. Whether they're interacting face to face at 'networking' events or connecting through online networking sites sites such as Twitter, LinkedIn or Smarta, they're looking for more than a simple contact.

They don't measure their networks by the size of their business card stacks (in fact, more and more of them aren't bothering with cards any more, if they're honest), their follower-to-following ratio on Twitter or the number of people stored in the Microsoft Outlook contacts. They're not interested in merely collecting names to

> **❝Smart business people don't measure their networks by the size of their business card stacks❞**

add to a list of all the other names, they want to get to really get to know people.

Smart business people are obsessively building relationships online with people they haven't met, they're meeting people at networking breakfasts in their area, they're using spare half hours for a catch-up in a coffee shop with someone working in their space, they're chatting on the phone, they're attending events in completely different sectors where they stand out, attract attention and then meet a handful of useful people they wouldn't otherwise have crossed paths with.

They're using social media such as Twitter to find out about people in their space and, crucially, building bonds beyond that simple exchange of essential info that's just raw data – they're digging deeper to get to know the person. They're blurring work and home life and not giving it a second thought. Scary? Not if you're talking about people you genuinely like and trust – and why would you want to do business with people you don't like or trust?

Smart business people are continually doing whatever it takes and using any combination of physical, face-to-face or technological communication to build relationships with people who they think are like-minded and connected to other people they respect.

Why? Because they get the value of working collaboratively with people to achieve more collectively than they can individually. Such a relationship can look like anything. Indeed, it can just be that they have a single shared interest, often even removed from their respective businesses, but by the very nature of being connected, social people, they are at some point in the future able to help each other.

The smart business person gets the number one rule of networking: it's not what someone can do for you, it's what you can do for them. Really. Because that's how collaboration works. But also because it's so rare that you'll walk straight into the person who holds all the answers to the problem you're looking for.

> **❝The No. 1 rule of networking: It's not what someone can do for you, it's what you can do for them❞**

So many business people make this mistake at networking events. You've seen them. They abruptly interrupt your conversation, ask who you are and what you do, then huff with disappointment and shuffle off to the next person. You don't quite fill their bill for a useful contact. That is as it may be, but this same frustrated business person is usually seen sipping wine on their own at the end of the night, mumbling about what a waste of time the evening has been.

WWW

Take a break here and talk to someone real:
www.smarta.com/network

The smart business person went with the expectation of meeting some cool people, getting their business known and maybe being able to help a few people along the way. Funnily enough, while chatting about their shared love of Greece and mutual problems getting planning permission for their respective retail units, they discover that the other person's sister's husband's former business partner is an expert in restoring fire-damaged buildings.

Smart business people realize it's not how many networking events you attend, how many cards you stack up or how many followers you can flatter your ego with, it's the level of connection, engagement and building of quality relationships that is more important, and it's the conversations that come out of those relationships that deliver the ultimate business value.

To become a connected, people person, you need to put yourself out there and do all you can to engage with the people you meet.

Smarta in Action: Huddle

Founders: Andy McLoughlin and Alistair Mitchell
Company: Huddle
Company profile: Huddle is a network of online workspaces that brings together project management software, online collaboration and document sharing.
Founded: 2006

Overview
While many of IT's more stringent evangelists maintain starting a technology business outside Silicon Valley is a fool's game, braver souls have ventured to Europe and found that in fact it's not a bad place to start up. But when Andy McLoughlin and Alistair Mitchell started their online collaboration business Huddle in London, they found one thing missing: networking.

How they did it
Taking time out to have a glass of wine and a chat with a few fellow London tech entrepreneurs during internet conference Le Web in Paris in 2008, Mitchell and McLoughlin realized they only rarely had the opportunity to socialize with their peers in such a relaxed setting. 'I thought, this is absolutely ridiculous,' explains McLoughlin. 'We've had to come to Paris to hang out and have a chat with our mates.'

The pair realized that while London had lots of formal networking events designed to connect entrepreneurs and investors, it lacked a social event where technology entrepreneurs could meet, socialize and collaborate.

The Huddle team knew that if they weren't going to do it, no one else was, and so three months later, networking event DrinkTank was born, and it proved a massive success. 'We came up with a list of people we wanted to invite,' says Mitchell. 'We assumed we'd get 45 people. I think at the first event we had 100.'

Tips

Building relationships with other entrepreneurs is essential to grow your business, so attending networking events like DrinkTank, where you can have an informal chat with other entrepreneurs, can be very helpful. If there isn't an informal networking event around near you, start your own. Venues are often free if you can guarantee a certain expenditure at the bar, and local businesses may be willing to sponsor the event.

Smarta in five

1 Smart people are building networks of powerful contacts to call on

2 Take online contacts into the real world

3 Offer to help people you meet, even if they can't help you

4 Like-minded people are teaming up to solve problems in cheaper and quicker ways

5 Our networks are our support mechanisms

3.5
Work hard, be nice

"When we first started out, one of our prime goals was to create a company that we would want to work at. The kind of place that you'd actually enjoy coming to work at. We'd have nice people, we'd have music playing all day, there'd be table football, we'd have a Nintendo Wii, we'd have a great coffee machine and fruit laid on, we'd give breakfast away, and all that kind of stuff. When you think about the overall cost to a business, putting on these little things is tiny but what it means to the staff is huge, it's massive."

—Andy McLoughlin, Huddle

"Tutting, face-pulling, coming off the phone and saying 'silly so-and-so' – I won't have it. It's an absolute no-no. It's dishonest. It's pretending to be one thing, and behaving in another way – and that's a lesson I have always carried with me."

—Deborah Meaden, *Dragons' Den*

> "We were very busy. We weren't sitting around, flicking through the paper thinking, look at me in that double-page spread in the *Daily Mail*. We were just working hard, talking to airlines, talking to technology partners, recruiting people, getting tickets to customers, trying to sort out terrible cock-ups that there'd been with their tickets being collected – it was normal business stuff."

—Martha Lane Fox, Lastminute.com

Warning: we're about to state the obvious. Starting and running your own business is seriously hard work. As we go on to discuss in Chapter 3.8, you're going to have to make some pretty serious sacrifices. At times you'll work on pure adrenalin and at times you won't even have that to keep you going. But no matter how tired you get, no matter stressed you feel, no matter how much nobody understands the pressure you're under, the one thing you have to do as the leader of your pack and face of your brand is to keep smiling and be nice.

The very notion that this could be a serious business maxim would have been sneered at 25 years ago and dismissed as hippy life coach drivel. There are probably some of you sneering at it now; if you are, you're wrong. Seriously, spectacularly and gloriously wrong. Being nice does matter and it's going to matter even more in the future.

> **" Being nice is a serious business maxim "**

If they ever truly existed, the days are long gone when to succeed in business you had to be ruthless, hard-nosed and rude to people. The outmoded throwbacks to the 1980s who still believe this to be true are quickly becoming dinosaurs, either dying off or being usurped by smarter businesses who'd prefer to work and collaborate with people they can trust.

Smart business people realize that if you're nice in business you get ahead more quickly because you more easily connect and form partnerships with other companies. People who are rude aren't liked and are resented by the people who work for and with them.

You absolutely don't have to be hard-nosed to succeed any more. Indeed, as much as we're seeing developments in technology changing the shape of business for ever, we also seem to be taking a path back to an appreciation of the values of integrity and politeness, and customer service is once again coming to the fore of the consumer's consciousness.

> **" Lose a sale rather than a contact "**

Smart business owners have realized that competing on price alone is a downward spiral with little room to manoeuvre and so are looking for different ways to compete. In turn, if the choice-spoilt consumer is buying on any other criteria than price, they're expecting more and more for electing to spend their money with you.

The simplest, oldest and most powerful way to secure long-term sales is to build relationships and trust with your customer, and the smartest business owners are busy doing that. From high-street stores such as John Lewis who put people right at the core of their strategy to the small business owners who follow up on sales personally to ensure the customer is satisfied, it's all about working hard to go that extra mile and, of course, being nice.

> ❝ *The owner's personality is an integral part of a business's brand* ❞

In many cases and increasingly with the explosion of social media, the owner's or owners' personality is becoming an integral part of a business's brand. The really smart business owners are leveraging that to build a personal bond with customers, or their loyal tribe of followers.

It kind of goes without saying that if you're to have any hope of building such a bond, you need to be nice and quite a bit more. It's not unusual now for the owners of small businesses to have Twitter accounts followed by tens if not hundreds of thousands of people who will message several times a day – and those people will expect a certain degree of engagement.

WWW

Don't believe us that business is based on people supporting each other? Be proved wrong here: www.smarta.com/q+a

Some entrepreneurs merely set up social media accounts, send out some messages and then let incoming messages pour in, but the really smart ones are engaging and replying to as many people who message them as possible, if not all. And they're continually looking to go the extra mile to help make their tribe feel special, valued and appreciated.

It's an old notion that everybody is out to get you and that to succeed you have to walk over everyone else to get there – and it's not true. If you do, you're doing the wrong thing in the wrong business.

Being nice stretches beyond customers and partners as well. As a leader, if make yourself unapproachable and rule by fear, your employees will be far less likely to flag problems or come to you with suggestions or opportunities they spot. It doesn't mean you should be a pushover or blur the boundary between employee and employer, but respect and motivation need to be earned on both sides.

Smart businesses work hard at being nice and being fair. While we wouldn't go as far as to say they reap good karma as a result, they simply connect with more like-minded individuals who want to work with them or for them.

The smartest businesses don't just rely on staying calm in the heat of the moment though, they instil the need to be nice to customers and fair to employees at the heart of their ethics and their business's values. They put being polite, courteous and helpful at the centre of their brand, staff training and assessments and ask customers if that's how they were made to feel. Likewise, they create an environment where staff feel valued, invested in and trusted and which encourages fun and creativity.

They don't just work hard and be nice – they work hard to be nice.

Smarta in Action: SnoozeShade

Founder: Cara Sayer
Company: SnoozeShade
Company profile: The UK's first blackout blind for prams and pushchairs.
Founded: 2009

Overview

Cara Sayer had spent years working in PR, marketing and user experience testing before she started her business, SnoozeShade. Although she had a huge amount of experience on the front end of business – getting the word out, getting customers excited and building brands – the more technical end of building a business was a bit of a mystery. And when it came to pricing her product, Sayer was at a loss.

How she did it

Attending trade shows up and down the country, Sayer found she met people and began to create a network for herself. Chatting to other vendors around her, she began to recommend them to customers who approached her stand.

At one show, Sayer met the organizer of a baby products show, who was also a distributor. He was more experienced in the industry than her, but speaking to him, he confessed he needed help with his website. 'I suggested we do a swap: I spent time looking at what worked on his website and what didn't. It was really, really badly written, so I rewrote bits of it for him.'

Later on, when Sayer was having problems working out how to price her offering, she turned to the same person, who could use his experience as a distributor to tell her how much to charge her retailers. 'I had heard retailers talk about percentages, but I was confused – I was thinking, if they want 41%, I'll give them this price, or if they want 45%, I'll give them that. He sat me down and told me to keep it to round numbers, to give them a certain percentage off if they order over 100 units.

'And that's the same pricing structure I've got to this day.'

Tips

'Be nice to people on the way up,' says Sayer, 'because they're the people you'll meet on the way back down.' Even if it looks like you might not make a sale to someone, it's worth making friends. 'I'd rather lose a sale than a contact,' she adds.

Smarta in five

1 You don't need to be ruthless to get ahead any more

2 Nice people prefer to work with nice people

3 Being nice builds trust, the foundation on which all successful relationships stand

4 Nice people build tribes more easily

5 A fair deal or sale is one both sides will want to do again

3.6
Take calculated risks

"People like to call entrepreneurs risk takers, but that's not the case. They calculate things and then they'll do things. Calculating, what does that mean? Does he add it all up? He does add it all up, but then he does things without any fear of failure – now that's a very special trait. That's confidence."

—Theo Paphitis, *Dragons' Den* and Ryman

"I reckoned we needed about £20,000. The bank said they'd match whatever I got, so I only needed to get to £10,000. I sold my car, borrowed some money on my Barclaycard and remortgaged the house. Everything was on the line – if the business didn't succeed, I'd lose everything."

—Mike Clare, Dreams

—Simon Woodroffe, YO! Sushi and YO! Group

Most people at some point are attracted to the upsides of starting a business, yet they'll never do it. The reasons are numerous, but the overriding one is that they'll simply never be able to satisfy themselves that the reward is worth the risk.

For the average Joe (or Joanna), quitting the comfort of a safe salaried job and putting all their savings into something that has a 70% chance of failure just stink of risks. To normal people, risk is an alien concept which is associated with danger and which they've been conditioned to avoid.

If there's anything which stands business people apart from the rest of society, it's their ability to see opportunity in risk where others see danger. None of the household names littering our high streets would have been established if at some point one individual hadn't taken the decision to turn their back on the easy route of paid employment and take a chance of making their own way in the world.

Before we evangelize too much over the amazing bravery of those who start businesses, let's be clear there's a huge distinction to be made between the opportunist risk taker or chancer and the calculated risk taker.

> **" Smart business people realize the difference between calculated risks and stupid risks "**

Smart business people realize the difference between calculated risks and stupid risks. Stupid risks are where there's far more downside than upside. But a calculated risk is where there is more of an upside than a downside. The rewards seemingly outweigh the risk.

Smart business people believe they will make money or achieve more happiness by taking calculated risks than not risking anything. For normal people that's still a stretch too far, but that's because their fear prevents them exploring the challenge further and trying to turn what looks like danger into a meaningful and controllable decision.

That's how smart people manage risks – by doing everything in their power to make them calculated. Calculated risks are about ensuring you have as much control as possible over the outcome and leveraging the risks you take to your favour. Smart businesses take more calculated risks than your average Joe because they have confidence in the outcome. The reason for that confidence is that because they're smart, they've planned their business properly so they know how they're getting to profitability and when; they know what the current state of their cashflow is; they're always aware of the market and what competitors are up to; and they have a tribe of people they're continually talking to keep abreast of their customers' expectations and sentiment.

When smart businesses take a risk they are confident of something happening because they feel they're the one in control of the outcome. They're not just throwing caution to the wind and taking a blind leap of faith.

They know that in order to win a contract they'll have to add an extra person immediately, but they'll make it a calculated risk by hiring a freelancer not a full-time employee until they know they've won the contract. They think about the risks, they weigh up the options and they do take the risks, but only after building the biggest safety net they can under themselves.

Smart business people know that not all risks can be converted into calculated risks, however. They realize that not all risks are worth taking and when to say no. When too high a percentage of the outcome is outside of their control, they'll walk away no matter how mouth-watering the opportunity.

In turn, they'll never bet the farm. Even if a deal is 99% in their favour, they won't take the 1% risk if they can't stomach the outcome turning against them. Regardless of how much you've tried to cover the risks, any opportunity which risks everything isn't worth it. To a sane mind, a bigger business at the risk of no business at all is a simple equation. Only greed is likely to skew that vision.

> **" Never bet the farm. Any opportunity which risks everything isn't worth it "**

Finally, and we'll explore how to nurture this in Chapter 6.9, smart business owners trust their gut. They understand that fear and intuition are not the same and that if their instinct tells them something isn't right, it probably isn't.

Smarta in Action: ekmPowershop.com

Founder: Antony Chesworth
Company: ekmPowershop.com
Company profile: Enables anyone to build their own easy-to-use online shop.
Founded: 2002

Overview
Having worked as a freelance web designer throughout his student years, Antony Chesworth saw a niche for an easy-to-use online shop system which allowed businesses to build a shop through their internet browser, rather than installing complicated software or paying a web designer thousands of pounds to build a custom one.

But when it came to funding the business, Chesworth found that few people were as passionate about his idea as he was.

How he did it

Without funding, Chesworth had to take a calculated risk. After months of cold calling ekmPowershop only had one customer, and he was faced with a choice between giving up on the business, or ploughing on in the hope of making some money.

Even though various business organizations told him his idea wasn't going to work, Chesworth chose the latter. Surviving on the dole, he began to sign up for credit cards with large limits, which gave him the money he needed to spend on marketing, web hosting and the various pieces of software and hardware he needed to get his business up and running.

Even though he was taking a chance by getting into debt, the risk paid off. Three years later Chesworth had more than 100 customers – and eight years on, the business now processes more than 500 new customers each month.

Tips

Almost every successful entrepreneur has had to take a risk at some point in their business career. So if the numbers add up and you think your idea is going to work, persevere.

Smarta in five

1 Normal people see risk as danger, but entrepreneurs see opportunity

2 Smart business people only take calculated risks

3 Risks become calculated when you can control the majority of the outcomes

4 Never bet the farm

5 A leap of faith isn't a calculated risk, it's a gamble

3.7
Kill negativity, nurture creativity

> "Reawakening creativity in people is hugely important, having a creative space is hugely important, giving people the time to think is hugely important. When we have to brainstorm, we get as many different people from across the company as we can, people who wouldn't normally think they were creative. We have as much of an open opportunity to share thoughts and ideas as we possibly can. Creativity can come from anywhere."
>
> **—Sam Conniff, Livity**

> "The fascinating thing about ideas is you just can't tell if an idea is going to be a good idea or not to begin with. It's a little bit like finding a little green shoot in your garden, and not knowing whether it's a weed or a flower. We have to nurture it, and after a while that little green thing will come up and it will a horrible weed or it'll be a beautiful plant. It's the same with ideas. At the very early stage of innovation, it's absolutely crucial that we are very careful with our ideas – if we ask too many harsh commercial questions too early, the idea will probably die."
>
> **—Matt Kingdon, ?What If!**

"Our engineers want to work for a quality company. They want to stay busy and, you know, we happen to have a nice clientele base that's comfortable to work for. You want to make sure you are drinking at the same teapot. And I think that's one of the things that we do very well at Pimlico."

—Charlie Mullins, Pimlico Plumbing

"We want our people to run our courses entrepreneurially, so we want them to be entrepreneurs. We can't ever say, 'We never want you to leave us' – that's not particularly entrepreneurial. So if somebody says, 'Well, actually I'd really like to be running my own business', we go, 'That's really interesting. Perhaps we can work with that.'"

—Tristram Mayhew, Go Ape

"If you have a curious, proactive, helpful person, that's the best employee in the world. Because no matter what you ask them to do, they'll do their best at it and be friendly and helpful in the process."

—Ryan Carson, Carsonified

Smart business people move quickly to kill all negativity, both their own and other people's. Instead, they encourage positive thoughts, seek positive viewpoints and explore positive outcomes. Not because they don't appreciate the virtues or the need for caution, but because they realize the value of creating a positive and creative working environment.

We're satisfied that in education and in sport, positivity breeds confidence and confidence is almost always attributed to an upturn in performance. Yet we wrap so many business processes in negativity. While business owners and entrepreneurs are often viewed as inspirational, ideas people, they're bombarded by internal and external negativity from the minute they utter the very notion of going into business.

The whole start-up process is steeped in negativity. Almost all business advice comes in the form of caution and we seem to focus as much on dissuading people as encouraging them, let alone assisting them.

If your business idea itself isn't questioned, your business model almost certainly will be, and then there's the economy and the lack of bank lending. Compound this on a personal level with the fear and risk of jacking in a regular income and supporting any dependants and it's a wonder anyone ever takes the plunge.

Smart business people resist this internal and external negativity. Instead of following the first instinct of most people to dissect every reason why an idea won't work, instead they focus on why and how it could.

It's actually harder and scarier to be positive. It's easy to be negative. Pointing out the dangers and pitfalls, considering all the downsides, thinking how to minimize risks and considering resource/time implications makes us feel grown-up, sensible and business-like. Persevering with positivity is harder, much tougher. Going out on a limb and challenging convention and disapproving voices is uncomfortable and often unnerving. It's the rough ride.

It's also how all progress, creativity and innovation are born too, and that's why smart businesses pursue this difficult path and banish negativity in order for positivity and creativity to flourish.

Smart business people surround themselves with positive people and dismiss negativity. But having someone around who's naturally quite sceptical or negative is actually really useful, especially if you're the type of entrepreneur who needs reigning in at times. However, there's a difference between constructive caution and destructive negativity.

"There's a difference between constructive caution and destructive negativity"

It's about striking a balance, of course, but smart business people actively encourage – even force – positivity to be heard and listened to.

Smart people don't hire negative people who confront all new ideas with 'no, but' and 'no, because'. Instead, they recruit people with expansive minds who are intrigued by the possibility of new ways to do things and instead reply 'yes and... And' and look to build on new ideas, not snuff them out.

"Develop ideas, don't dismiss them"

They encourage an atmosphere where anyone can put forward suggestions for the business and where no idea is a stupid idea. Ideas should be developed not dismissed. After all, even the least thought-out half-formed ideas can grow into really powerful concepts.

Smart business people also empower their staff to be creative and resist putting too many processes or too much bureaucracy in place to prevent people acting on what makes sense and is best for the situation or the customer. They seek entrepreneurial staff who thrive on autonomy and take it on themselves not only to fulfil their basic duties but to look at how they could help the company advance, perform better and evolve a superior proposition. The employees they nurture give substance to the term 'intrapreneur' and build a workforce of intrapreneurs with a shared vision, who are continually on the look-out for how their individual roles and the company as a whole could work better.

Smart business owners don't overassess staff and do realize that while targets and performance-related pay make sense in certain roles such as sales and marketing, they can prove prohibitive in more creative positions and environments.

Smart people are quick to move when they're working with someone who's spreading negativity or who always has a negative effect on their working environment.

WWW
Free advice on recruiting positive people:
www.smarta.com/recruitment

Whether it's an employee, director, contact or even a customer, they quickly remove them before the negativity spreads.

Smarta in Action: Carsonified

Founder: Ryan Carson
Company name: Carsonified
Company profile: Carsonified brings the web community together to learn, converse and connect, producing world-class web events to make this happen.
Founded: 2004

Overview
Having moved to the UK from the US in 2001 and worked at various creative agencies, when it came to starting Carsonified Ryan Carson knew that the best way he could build his business would be by bringing in the most exciting, talented and creative people he could find, and nurturing their creativity.

How he did it
To attract the most talented people, Carson did what any employer would do – he made the employment package as attractive as possible. Offering his employees a free MacBook and an iPhone was just the beginning; they are also entitled to 35 days' holiday and, crucially, the whole company has every Friday off.

To sweeten the deal, the Carsonified office is designed to encourage as much creativity as possible. With a giant blackboard and a circle of beanbags, one room is dedicated entirely to creative thinking, with a fridge full of free Innocent smoothies to boost the team's brainpower.

Team integration is essential to the atmosphere at Carsonified, and the entire team meet once a day, at lunchtime, to talk over what's happening in the business. Each day lunch is on the company as well, which means the team have no excuse not to apply their brains to coming up with creative ideas for new conferences or web apps.

Tips
Giving that little bit extra might sound like a large cost to you, but for Carsonified it's worked out for the best. 'We want curious, helpful, proactive people – and if they're happy, no matter what you ask them to do, they'll do their best at it and be friendly and helpful in the process,' explains Carson.

Smarta in five

1 Creativity breeds opportunity

2 If you're creative you find smarter ways to get ahead

3 Negative people kill team spirit

4 Caution is different to negativity

5 If you want to be better and smarter, be creative

3.8
Ditch the TV

"On the days I am working, I start work at 5:20 in the morning and pretty much start work immediately. I do a good 14-hour day, two to three days a week. But my family and my kids actually get the bulk of me. The other four days that are left out of the seven-day week, I am theirs."

—Jennifer Irvine, The Pure Package

"Set your expectations in terms of what you can achieve relatively modestly and overshoot them, rather than having expectations that are too high and being disappointed. Don't underestimate the amount of time it takes to get something off the ground."

—Karen Hanton, Toptable

> "I work five days a week. I send my kids to school and I get to the office very early. I'm very fast. I get a lot done in a day – so when I go home, I like to cut off."

—Millie Kendall, Ruby & Millie

Starting a business might be something anyone can do. There might be more free advice out there than ever before. Technology might be taking the pain and time out of the more laborious tasks of running a business. But let's not kid ourselves, starting or running a business is going to cost you in other ways than money. It's sheer, damn hard work and quite frankly, no matter what we put in this chapter to discourage you, you could easily spend every waking hour making it work.

The smart business owners out there realize that something has to give and they take action to ensure it's the right thing. A smart person doesn't give up their family or stop working hard (both of them just aren't options), a smart person gives up the TV. Or the cinema, or the pub, or football – whatever it is they do in those valuable 'extra' hours.

> **A smart person doesn't give up their family or stop working hard, a smart person gives up the TV**

Whether you've already quit your job and are working on the business full-time or are still in the world of employment, let's assume the normal 9 to 5 is a given. One way or another, you're working.

So, what does that leave? Well, in some respects not a lot, but if you're serious about making your business a success and achieving your dreams then everything from 5 to 9 can actually be highly productive.

Smart people don't give up sleep, it's worth adding. But they do develop a firm understanding of how much sleep they need and, medical daily recommendations aside, we're all different. As a rule, the amount should be enough to keep you charged and efficient, but little enough to ensure you're alert and maximizing those crucial witching hours.

If we assume the average person can get away with six hours' sleep a night, then if you really look for it, there's a decent amount of time after the end of 'normal' work at 5 p.m. and before the start of 'normal' work at 9 a.m. to fit in a good four or five hours' work on the business – and you can do a lot in those hours.

Which hours you spend working is of course completely down to you, but smart business owners are clear in their head about their priorities and set themselves clear periods of time to work – and, more importantly, clear periods they'll spend with their family.

As we've already mentioned, though, this almost always means sacrifices for you and your family. It's fairer all round to plan how you're going to do this and what's going to change so that everyone is clear.

It may be important to you to spend family time between 5 and 9 eating together, talking, helping do the children's homework, whatever family time involves, and so 9 to 12 becomes your time. Or you may find it easier to go to bed earlier and get up at 5 a.m. to cram in a good few hours' work in the quiet of the early morning before the world – and usually the sun – rises.

> **Smart business people come to an agreement with their loved ones and pick the right sacrifices**

Smart business people think out how they're going to make this happen, come to an agreement with their loved ones and pick the right sacrifices, whether it's TV or something else.

But equally, they don't set themselves any hard-and-fast rules about their family and work balance, and they don't beat themselves up on the odd occasion everything doesn't go to plan – which will probably be fairly frequently. After all, are there two things more unpredictable than families or businesses?

Working parents in particular tend to feel guilty about everything. They feel guilty about their work and they feel guilty about their children. They feel guilty that their work is suffering when they're with their kids and that their kids are suffering when they're working.

WWW

Check out Smarta's video interview with time management master and author of *The 4-Hour Work Week* Tim Ferriss: www.smarta.com/tim-ferriss

But that's a hopeless spiral to misery. You please nobody and are continually frustrated. So let your happiness be the judge and stop beating yourself up. If you spend too long at work one day your kids will be fine, provided that overall the balance is right.

The key isn't to have a rigid schedule of what you do and when, it's to appreciate that you can't do *everything* and to prioritize what's truly important to you.

Smarta in Action: Claire Dances

Founder: Claire Novis
Company name: Claire Dances
Company profile: Egyptian-style belly-dance classes and performances.
Founded: 2006

Overview
Ten years after Claire Novis started belly dancing in her spare time, she realized she was so passionate about it, she wanted to make money out of it. She set up Claire Dances, teaching classes, running workshops and performing around the

UK. But passionate as she is about it, Novis knows her belly-dancing business won't pull in enough to keep her afloat, so she juggles it with her 9-to-5 job as a senior geologist at a firm of consulting engineers.

How she did it

Bizarrely, Novis says the two jobs complement each other. 'I love the fact they combine to challenge me intellectually, physically and creatively,' she says – but it does mean she's busy.

To maintain her sanity, Novis sets aside time each week to manage her business. While she gives herself a few hours in the evenings and at weekends, she needs to be able to respond to clients and students quickly, so she uses time that would otherwise be wasted – travelling time, for example – to do a lot of the administration for the business.

The key for Novis is not to neglect either job. 'Professionalism is very important to me in both of my jobs, and it's essential to me that I don't compromise on this.'

Tips

To manage her website and email address, Claire uses remote software. This means she can access emails and make changes to her website wherever she is, as long as there's a computer. 'This is invaluable for managing my business in the time I have available and also keeping my outgoings low,' she explains.

Smarta in five

1 Every business person makes sacrifices: pick the right one for your company and your family

2 Understand your sleeping pattern, then be consistent

3 Make the most of the witching hours

4 Set yourself ground rules but build in flexibility

5 Work hard but don't make yourself unhappy

3.9
Make success personal

"It's important to ask why you are doing this. Decide whether you're going to build a $100m company, or a $10m company – or a company that's just you. A lot of people think they need, in order to be respected, to build a $100m company – and I think that's bullshit."

—Ryan Carson, Carsonified

"In terms of profitability, all my businesses in the southern hemisphere are probably the most successful in the world."

—Darryn Lyons, Big Pictures

"The idea of being a pioneer and revolutionising the diet industry in this country appealed to me."

—Jennifer Irvine, The Pure Package

Smart people don't get hung up on other people's ideas or measurements of success. They understand what success means to them and gear their businesses around fulfilling their personal goals and ambitions. Clearly focused on what they're aiming to achieve, they're a lot more likely to 'succeed' in doing it and tend to get more satisfaction when they do.

Sure, most of us would like to be wealthy and yep, a fair percentage of us wouldn't mind being stinking rich, but very few people start a business with the accumulation of piles of filthy lucre as their chief objective. It's a welcome by-product, but it's not what drives most people and so that alone won't be what would make them happy, either.

The two don't need to be mutually exclusive, of course. But if they're honest, most business owners have more sober reasons for starting up and expectations of what they'll achieve than simply to 'get rich quick'. In reality, especially in the early days, 'success' is quite far removed from financial reward. Establishing the business and paying the bills is usually as close as the two get, in fact.

While they're definitely driven by profit and money motivated, smart business people don't measure their 'success' by material possessions for some time, often until they exit. It's true to an extent that most people have a personal benchmark of what comforts and wealth they expect, but beyond that success is about being happy.

For some being happy is about having that Bentley or Aston Martin on the driveway and there's nothing wrong with that, but the smart business owner is motivated and made happy first and foremost by making their business work, thriving on the excitement that brings.

For others, success is measured very differently. For those who have overcome personal and physical barriers to establish their businesses, simply trading is a success they're proud of. Likewise, entrepreneurship has long provided incomes for those who have found themselves unemployable and for ex-offenders, those made redundant or immigrants who find it hard to find work, simply earning a crust on your own is an enormous achievement.

Starting a business can be a means to an end, a challenge, an addiction, a life goal, the ambition to create a legacy – any number of things. It is these motivations that drive smart business people, not money. Money might be one way of measuring success, but it's rarely representative of personal fulfilment. If it were, why would so many wealthy entrepreneurs who've made their fortunes be champing at the bit to jump back into the action weeks after landing that big exit?

> **"Money is rarely representative of personal fulfilment"**

WWW

Check out Theo Paphitis's 10-step guide to success: www.smarta.com/theo-tips

The smart business owners set personal goals which represent their idea of personal success and focus on achieving them.

Smarta in Action: AnyTackle Sports

Founder: Admir Rusidovic
Company: AnyTackle Sports
Company profile: One of the UK's most popular fishing and sports shops.
Founded: 2007

Overview

When Admir Rusidovic was five years old, he fell in love with fishing. Fast forward 23 years and, stuck behind an overpiled desk in a stuffy IT management company, he realized something profound: he still loved catching fish. So he decided to jack in his career and make money from his hobby instead.

How he did it

Enjoying your hobby and making money from your hobby are two separate things. Because Rusidovic had already had a career in IT, he could bring those skills across to his new venture. His IT know-how allowed him to build a simple website that fulfilled all his business needs, without having to fork out for developers.

Starting a fishing business tested Rusidovic's commitment to the limit, though. At the beginning, it was almost impossible. 'You have to have a passion,' he says. 'I worked non-stop and there were times when I didn't get a penny for it. If I hadn't had the passion, I wouldn't do that.

'Sometimes you work and work and work and you just don't see the end. It's back-breaking. You have to try so hard to keep yourself motivated.'

Tips

Starting a business from your hobby may sound like the easiest thing in the world, but there might be times you feel your passion begin to wane. Stay motivated by taking time off to think about something else and keep the bigger picture in mind. Once you've got your business up and running, you'll have plenty of time to indulge in the more enjoyable aspects of your hobby again.

Smarta in five

1. Business success isn't measured in material items, it's what makes you fulfilled

2. Be clear why you're doing this and what you hope to achieve

3. Smart business people set personal targets and work towards those

4. Have business goals and life goals

5. Don't judge yourself on other people's terms

3.10
Ask for help

"Mentoring can be very useful, because it draws on experience from other people. Usually all I'm doing is asking the right questions. But mentoring can also be dangerous – a mentor's job is not to become a crutch. And it can very easily slip into that."

—Deborah Meaden, *Dragons' Den*

"Mentoring is all about building a relationship. If it's not a great relationship, they could be limiting your performance."

—Will de Lucy, Amplify Trading

"Having seen an entrepreneur work first-hand, it was the catalyst for me to do the same. Lord Sugar was my inspiration."

—Tim Campbell, Bright Ideas Trust

The chief reason that Smarta spends its time going out and collecting the views of as many different business owners and entrepreneurs as we can manage to push our camera in front of is because we realize one simple fact about business: the very best way to learn is from experience.

That is how entrepreneurs have learnt for centuries, either by themselves or by sharing their knowledge with other people.

No matter how many business books or website gurus might try to convince you otherwise, there's no one right way to do anything in business and indeed, most of the time you've got a number of routes open to you.

Having people you can seek advice from and bounce ideas off is absolutely essential, unless you're adamant you'd rather go it completely alone and not benefit from hearing about other people's mistakes and wrong decisions (not something we'd recommend).

Smart people realize that no man (or woman) is an island and are quite comfortable asking for help. Indeed, they are continually looking to build new relationships that broaden their knowledge and the circle of contacts they can draw on.

No matter how smart you are, you're only one person and running a business can be, especially when times are hard, a lonely and isolating experience. Surrounding yourself with a network of like-minded business people and ideally one or two wiser heads who've seen it all before can be enormously reassuring and comforting.

Mentoring is a bit of a buzzword and it's certainly a smart move to team up with a more experienced entrepreneur who's able to pass on tips and their knowledge of growing a business; even better if they've got relevant sector or industry experience.

But mentors can be hard to find and there's no official government matching scheme for mentors and those looking for mentorship. Smart business people are resourceful in proactively seeking out mentors, often putting out the word that they're looking for someone to help among their networking circles, through their accountant or lawyer or by approaching people directly.

> **" Smart business people are resourceful in proactively seeking out mentors "**

Experienced business people are likely to have had similar help along the way themselves – or wished that they had – and you'll find they'll be surprisingly receptive to helping you out if you're clear about why you need their assistance.

Some mentors work free of charge, for some there's a small fee, others take a small stake in the company. It depends entirely on the relationship and the level of interaction, but if you find someone really useful who you respect and value, it can pay to give them some equity even if they don't ask for it, as a sign of your appreciation and their commitment to the business.

Mentors aren't the only way to surround yourself with valuable business advice, though, and in truth there are very few mentoring relationships. Instead, smarter business people build safety nets around them made from relationships with people they can trust.

It might be with a fellow business owner in the same sector or just somebody you've made a connection with, but the more solid personal business relationships you can build, the more people you'll have to turn to in times of need, when you want a second opinion or need fixing up with a favour.

Smart people are always looking for new contacts, whether it's through physical networking or connecting with people across social media. Taking relationships face-to-face can turn contacts into valued friends. But remember, choose your advisors wisely: it's pointless taking advice from someone you can't trust and respect. You won't listen to them.

> **Shout if you need anything**

Even the least sociable smart business people in the world (there are a few) are still learning from other people. If you're stumped, feel boxed into a corner, don't know what to do and don't have anyone to talk to, you can still learn from your fellow entrepreneurs.

WWW

Find a mentor on Smarta.com: www.smarta.com/mentor

Go to Smarta.com and watch one of our thousands of small business videos and discover what 10 entrepreneurs did in your predicament. Read business blogs or any of the million business biographies out there. Ask for help on Smarta or Twitter or LinkedIn.

There have never been so many ways for you to connect with other people and get free business advice. The smart people are embracing that and you should too. There's no longer any excuse for burying your head in the sand. Shout if you need anything, because there's a whole crowd of people ready and willing to lend a hand.

Smarta in Action: DaisychainBaby

Founder: Lindsay Drabwell
Company: DaisychainBaby
Company profile: An eco-friendly online boutique for organic and ethical clothing and gifts for children.
Founded: 2008

Overview
When Lindsay Drabwell started her business in 2008, she had a budget of just £5,000. Once she had paid for her website to be designed, stocked up and covered all the other costs involved with starting a business, there wasn't much left to get the word out about her company.

How she did it
'I hadn't got as far as thinking about PR,' confesses Drabwell now. 'I thought I'd spread the word myself.' But when it came to it, Drabwell realized she would need the help of a professional. Without the budget to spend on a PR agency, though, she had to turn elsewhere, and found help from a friend who ran his own PR company. He guided her through the basics of doing PR, helping her to write

press releases and even accompanying her to interviews to make sure she said the right thing.

For Drabwell, getting a friend involved was easier, because he knew her back story and he knew the company. 'I wouldn't want to consider anyone else now, even if it did get really big,' she explains.

Tips

Starting a business means there will inevitably be times you'll have to turn to friends or family for help. For Lindsay it was easy – her friend never mentioned payment – but for you it may be more difficult. If your friend is offering you a skill they use in their professional lives, they are effectively giving away their service, and simply expecting them to do it for free may devalue them. Always offer to pay what you can – and if you can't, offer to swap skills or give them something else to say thanks, even if it's just offering to babysit for a couple of evenings.

Smarta in five

1 No man is an island – learn to share!

2 Build a team of people you can turn to

3 Listen to people who've been there, done it and understand

4 Smart business people are always asking questions – and giving answers

5 Listen to everyone, then form your own opinion

3.11
Work on the business, not in it

"I'm a person who tends to evaluate businesses first, and then get passionate. It worries me when people think passion is enough to make a business work, because it isn't."

—Deborah Meaden, *Dragons' Den*

"In the beginning, I did all the driving, pretty much all the cooking, answered the phones, did everything. Then I had this quite traumatic step back from the business where I let my team get on with their jobs – and they stepped up to it and I haven't looked back since. It's meant that I've been able to take a much more strategic role and push the company forward."

—Jennifer Irvine, The Pure Package

> "It's really important to have, from the beginning, a fundamental idea of what it is you're trying to do and what it is that's different – to look at the big picture and see if what you're trying to do makes sense or not."
>
> **—Sokratis Papafloratos, TrustedPlaces**

One of the aspects people most look forward to about running their own business is being able to call all the shots, make all the big decisions and shape where the company is going. Then they realize once they're doing everything else how little time there is even to think about future, let alone sculpt it.

Smart business people make space right from the very start to work *on* the business and not *in* it. When you're snowed under with a million tasks to do and every one of them seems urgent, that's no easy thing to do. But if you don't take time out to look at the bigger picture, it's likely your business won't ever move on from first base. If you're making the orders, stocking the shelves, opening up, manning the till, cashing up and dealing with any staff, when will you ever get the time to analyse which stock is selling best, which lines are most profitable, where you can negotiate a better supplier deal and when you could possibly open a second shop?

> *If you don't take time out to look at the bigger picture, your business won't move on from first base*

Smart business people realize that the only way to stop continually fighting fires is to look at how you can move on from the survival situation and grow the company to the stage where it can sustain extra resources, and then free themselves up to use their skills more powerfully.

In many cases, especially early on, nothing can realistically be done to alleviate the strains, so it means working even harder in order that in future you can work smarter, not harder.

For example, a regular plumber will fix your washing machine and spend all his working hours fixing things he can bill his customers for, but smart plumbers will do all of that and then give up all of their time they spend watching television to work out how they can grow the business, when they can subcontract some of the jobs so that they're doing less of the actual work in the business, what job type gives them the greatest profit. You only know that by working on the business and not just in it.

They make a plan and over time they're able to take on extra plumbers, extra work and slowly start to grow the business with more of the owner's time spent on what they're better than the average plumber at: spotting opportunities, promoting their business and securing more work.

In order for you to take a step back and look at where the meaningful opportunities are for your business, you'll need to drag yourself away from the minutiae. Even if you're putting in the extra hours, it can be hard to pull yourself away to focus on the business.

Smart business people force themselves to do the following:

1 They analyse the business to discover where the profitability and inefficiencies are so they know where to focus sales and attention.

2 They spend some timing testing their own service and speaking to customers. Are you really providing as good a service as you think you are?

3 They revisit their business plan, measure their progress and revise targets and goals accordingly.

4 They scrutinize their own time and force themselves to let go and delegate some jobs to other people or, if they don't yet have staff, assess what could be outsourced as projects for freelancers.

5 They set short growth goals and outline actions to help them get there: secure five new contracts, or start marketing activity, for example.

Smart business people who carve out the time to work on their business could just as easily be labelled people who get things done. It's the same as in any office: there will be people who appear to work harder and longer than anyone else, they're the first in and last out, yet when you analyse their actual output and results, there's often someone working a lot smarter by getting just as much if not more done in fewer hours and with less sweat.

It's rarely that the person putting in the hours is trying to pull the wool over anyone's eyes, it's just that they're not working efficiently or aren't as suited to the position as their counterpart.

> **"Smart business people work where it matters and where it makes the biggest difference"**

It's the same with those business owners who get ahead and start growing their businesses: they're not always the ones who work hardest. The smart business people are just working where it matters and where it makes the biggest difference.

If you intend to grow your business you've got to give yourself the breathing room and, more importantly, the thinking time to let it happen. It might be more painful in the short term, but it's the answer to scaling your business in the mid to long term and eventually making life a lot easier.

Smarta in Action: Ruby & Millie

Founder: Millie Kendall
Company: Ruby & Millie
Company profile: A cosmetics brand with personality, available exclusively at Boots.
Founded: 1998

Overview

Having launched Ruby & Millie in 1998, entrepreneur Millie Kendall and her partner Ruby Hammer launched their brand consultancy, Hammer and Kendall, a few years later.

With two businesses and more due to launch shortly, Kendall had to take a step back from the business so she could make the big decisions, allowing her employees to concentrate on the details.

How she did it

Getting a contract with Boots meant that Kendall had to learn to step away from the business early on in her career. 'When it was a baby, and it was just evolving, we needed to be at the forefront. But because it's so big and there are so many people working on it, we're not as involved as we were when it was smaller.'

Kendall is also very emphatic on how she manages her time: 'I work five days a week. I get to the office very early, but I don't like to work late at night and I do not work at the weekends – don't call me on a Saturday or a Sunday. I'm not interested.'

Instead, Kendall makes sure her employees are empowered to make their own decisions. 'I've had a lot of years running businesses with a lot of women underneath me. I keep in very good contact with the girls, but I like to give people a bit of control and a bit of power of their own.'

Tips

Learn to trust your employees and concentrate on the wider picture. Kendall has stringent quality-control measures in place – 'very little leaves the office without my stamp on it' – but she knows that by empowering her employees, she is taking the onus off herself.

Kendall also knows most employee mistakes are reversible. 'Anything that goes wrong can be fixed,' she says.

Smarta in five

1 Make time to take a step back and assess your business's performance

2 Outsource anything non-essential

3 Prioritize what will make you money

4 Limit the time you spend on emails

5 Take a long-term view of short-term problems

3.12
Understand what people want

"You can't force someone into a sell and you can't bore someone into a sell. People come to me in the office to do presentations, and after two or three slides, I stop them and say, 'Just tell me.'"

—Brad Burton, 4Networking

"Are the customers who have been with you longest the most important, or is it those who spend the most?"

—Gavin Dein, Reward

> "When we showed them what we were building, they said, 'That will solve all our problems.' So really, it wasn't a sell – we were answering one of their needs."
>
> ## —Alistair Mitchell, Huddle

If you're going to succeed in business, you have to be able to sell, there's no escaping that. But it really doesn't mean you have to be a silver-tongued negotiator. Smart business owners sell their business in a variety of ways, but chiefly by getting to the very bottom of understanding three things: what their business does for people, why people will want to buy from them and how not to put people off.

> **You have to be able to communicate your vision or you can't expect anyone to share it**

It's true that if you're not a natural sales person you can get someone in to do this for you, but you can't avoid it entirely if you're going to be running the business. Selling isn't just about closing transactions. You need to be selling your business all day, every day, whether it's to customers or suppliers, the bank manager, investors, the press or even your employees. You have to be able to communicate your vision or you can't expect anyone to share it, let alone buy into it.

Smart business people realize that the easiest way to sell anything is to make it good enough that people want to buy it – and of course, if you make a product or service genuinely superior to anything in the marketplace it should sell itself. That said, half the sell for a new business can lie in capturing people's attention for long enough for them to understand it's a superior proposition.

We'll get onto some hot tips for selling and closing sales, but what smart business owners do best before any of this is create an environment where people want to buy.

1   Do your homework

First things first: be sure you're talking to the right person. You might not be able to figure this out until you're in your initial meeting. If someone more senior is mentioned, you know who to call next.

The more you know about your target customer, the better chance you have of understanding what they want – and how you can meet their requirements. Homework allows you to make suggestions that help seal the deal: pointing out you have a warehouse near their biggest retail outlet, for example, which would save them delivery times and costs.

Scrutinize your target's website, ask mutual contacts what they've been up to and swot up on industry news.

2 Build a personal relationship

People buy from people first and we all make decisions based on emotion. If your prospective buyer likes you, they'll find it to harder to squeeze you on payment or terms. And they'll want to do business with you rather than a competitor.

Invite your target to drinks or follow them on social media before the hard sell, and find some common ground.

3 Killer questions

Open the meeting by asking questions, rather than rushing straight into a sales pitch. Find out what your target buyer wants and what they dislike about their current supplier. Pull out the pain and the hurt that the prospect is experiencing and provide them with a solution.

You can then start giving the problem more weight in their mind. Ask them what the long-term effects on their business would be if that problem carried on. Ask them how quickly they'd need it resolved to prevent lasting damage. Sowing seeds of worry and urgency in their mind will help open them up to the solution you're offering, which you can now tailor exactly to their needs, having found out what they want.

4 Make it win–win

The days of trying to completely screw over the person you're doing business with are long gone. These days it's all about reputation. So talking someone into something that's not right for them is a mistake.

Instead, smart business people look to make everyone a winner. It makes your sale a heck of a lot easier if you can prove that your service will help your customer. Plus, you can look forward to a few referrals if your buyer leaves the room feeling good about the deal.

Come prepared with numbers and arguments that show this will be a good move for both of you.

5 Live the dream

Convincing someone your product is brilliant is hard work. You need to come loaded with enthusiasm. You're selling your vision of the business as much as anything.

Know your product inside-out and practise your explanation of its wonders non-stop. Be armed with long and short versions of your pitch, so you can cut yourself short if they're looking bored, or carry on if they're engaged.

A few client testimonials neatly printed out never go astray either, and don't forget to casually drop in the fact you're in talks with other businesses too. There's nothing like a bit of demand to stoke the fire in a buyer's belly.

And go in to the meeting expecting a yes. That optimism is really appealing and will make you shine with confidence.

6 Watch their feet

It's unlikely your target will be 100% honest with you throughout the pitch – they want to keep their cards close to their chest just as much as you do. Grasp the basics of body language and you'll have a much better insight into what they're really thinking.

If someone's interested in what you're saying, they'll make direct eye contact, have a relaxed brow and their feet will be pointing towards you. Their mouth may be slightly upturned at the corners. If they're leaning back with their hands behind their head, they're incredibly relaxed. If they're still, they're pretty much captivated. Good news: you're in.

But you need to back off if you notice someone tapping their fingers or fidgeting, looking around the room, bouncing their legs or with their arms crossed. If their posture or face seems tense, pull back. Ask what they think and give them a chance to talk themselves into a more relaxed state, when they're more likely to be open to your suggestions.

You need to be aware of your own signals too, so your buyer trusts you. Try not to go up at the end of your sentences or nervously half hold your breath – it makes you seem uncertain. Keep your posture as relaxed as possible and don't cross your legs or arms. Nod when they speak to show you understand and aim to keep your voice measured and calm.

Mirror the other person's body language if you can. It builds rapport.

7 Make them think you're a martyr

You want your buyer to feel they're getting a fantastic deal. So create the impression you're making sacrifices for them.

Pitch your price higher than you expect to them to pay, and gradually allow them to bargain you down – but only give ground when they do. Gradually decrease the length of time of the contract or the quantity of what you're selling in sync with the price drop. And make it seem like you're stretching yourself to give them that, adding in the occasional, 'Well, I wouldn't normally, but …' so they feel they have the upper hand.

8 Play good cop, bad cop

You might be the only person in your business, but you can still defer to a higher power when things are getting hairy to give yourself extra leverage. Say you need to consult your accountant or executive board (whether or not you have one).

By telling your target that you'd love to do the deal but you're not sure if your board or accountant would go for it, you stay on their good side but still keep the boundaries you want to, protecting your position.

9 Don't close

Rushing the close of a deal (the bit where you get them to agree final terms) is a huge error.

Always act patiently. Make sure you leave yourself a free window after sales meetings in case things overrun. You can guarantee you'll lose a sale if you have to rush off.

WWW

Insider selling tips for sales pros: www.smarta.com/sales-tips

Everything should be about making your prospect feel like they're buying wisely rather than being sold to. So give them some breathing space if you sense they're feeling suffocated of if things are tense. Say you understand this is a big decision and ask if they'd prefer to meet at a later date, after they've had some thinking time. It shows you empathise and gives the impression you have their best interests at heart.

Stretching things out can also save you if you start feeling out of control. It's far better to do a deal slowly than hurry a deal that leaves you short-changed.

Smarta in Action: 4Networking

Founder: Brad Burton
Company: 4Networking
Company profile: The only truly joined-up UK business network with 200+ vibrant, unstuffy breakfast groups across the nation – making business appointments easy.
Founded: 2006

Overview

When Brad Burton set up 4Networking in 2006, it was during a change in consumer attitudes. Social networking was beginning to empower the consumer. Burton realized that with this business, he would need to do away with the traditional attitude of the super-slick sales person and take advantage of the new levels of honesty brought on by platforms like Twitter.

How he did it

'You can't force someone into a sell any more, and you can't bore them into a sell either,' says Burton. Forcing your way into an appointment with a potential client even through it's clear they won't want to buy no longer cuts it.

'If I sort you with something today that's not appropriate for your business, you're going to go and Tweet about that. I'm actually doing myself a disservice.'

Instead, Burton says you need to find someone who already wants to buy. 'When was the last time you went into Dixons and said, "Excuse me, young man, can you tell me the benefits and features of an iPod?" No. You go, "Can I buy an iPod, mate?" and he says, "Yeah, we've got white, black or red." The sell has happened before you walk in.'

Instead of employing pushy sales people, Burton looks for situations where the sale will be mutually beneficial. 'These days it's about reputation. Talking someone into something that's not right for them is a mistake.'

Tips

The days of slick sales people screwing over those they are doing business with are over. Instead, use your contacts to find people who have a need for your product or service.

Smarta in five

1 Smart sales people understand why people want to buy

2 Make your sell a common-sense buy

3 Strike a fair, win–win deal and you'll sell again

4 Never rush to close a deal

5 Sales talk rarely leads to sales

Part 4
How to build a smart business

4.1
Know what you're doing and why you're doing it

"If you understand what you're going to do before you start doing it, it's going to save you an enormous amount of time."

—John Paleomylites, BeatThatQuote.com

"You believe you have a key to unlock a door, and you're excited by that – it's that creative flow of energy. You can see the Sistine Chapel, you just want to paint it: the rest of it is just execution."

—Julie Meyer, Ariadne Capital

"The first few months were a period of intense research, paperwork and admin. At the same time, designing a plan of how things were going to be done. It was a bit like the big bang – an explosion, a multiplication of things to be done. It was an amazing, buzzy time."

—Richard Moross, Moo

"A new idea starts as complete inertia – it's got no momentum. But by plucking at it, by tweaking at it, you give it momentum. You just have to keep working at it."

—Sahar Hashemi, Coffee Republic

"We realised if we were to be sustainable we needed to have clear goals and objectives and stick with our business plan. That was something we learned early on."

—Kanya King, MOBO

It's a tired cliché we would usually avoid: 'Failing to plan is planning to fail'. On this occasion, though, we can't avoid it because we can't better it – it's just too true. Let's try instead to bring back to life the notion of business planning, the point that tends to bring the budding entrepreneur's enthusiasm to a shuddering halt.

> ❝ **'Business planning' is the most searched-for business term on Google** ❞

It's no coincidence that 'business planning' is the most searched-for business term on Google. It's the common pain point where anyone who's ever thought about starting a business realizes that to act on the idea burning away in their head, they're going to have get it down on paper and prove it's really as good as they've convinced themselves it is. But where to start? And why, oh why is that a negative?

Proving to yourself before anyone else that your idea works on paper and in the real world and not just in your head should be embraced, not dreaded. It's really not that painful either and you should view it as validating the vision and dream you're so excited about.

Business planning is simple: it's about building a map to where you want to go and charting out how you're going to get there. Before you start, you've got to have some sort of end in sight. And before you start panicking, that doesn't mean an 'exit plan'; we know most people don't want to think about selling before they've even started.

The 'end' you'll plan towards might be as simple as 12 months on, when the business is established and trading in profit. Indeed, you might have several 'ends' you plan to, starting with the first day of trading, through to the first six months, then your 12-month target, a second and maybe even third year (although that might be increasingly optimistic to foresee in today's fast-paced world).

The most important thing is being clear about what you're trying to achieve and then mapping out your journey: how you're going to get there, the route you're going to take and what needs to happen to get to all the stops along the way.

Let's get one thing clear: planning your business is completely different to writing a business plan. We'll come to business plans all in good time, but for now you're charting out what your business is, why it's going to work and the milestones you're going to pass along the journey. It's also about ensuring you don't fall on your ass, so listen up.

> **Embrace the idea of proving to yourself that your idea works in the real world**

WWW

Business planning help and 500 free business plan templates: www.smarta.com/business-planning

It's common for people to have a great idea but not know how to turn it into a great reality. How can you take what is just a concept and turn into a real, revenue-generating, going-concern reality?

It sounds obvious, but start by simply writing the idea out. What is this? Why is this a good idea? What's it going to look like? What's it going to sell? Who's going to buy what you're selling? How much will they pay? How much will it cost you? How are you going to make money? Literally draw it out – yes, we mean pencil, paper, scribble. Then keep looking at it.

Next, contrary to what the old school say about hoarding your idea away from the world, speak to a few people you trust about it and use their views as a sounding board. You don't have to follow what anyone has to say, but it'll be useful to hear their initial responses as well as their more processed views. Find out what people think. The point is that you continue to look from different angles.

Once you've done that, set yourself a period of time to research the idea and prove that it's viable.

Crystallize your concept. Be clear what your idea actually is.

Exit The point at which you intend or foresee that you'll sell or leave the business.

What's your elevator pitch? Could you say it in a tweet? If you can't explain your business in a sentence then you're doing something wrong. It's not compelling or clear or focused enough.

At the same time, don't overplan. As much as you shouldn't dive blindly into any business, you can spend too long looking for reasons not to do it. (Incidentally, if you are, that's possibly a good sign that you shouldn't be doing it.) Good enough is usually good enough. Sooner or later you have to just do it, or stop pretending and accept you're not going to. Do plan but don't plan yourself into paralysis.

Every day should be about delivering a result, finding another piece of evidence this will work. If you don't plan you face unexpected costs; you'll typically assume you'll make more; you won't know the most profitable areas of your business and you'll continually be fire-fighting. If you do plan you'll have a greater and better-informed perspective and vision.

View the business planning process as a way of proving to yourself and everyone else that what you're doing makes total sense. Take the time to look ahead for all the potential icebergs on the horizon now and there's a far greater chance one won't catch you by surprise once you've set sail.

Smarta in Action: Green Hands

Founder: Naomi Andersson
Company: Green Hands
Company profile: Award-winning experts in natural nail care, selling products free from harsh chemicals and not tested on animals.
Found: 2005

Overview
Having come up with the idea for her natural nail care brand, Green Hands founder Naomi Andersson wasn't sure there was a market out there – or even any products for her to sell. She decided she would need to do extensive research to determine whether she should start her business.

How she did it
With a 9–5 job on the go, Andersson had to use her spare time to look into her business. What followed was two years of extensive research, speaking to potential competitors, suppliers and manufacturers both at home and in countries such as Germany, where the market was already established.

With the eco-craze yet to take hold in the UK, Andersson had to convince herself people were likely to choose a sustainable alternative to established nail care brands. 'The people I was speaking to were doing it because it was their passion. Now, the natural beauty and nail products industry is worth millions of pounds. The nice thing is, those little companies that were so passionate are now much bigger and have huge distribution deals,' says Andersson.

Having made plans around an industry that was yet to take shape, Andersson realized there was a real niche for her business.

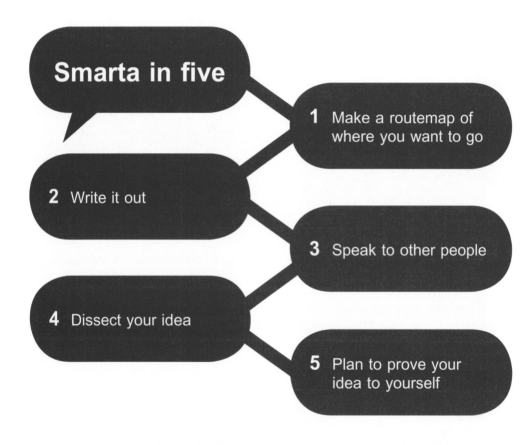

Smarta in five

1 Make a routemap of where you want to go

2 Write it out

3 Speak to other people

4 Dissect your idea

5 Plan to prove your idea to yourself

4.2
Remember ideas are cheap

"You're constantly trawling. You're always trying to piece bits together in your mind, looking for trends, looking for ideas. You always have your radar on."

—Eileen Gittens, Blurb

"Entrepreneurs have ideas by the dozen. It's almost a way of life – everywhere you look you can see an opportunity."

—Karen Hanton, Toptable

"It came to me at about four o'clock in the morning. I had a friend who was brilliantly game for being set up with people, but I'd set her up with everyone I knew, so I thought I need to find more. All I needed to do was to get all my friends' single friends to meet all my single friends. I was sure some of them would like each other."

—Sarah Beeny, MySingleFriend.com

> "I was watching a dreadful programme about the spread of HIV/AIDS in Africa. They said the only way they could stop it spreading was by the use of radio. It takes me longer to describe my having the idea than the event as it occurred."
> **—Trevor Baylis, Baylis Brands**

> "You just can't tell if it's a good idea or not to begin with. It's a bit like if I come across a green shoot poking out of the ground. Is it a weed, or is it a flower? We just don't know – we have to nurture it, and give it some love."
> **—Matt Kingdon, ?WhatIf!**

If you're searching for that billion-dollar business idea we've got one piece of advice: stop. Billion-dollar business ideas don't exist. Ideas exist and billion-dollar businesses exist, but there's a hell of a lot more than a eureka lightbulb moment for the one to become the other.

It's true that every now and again someone invents a genuinely innovative proposition, but they're few and far between. What is more, it's not the creators of new products or markets who profit from them.

Almost all of the most successful companies and household brands of the past 100 years – including right now – weren't 'new' ideas. The billion-dollar businesses certainly weren't billion-dollar ideas on day one. And a 'smart' business idea isn't necessarily a 'new' business idea.

> **A 'smart' business idea isn't necessarily a 'new' business idea**

Of course there is the occasional mega idea that makes everyone sit up and ask, 'Wow, where did that come from?' These are the ones that don't bother blowing away the existing market and just go straight to creating their own. If you've got one of those you can probably skip this chapter.

Then there are the smart ideas which have big customer appeal, a readymade market, and are cost-effective to operate with high margins and low overheads. These are the

> **A smart business idea is quicker, smoother, more reliable, better looking or cheaper**

ideas you should be searching for. The good news is that you don't need to reinvent the wheel to meet the criteria of a smart business idea, you just need to make it quicker, smoother, more reliable, better looking or cheaper than what's already there.

> **❝ Ideas are cheap – they're everywhere ❞**

Once you stop searching for that big idea, you'll soon realize that ideas are actually cheap: they're everywhere. We live a world where consumers are continually demanding instant gratification and more for their money or time. There's no shortage of opportunities, you've just got to find your own angle on a business where you can make a big enough difference.

There are very few monopolies in today's business, so no sector is off limits for new entries. McDonald's has been at the forefront of the fast food industry for decades, but it hasn't stopped a whole host of brands establishing themselves in the same space. You just have to find your niche and the market for which you can make a difference. If that market is big enough and you can get to them, then you might have a viable business on your hands.

At the risk of contradicting every message we've given you in this book, you don't always have to be different. There are some excellent examples of copycat businesses which have created rich trade by simply being No. 2 in their market. John Paleomylites, the founder of BeatThatQuote.com, fully admits he was so impressed by the way MoneySupermarket.com cornered the online comparisons market that he thought he'd join the party. He simply looked to be very good at what he did and within three years had a £20million-plus, award-winning business on his hands.

> **WWW**
> Watch a host of top name entrepreneurs reveal how they came up with their business idea: www.smarta.com/videos

Where do you start looking for business ideas? Start in the mirror. What do you know, what are you good at, what's your passion? Think about where you could make a difference.

Great businesses usually solve problems and address challenges, so think about frustrations you've had or have heard about and how you could fix them. If you know the electric trade and hear people complaining that they have to wait three months to get their satellite dish installed because there's a shortage of contractors, your ears should prick up. Alternatively, if the same people are complaining that they won't renew their TV packages because all the engineers were sloppily dressed and rude and included hidden charges, there's another way for you potentially to fill the proverbial gap in the market.

> **WWW**
> Visit Smarta's ideas centre for all the help you need on finding and developing a business idea: www.smarta.com/ideas

Be creative. There are plenty of ideas that work because they improve what's gone before in their own right, not just because the alternative wasn't performing.

Once you've got an idea – and especially if you're generating them on an almost hourly basis – you need to apply some mental criteria in order to decide which ones are worth pursuing and exploring, and which, for any number of reasons, aren't. Ask yourself the following five questions:

1 Who is the customer and is there a big enough market?
2 How is this going to make money?
3 How much money do you need for this to happen?
4 How quickly can you make it happen?
5 How suited are you to this?

Be really honest in answering these questions and answer them from the heart. You've got to run this business and so it has to work for you. It's very conceivable that you might have stumbled on a great business idea, just for someone else rather than you.

If it's going to cost you more money than you can access to launch the business then you need to think twice. Without the cash could you get to profitability in time for it to work? Is it an idea for someone with more capital? If you don't have any expertise or experience in the space, how important is that? Can you afford to hire the expertise in? Is that viable? Have you come up with a brilliant proposition for a market that's so disparate that reaching customers is going to be a problem?

This book aims to provide you with a plethora of reasons why your business can survive and prosper if you act smart, but there are also quite a few reasons why certain businesses won't. The checklist below outlines why even what might seem like a gem of an idea might not sparkle so brightly on closer inspection. Check out these common pitfalls and start-up killers and make sure your idea isn't vulnerable before exploring it further:

● Does it have killer costs that will prove problematic early on? Will it cost too much to scale up? Are you able to control costs?
● How susceptible is it to market forces: shifts in the property market, the value of the pound, the cost of raw materials?
● How big are your margins? Can you cope with fluctuations in market conditions or a rise in overheads?
● If revenues are tied to a critical mass of web visitors, then how long will it take you to reach that total?
● How many revenue streams do you have? If only one, what degree of risk does that entail?
● Is the market big enough? Can you target people cost-effectively? Will they pay enough? Who is the competition? Is there room for you?
● How reliant is the business on certain suppliers or buyers? How easily can they change their terms and squeeze your margins?
● Do you have the right location? Can you afford the right location?
● Is there an angle and room for you to differentiate your offering?

If you're sure in your mind that your business idea is safeguarded against all of the above, it's time to start gathering evidence to prove it to yourself and anyone else who needs to see your business plan.

Smarta in Action: PlayMade Energy

Founder: Daniel Sheridan
Company: PlayMade Energy
Company profile: PlayMade Energy's mission is to bring playground equipment and renewable electricity to schools in the developing world to enhance the lives of underprivileged children.
Founded: 2008

Overview
Half-way through his time at university, Daniel Sheridan was at a loss over what to do with his life. Having done an industrial placement year, all he had learned was that he wasn't suited to sitting behind a desk. But it was while he was on a trip to East Africa during the following summer that he was inspired to start his own business.

How he did it
During his time in Africa, Sheridan took part in volunteer work at a Kenyan primary school, where he helped to build a classroom and teach. He was inspired by the experience, so on his return to the UK to complete the final year of his degree, he used a design project he had been set to create an 'Energee-Saw', an electricity-generating see-saw for African schools. 'There was a clear connection in providing school playground equipment to underprivileged children, as well as creating some electricity from their play which could benefit their health and education,' explains Sheridan.

So inspired was his idea that when he entered it into a competition at his university, he won the £1,000 prize, giving him enough money to create a prototype and send it to Kenya. 'The excitement on the faces of the children made me realize that to be able to install more see-saws at schools in the developing world could bring benefits to many underprivileged children,' says Sheridan.

Tips
Look to your passion for inspiration. Sheridan says his idea came from his passion and he's never looked back: 'I realized that by combining my desire to work in international development with a product design degree, I could have my ideal job.'

Smarta in five

1 Very few successful businesses are born from eureka moments

2 Finding a niche and executing it powerfully is more important than a 'new' idea

3 Seek opportunities where you're passionate and can see frustration

4 Check this is a business idea that's suited to you

5 Consider how vulnerable your idea is

4.3
ID your business – make people care

"There was always a link between SuperJam and Superman, so I created a brand around a comic book theme. When we presented it to the buyer, he said, 'This idea doesn't really work.' It was probably a bit childish, even though it was a lot of fun. So we went back and redid the labels and went through the process a few times until we came up with a set of labels, a factory and a price that worked for everyone."

—Fraser Doherty, SuperJam

"What we're trying do is build a brand, and we're building it for longevity. We're not going to be a flash in the pan. If the company is still around, I want my children to have the opportunity of working for it."

—Laura Tenison, JoJo Maman Bébé

> "We didn't want to scream our brand from the rooftops, we just wanted people to organically begin to know about us and talk about us. And it's worked: we've developed this range where they are discreet – it's about being sophisticated and elegant. It's about being in the know. That's what our very minimalist branding actually achieves."
> **—Tremayne Carew Pole, Hg2**

> "If entrepreneurs don't believe that they have a unique contribution to make to whatever they're trying to achieve, people will suss it out."
> **—Julie Meyer, Ariadne Capital**

It's crucial to develop an engaging brand and the smartest businesses have strong identities that their customers relate or aspire to. This isn't some marketing spiel about the messages your logo sends out, it's about the whole identity and personality of your business. It's about who you are and what you stand for as a business. You need to know this from day one, because it's the fundamentally best way of establishing loyalty from your customers and a tribe of people around you.

If you're going to open a café, what does your café stand for? Is it the coffee? Is it the free wifi? Is it the magazines lying around? Is it the food? You can't be all things to all people, so you have to be something that hooks customers in and convinces them to keep coming back to you instead of the 100 other cafés on the high street.

Sculpting the identity of your business should be one of the most enjoyable elements of starting the business.

> **Sculpting the identity of your business should be enjoyable**

Job number one is to be clear what your unique selling points (USPs) are. What do you stand for? What will people pick you out as representing? What is the chief reason for doing business with you and not somebody else?

A USP needs to put clear blue water between your business and those of your competitors. The vast majority of companies operate in highly competitive markets and whether you're selling software, paperclips or package holidays, your customers have a choice. It's vital to give those customers a reason to spend their money with you rather than with your rivals. That is the role of the USP.

Save 25% on Business PlanPro

the alternative workspace

Save 50% on membership

eOffice is a world-class operator offering the ultimate in workplace solutions. Its members benefit from stylish, fully furnished serviced offices available on a daily, weekly, monthly or yearly basis, plus impressive meeting and video conferencing rooms and cost-effective virtual office services. eOffice is offering Smarta Members 50% off its eCard membership, which gives access to over 100 locations at preferred rates, plus 25% discount on all meeting and conference rooms. You can also claim one month's free virtual office service.

Free 2-week subscription to UK grants database

Search over 1000 grants and funding opportunities available to UK businesses by sector and location. It's **completely free to search the database** and you only need to pay a subscription for full reports and details of how to apply for the grant. However, with this offer you will get **2 weeks** of access to full information.

10% off Moo business cards

moo.com

MOO was born out of a love of beautiful, high-quality print. MOO want to set a new standard for print, with remarkable new products that bring great design and uncompromising, high standards to the web.

Design is key to everything MOO does. They believe design helps us stand out: from the clothes we wear, to the homes we live in, to the business cards we use. Design tells a story about us and what we stand for.

But professional-quality design has traditionally been expensive or out of reach for most people; MOO want to change this. They're passionate about helping people of all abilities design the best looking and highest quality print products: products that will help them or their business look great.

MOO are offering smarta readers a great 10% off all their business cards.

TO CLAIM THIS OFFER GO TO: www.smarta.com/bookoffers/businesscards

intuit ®

Claim 15% off Intuit Quickbooks accounting and tax software

Quickbooks is Smarta's choice for accounting and tax software. Really easy to use, it grows with you as your business grows. Choose the product that is most suited to your business from Starter, Pro and Professional. Intuit is offering an amazing 15% off all its award winning products.

B.HIVE™

One month FREE MEMBERSHIP worth £25

B.Hive Women's Business Club, opened by Lynne Franks together with Regus, offer one free month membership worth £25 plus Vat when buying a year's membership.

It's clear that more women than ever are starting their own businesses, freelancing or taking leadership roles in large companies. But until now there just hasn't been anywhere to go where we can have meetings, catch up with our e-mails and hold events in a space that reflects 'the feminine way of doing business.'

In collaboration with Regus, the world's largest work space provider, we have now created B.Hive, a stylish, feminine environment with the practical, professional support that you need.

an **Office DEPOT** business

10% off all Office Furniture

Welcome to your perfect new office ... As a Smarta customer you'll receive 10% discount across Viking's entire furniture range – just enter the exclusive prefix 2SB when you place your order. (Example: instead of ordering F29-BSH57, order 2SB-BSH57.) It's that simple.

TO CLAIM THIS OFFER GO TO: www.smarta.com/bookoffers/vikingdirect

4 NETWORKING
meet > like > know > trust

Get 1 free extra month with 4Networking

The most difficult thing about running your business is getting appointments.

Not any more!

4Networking is the largest joined-up business breakfast network in the UK, with access to 200+ groups and 30 000+ members. 4Networking provides real-world appointments and support for microbusinesses/SMEs. Joining through the Smarta portal offers even greater value, with an *additional* month added free on any initial membership.

A USP can relate to the quality and price of your products, the branding of your company, the service offered to customers, or the way that you run on ethical grounds. Given that very few companies are offering products that can't be bought elsewhere, the USPs are often woven around the way the product is sold, packaged and serviced.

For instance, a mail order company could distinguish itself from rivals by offering no-quibble returns, a 24/7 helpline and guaranteed delivery. A café selling almost identical coffee to a rival sitting across the road could entice customers through décor, speed of service, internet access and a wider range of food.

The key is to establish USPs that are genuinely distinct from those of your competitors and in line with what is useful and attractive to your customers. So ask yourself why customers should buy from you, rather than your rivals.

Your product may not be unique in terms of function – a can opener is, after all, a device to open cans – but it can be differentiated in a range of ways. It might be easier to use than rival products, more pleasing on the eye, cheaper, made with better materials or easier to assemble. Increasingly, ethical or environmental factors can be effective USPs. For instance, a significant number of consumers are prepared to pay more for Fair Trade products or goods that are seen to be environmentally friendly.

WWW

For a list of 50 USPs you can apply to your business: www.smarta.com/usp

A unique service proposition can be hugely compelling. Once you understand exactly what your customers want – or what they would like in an ideal world – you can begin to tailor your service accordingly. In practice that may mean longer opening hours, delivery options that suit the needs of the customer or multichannel ordering via phone, web, in store, mobile and so on. Equally, a high level of customer support via a 24/7 helpline or genuinely expert staff can also be a USP.

Your USPs should be integrated into your company's marketing message. For instance, in the competitive logistics sector FedEx established that a key USP would be next-day delivery on a global basis. This was captured in the advertising slogan: 'When it positively, absolutely has to be there overnight.' The key selling proposition also became a memorable strapline to grab the attention of customers and arguably also a key performance indicator.

> **The key to establishing your USPs is to establish the true identity of your business**

USPs should be communicated clearly to customers using your preferred marketing channels: advertising, email, face-to-face meetings and so on. You should ensure that all staff are aware of the importance of the USP. If next-day delivery is the selling point, it's vital that the business honours that promise.

Identity The who, what, where, why (should we care) of your business.

The key to establishing your USPs is to establish the true identity of your business. It's the point at which to the outside world and to your target audience, your business goes from being a 'marketing agency' to a 'digital social media agency specialising in working with public-sector clients', an agency that guarantees 24/7 contact with a dedicated account manager, with results-driven pricing and one month's free consultancy.

At this point you can also develop your internal and external vision, a clear focus on what you want the business to achieve, what it stands for, how it will operate, how it will behave, how it will treat customers: and its staff, and what is important to it. At one extreme this can be the dreaded mission statement, but at the other it's a case of scoping out exactly, in the simplest terms, who you are.

If you haven't yet chosen a name, logo and company branding, this should be the point that these identity values start to emerge.

USPs (Unique selling points) The key features or functions that differentiate your business from the rest.

Smarta in Action: Mr & Mrs Smith

Founder: James Lohan
Company: Mr & Mrs Smith
Company profile: A publishing company and hotel booking service which hand-picks the best boutique hotels and luxury accommodation to ensure you find the perfect romantic getaway.
Founded: 2003

Overview
Having previously owned a bar, restaurant, and events production company, James Lohan was familiar with the steps it took to build a brand. But when he launched Mr & Mrs Smith, originally as a series of nice hotel guides, the positioning of the brand was crucial.

How he did it
Lohan knew exactly what he wanted the brand to be, best described as understated luxury. Lohan knew if he overdid it, the subtlety of the brand would be lost.

A friend came up with the name Mr & Mrs Smith. 'It was a master-stroke,' says Lohan. 'It gives a real personality to the brand – it makes customers feel like there's a sense of fun.' Although the name is understated, he says it differentiates the brand from other 'high end' products. 'We're not just another ultimate luxury this or a wonderful luxury that.'

A second stroke of genius came during the first PR campaign, when the need to win over consumers was paramount. 'We PR-ed it as a lifestyle brand, rather than a publishing brand,' explains Lohan – and it worked. It may have been brand new, but the business saw 'the most phenomenal reaction', with headlines in major newspapers and magazines.

Lohan says PR is one of the most important ways to get the word out. 'If you can get column inches, that's the quickest route to building your brand. If people read editorial about you, they believe it.'

Tips

Building a brand is about more than just coming up with a nice logo, it's about positioning. 'People adopt brands,' explains Lohan. Everything you do has an effect on your brand, from your design, to your promotional partnerships, to where your office is, and down to the people in your team. To create the most convincing brand you must learn to live it – put a foot wrong and your brand could be at risk.

Smarta in five

1 Customers don't just need to know what you do, but what you stand for

2 Give people a compelling reason to shop with you and not anyone else

3 Different does not have to mean wacky

4 Make your USPs purposeful and focus on delivering value

5 Don't just be different, be better

4.4
Know your customer inside-out

"Customers are the lifeblood of the business. Try and imagine you're a customer."

—Mike Clare, Dreams

"We actually decided to target Bebo at me – but we missed, because people using it were not my demographic. But we had literally designed a site we thought was useful for me to stay in contact with my family in the UK, so it's very much designed around things we thought were useful and fun."

—Michael Birch, Bebo

When you're planning your business you can focus all you like on evolving your product or service and establishing a power brand, but more than any of that, absolutely everything hinges on thoroughly understanding your customer. Knowing your customer is absolutely everything. It's the single most important thing in researching your business.

> **Knowing your customer is absolutely everything**

Seriously, if you ignore every piece of advice all these great people are giving you in every other chapter but you still listen to this one and you focus on nothing but getting to know who your customer is and what they want, you'll screw up loads but you'll still have a real chance of putting it right again and succeeding.

Ignore this chapter and even though you listen to and follow the advice in every other section of this book, you're finished – before you've even got started.

You need to know your customer to do anything constructive in business. How can you possibly design a product or service or build a brand or market it if you don't know who the audience is? How can you forecast how many sales you'll make if you don't know how many potential customers there are? It's a non-starter.

Don't fall into the trap of believing you've got a product for everyone. Categorically, you haven't. If companies the size of Tesco and Waitrose can differentiate their customer bases, then it's safe to assume that you haven't stumbled on the product the whole world wants.

Even if you're adamant you've got a world-beater of a product or service, you still need a target audience to focus on, otherwise you'll end up targeting everyone and reaching and appealing to nobody.

You need to get up close and personal to your customers to understand exactly who they are. Whatever you do, don't assume you know who they are either. Get out and meet them. If you're product or service testing you have to record the demographic of the people you're working with or it's absolutely pointless.

> **Don't fall into the trap of believing you've got a pro- duct for everyone**

If you're still in development you've got two choices: either you target a certain type of person that you want to sell to or, just as realistic, a certain price point you want to hit, and adjust your product or service according to what your customer research tells you. Or you set out to identify who will buy the product or service you've outlined and then market it accordingly.

The smartest businesses are likely to remain open to a combination of the two: basing their marketing approach on a firm understanding of how their target customer behaves and also developing services and products based on the information they've gleaned.

What to find out
Begin by looking at your customer demographics, find out what their profiles are. Look at:

- age
- income
- level of education
- gender
- race or nationality
- family status and size

Your customers' behaviour is also crucial to how you present your business. Find out:

- what they spend their money on
- what their habits are
- how loyal they are to other brands
- what their interests are
- how often they spend their money and how much they spend

Knowing your ABCs – the official demographic consumer scale – can help. Some investors will want to know if your clients are ABs or C1s.

Depending on what type of business you're running your customers' location will also be a big consideration and could affect how much they spend and how frequently they buy. Find out:

- how far they live or work from your premises
- what sort of area they live in
- if it's further afield, what the climate is like
- how many people matching your target customer there are in your area

You can pay companies to research this for you, but we wouldn't advise it. Most of the information is available publically and increasingly the most powerful customer research you can do is either face to face or online, with the only cost being the time you incur carrying it out.

Use social media such as the search facility on Twitter to find out what discussions are taking place around similar products to yours in your space. Look at the profiles and interests of those people – do they watch your target audience? Go one step further and join in the conversations. Ask people what kind of services or products would make their lives easier, how much they'd pay for the solutions and how and where they spend their money now.

The smart companies we've discussed who are harnessing social media to build tribes and evolve brands even before they've started trading have the most powerful understanding of their customers because they've developed that customer base purely on engagement and by appealing to them. It stands to reason that if they develop on the basis of that feedback, they'll have a proposition their ready-made target customer wants to buy and a captive audience to market it to.

Once you have collected data about your customers, you will need to break them down into different groups, or segments, based on information such as age, income, region and lifestyle. This is called market segmentation and allows you to determine specifically how you will encourage each group to buy into your brand.

> **" Effective sales and marketing flows from a knowledge of your customers "**

That said, the smartest small businesses are building customer bases built on loyalty and return visits. They're seeing value in focusing on delivering excellent service to the customers who are likely to repeat buy as loyal customers 20 times rather than chasing a quick-buck, one-off transaction.

Effective sales and marketing begins with a clear understanding of the customer. Your pricing, the service package, the advertising and marketing strategy – all these things flow from a knowledge of who your customers are, what they are prepared to pay and what their expectations are in terms of quality and service.

And there can be huge variations in customer expectations, even within a single business area. For instance, in the business-to-consumer sector a handbag manufacturer probably won't be addressing the UK's entire female population. Within that overall group, some will be prepared to pay hundreds or thousands of pounds for designer creations while others will be content with something from Top Shop or Primark. Equally in B2B, the software accounting solution that is tailored for a small business won't be suitable for a blue-chip company. It's vital to match what you're selling to a clearly defined market.

Smarta in Action: Bright Ideas Trust

Founder: Tim Campbell
Company: Bright Ideas Trust
Company profile: Provides an innovative package of business support services to 16–30 year olds in London who are looking to start their own business.
Founded: 2008

Overview
Former *Apprentice* winner Tim Campbell remembers the first task he was set by Lord Sugar: creating a line of anti-ageing products for women. Campbell had never even considered working in the beauty industry before, he needed to learn about his customers – and fast.

How he did it
Campbell says learning about his customers and their needs was relatively simple. It involved finding a whole range of data about his target market. 'We had to work out who our customer was,' he explains.

Campbell and his team mapped out everything they could think of about the customers' habits: their age, their occupations, the magazines they read, the newspapers they bought, where they shopped and how they lived their lives. Not only did all that information help them to determine what their brand would be, it also helped them work out how and where to target their advertising.

Campbell also discovered that the beauty industry was led by celebrities. The Amstrad team leveraged that by finding a celebrity from the same age range to endorse their products, increasing consumers' trust in their brand and helping them spread the word.

Tips
'It was really about finding out what the customer's needs were and meeting those needs,' explains Campbell. 'It really wasn't rocket science.' Once the team had created a product they knew their target market would want, all they needed to do was get the word out. 'We had a product we knew worked,' says Campbell. 'It was just a matter of letting people in the target market know about it.'

Smarta in five

1 Customers are everything and should influence every decision

2 Target everyone and you'll please no one

3 Pick your target audience, but treat them as individuals

4 Going the extra mile for one customer *is* worth it

5 Segment your customer base to be extra personalized

4.5
Test, develop, test, develop, test …

"It was important we tested our collection during a trial. We put in an order for 100 umbrellas and went down to Spitalfields market. That was how we launched and tested our first idea."

—Vivianne Jaeger, SquidLondon

"I decided to ask my friends if they'd taste the food for me and tell me what they thought. My friends are lovely people, which pretty much makes them useless at giving proper feedback because they'd just say, 'Oh Jenny, those muffins were delicious, send me some more muffins', which isn't very helpful at all."

—Jennifer Irvine, The Pure Package

> "In the early stages of a business, part of what makes an entrepreneur very good is worrying about the detail and to worry the detail you need to see it, you need to touch things, feel them, see that something's not quite right."
>
> **—Sara Murray, Buddi**

W e're going to be really blunt here because everyone we've spoken to agrees: whatever you're selling, you have to test it. What is more, you have to test, develop, test, develop, test… You can't not test. It's crazy not to.

> **There's a big difference between spotting a product people want and executing it exactly as they want it**

WWW
Free market research reports: www.smarta.com/market-research-report

Never assume you know what people want. Be clear: there's a big, big difference between having the business or entrepreneurial instinct to spot a product or service that people want and would pay money for, and executing it exactly as they want it. You can't do that on your own and you can't do it first time around.

Indeed, most ideas come not from the brains of business people but the needs of the consumer: fixing their problems, meeting their needs and desires. All anyone needs to do is observe and listen and then provide the solution. It's obvious stuff and you only have to examine how the consumer and market research budgets of big companies dwarf what they spend on research and design. They don't need to dream up new products, they just need to make them.

With the consumer increasingly vocal and amplified in their demands and those views more readily available for small business owners to absorb, it's madness not to be continually testing and adapting your business on the basis of feedback from your target customers.

It's seriously crazy how many people don't, though. People are so consumed by their product and service that they base everything on their opinion of it, often subconsciously. Unless you're planning to buy all your business's products or services out of your own money (which clearly you're not), then you really shouldn't be basing your decisions on your personal taste alone.

That might sound idiotically simple, but don't either assume that people share your taste or that you know what people want. Let us clarify: you don't. The biggest retail outlets in the world make catastrophic buying decisions every year and they base their decisions on mountains of their own and industry data. So how could you consider taking similar decisions without asking your customers?

Realized from day one that this is your business and your baby, but that if you're going to make any money,

> **Don't fall into a 'build it and they will come' trap**

whatever you sell has to be targeted squarely at your customer, not you. One of the safest and simplest ways to rid yourself of this misguided affliction is to ask yourself how many people you know just like you, with the same tastes and same spending habits, and then see if there are enough of them to make your business plan work.

Likewise, if you're assuming you've got a firm understanding of what people from a different demographic to you want, pick five subjects and go and chat to five of those people about them. Chances are you won't get five sets of answers the same. It's simply not that easy.

Don't fall into any of the 'build it and they will come' traps, either. That quote comes from the movies for a reason. If you build purely on instinct you're simply skewing the risk of success to failure and basing your probability more on chance than science.

> **The product you tested and that worked last year may need tweaking this year because of how the world has changed**

For a start, too many things are being built now for you to be able to assume that yours will be different. Trends are moving so quickly that even if it was what people wanted when you started building, it almost certainly won't be by the time you've finished it.

Product testing is increasingly relevant because things are changing so much. The way we live, the way we work, the way we interact, they are all changing on such a frequent basis that the product you tested and that worked last year may need tweaking this year because of how the world has changed.

Even the phrase 'If it ain't broke, don't fix it' is no longer true. Smart businesses need to test any product or service carefully before launching it and then make testing an ongoing process.

As consumers we are less loyal than we used to be. We have a huge desire for immediate gratification. The smartest companies will be those that are continually reinventing their proposition in line with their customers' tastes.

Testing and development should take many shapes and forms for many uses. First, be aware of what your target customer is talking about in the public sphere, in places such as on Twitter or Facebook and on media where they review products or services or even in physical spaces – in short, wherever the conversations about your proposition and industry are happening.

Here it's a case of observation and ideally interaction. If you're selling bird tables, then you want to be entering all the conversations people are having around buying bird tables: the ones that are well built, and more importantly the ones that are poorly constructed, too expensive or difficult to carry back from the DIY store. Then ask people how you could make their lives easier by improving the product.

WWW
Tips and advice on market research and user testing: www.smarta.com/market-research

At the other extreme, you should be user testing everything you release: give it to people, get their response, watch them use it, ask for brutal feedback. Learn to love criticism. Resist the urge to get defensive. Think about every poor review not as a setback, but as an advantage: you've shown you're listening. Hundreds or thousands of other sales will be saved because of the potential improvements you've taken on board.

Don't assume anything. If you're running a website, don't assume you know how people will navigate around it. The biggest mistake some web businesses make is to keep spending money on the display and design of their product without checking whether people are finding their beautifully photographed or laid-out pages.

Be sure to put product and user testing at the heart of and throughout your complete business process. It's the only way to be certain of what you're doing right and what you're not.

Smarta in Action: SquidLondon

Founders: Emma-Jayne Parkes and Vivianne Jaeger
Company: SquidLondon
Company profile: Beautiful, innovative umbrella designs that change colour when it rains.
Founded: 2008

Overview
Working on a project to create a protective overshoe during their degree in product design at the London College of Fashion, Vivianne Jaeger and Emma-Jayne Parkes came up with the idea of creating a Jackson Pollock-inspired design which changed colour when it rained.

Realising that clothing manufacturers hadn't managed to find a way to put ink that changed colour when it got wet into fabrics, Jaeger and Parkes approached an ink manufacturer which allowed them into its laboratories to develop an ink.

Having created a way to impregnate fabrics with colour-changing ink, Jaeger and Parkes needed to find a way to market their product.

How they did it
The pair came up with the concept of an umbrella which changes colour when it rains. Searching online they found a manufacturer in China, but they knew it was important they weren't too hasty. The pair put in a small initial order with the manufacturer.

'It was important we tested our collection during a trial,' explains Jaeger. 'We put in an order for 100 umbrellas and went down to Spitalfields market. That was how we launched and tested our first idea.'

The first order sold out in just 11 days. 'We had proved to the world we could produce it, so we could go on and produce bigger collections,' adds Jaeger. 'We knew people liked it – that's what was important.'

Tips
If you're designing a product, take your development process slowly. From developing the ink to having their first umbrella on the table took Jaeger and Parkes months, but it was important they got their product just right. If you're hasty with your development, there's a good chance you'll waste money.

Smarta in five

1 You don't know your customers better than they know themselves

2 Keep testing – what was right six months ago might not be now

3 Use social media to court opinion and stay abreast of market trends

4 Never assume 'If it ain't broke, don't fix it'. It might be broke and you just don't realize

5 Don't just test products, but the way they're displayed, packaged and marketed too

4.6
Make sure the numbers add up

"When you've got a business idea, play devil's advocate with every single item. What objections am I going to get to this? What objections am I going to get to that? Really try to answer all these questions for yourself."

—Eileen Gittens, Blurb

"I have never gone into a business because it is something that I wanted to do. Is it a good business first? And then I know I am going to love it because I love business for itself. So I know I am going to engage with it. But first off, is it a business proposition?"

—Deborah Meaden, *Dragons' Den*

"The crucial element is to try and make some educated guesses around the likely scenarios that could come out to play. Create a number of different scenarios, then run some figures through so you can understand your financing requirements and also understand things like cashflow and how cash is going to play a big role in the success or otherwise of your business."

—Alan Gleeson, Palo Alto

"If I build a nursing home or a health club or a children's day nursery, I look at the build cost and the return and that's it. Capital return, return on capital employed, whoever you want to employ, how are you going to use it, how are you going to talk about it, all these things are the most important thing for me. Really, my big criterion is just making sure I get a return on capital."

—Duncan Bannatyne, *Dragons' Den* and Bannatyne Group

Before you actually commit to starting your business and spend any of your – or anyone else's – money on it, you have to ask yourself some really tough questions, be brutally honest and act on the answers. You need to be absolutely sure that underneath the excitement of

> **You need to be absolutely sure that there's actually a business underneath the excitement of your big idea**

your big business idea, there's actually a business there: one that will attract revenues, make profit, sustain you and your dependants and pay the bills.

The truth is that even if you're not in it for the money, you still need to pay your mortgage and put food on the table. If the numbers don't stack up, it doesn't matter how good you think your idea is, it simply isn't if you can't show how you're going to make money. And regardless of whether you've started the business to enable you to spend more time at home, to control your own destiny or to save the whale, remember that first and foremost it's a business and successful businesses have one only thing in common: they make money.

You don't have to make profit immediately, of course, but you still have to have a very clear path to making a profit – and you have to have the buy-in of your investors and backers about when that profit period is.

The problem is that when you're making cash forecasts they can feel so intangible that you might as well stick a finger in the air. Everyone understands that, but it doesn't mean you shouldn't do it and it doesn't mean you shouldn't still try to be every bit as accurate as you can be.

It's always better to underestimate and overdeliver, even if you don't like the answer you get. Do the opposite of what comes naturally as an entrepreneur and an optimist and assume your glass is half empty. It's always preferable to be pleasantly surprised.

You can do middle-case scenarios and great-day scenarios, but the truth is you have to be able to prove you can operate this business on a doomsday. Don't treat the doomsday figures as a gesture that won't happen, treat them as what you think is most likely to happen and then enjoy the upside if you exceed them.

The really basic place to start is to work out how you'll bring revenue into the business. Until you've proved you can do that there's no point looking at your overheads, because if you have no turnover you really shouldn't be taking any on!

WWW

Get organized from day one with professional business planning and accounting software: www.smarta.com/business-builder

Focus on where your first customers are going to come from, how many sales you'll realistically make in month one, month two and so on. We can't emphasize the need for caution enough. If you think you're going to be selling from day one and then you're not, that's going to be a big problem and immediately set you into a negative cashflow cycle; unless, of course, you've factored the possibility in and dealt with it.

Only when you've established what revenues you can expect and when should you look at your outgoings: the cost of your sales and your overheads. Here you need to work out and prove a strong clear margin. Too many businesses have great sales but are selling at cost price and making nothing, at best. And it doesn't matter if what you're selling is £1 a unit or £100,000 a unit, zero profit is zero profit.

Taking into account market and industry conditions, the size of the business, marketing strategies and even geographical location, a financial forecast allows you to set goalposts and create metrics by which you can measure the success of your business.

If you're starting a new business and don't have any historical figures to make your predictions by, don't worry. Instead, use industry and local footfall figures to come up with realistic predictions (Companies House, the Office for National Statistics and the British Library are all useful resources for this). No one is expecting these figures to be watertight; realistic figures are all bank managers and investors will be looking for.

Once you've calculated your revenues and your outgoings, you should be able to calculate a projected cashflow. This should be used to work out how much cash you will have available for various parts of your business in the next month, three months and the next year.

Making a sales forecast

Sales forecasts allow you to predict and plan for peaks and troughs in trade. For example, if you're a retail business, there's a good chance Christmas will be one of your most busy periods, whereas February may be less busy. A sales forecast will give you a good idea of when to tighten your budget.

To begin with, make a set of assumptions:

- The current value of the market and its predicted value at the end of the trading period – what percentage is it likely to shrink/grow by?
- Your share of the market and your predicted share of the market at the end of the trading period – does a competitor have a particularly aggressive marketing campaign planned?
- The number of staff you have and the number of sales each salesperson is predicted to make.
- Marketing campaigns and the return on investment (ROI) you expect to get from them.
- Any factors which are likely to simplify making sales, whether you're launching a new website, moving to a more central location or stocking a new line of products.

Include the number of customers you expect to have and the number of sales you expect to make per customer. Don't forget to take into account that it's much easier to make repeat sales to existing customers.

Once you've written down your assumptions, break your sales forecast down – this could be by product, service, geographical location or market.

In a spreadsheet, put the months along the x-axis and your products along the y-axis and, using your assumptions, make the forecast from there.

Making a profit and loss forecast

Profit and loss accounts are very simple to draw up, although they're based on a certain amount of speculation:

- To begin with, identify what your gross sales are.
- Take away the variable costs of sales – the variable costs associated with manufacture, shipping and so on – and you'll be left with a gross profit.
- Take away the costs of your overheads – the cost of rent, business rates, utilities bills and so on – and you'll be left with a net profit.
- Take away your drawings – the amount you've withdrawn from the percentage of the business's profit you're entitled to – and you're left with a figure for the business's retained profit.

Your finished profit and loss account should look something like this:

	Jan		Feb	
Sales		£5,000		£7,000
Cost of sale	£2.50		£2.30	
Gross profit		£3,000		£5,500
Overheads	£3,000		£3,000	
Net profit		£0		£2,500
Drawings	£500		£1,000	
Retained profit		–£500		£1,500

Look at your outgoings. These should include the following:

- The direct or variable costs for each sale you make. This includes the per-unit or per-hour cost of materials or shipping, how much the materials and manufacture of the product costs or how much it costs to pay the people supplying the service.
- Your business's fixed costs. These should be broken down into:
  - rent
  - utilities bills
  - wages (including your salary)
  - business rates, service charges and so on
  - vehicle, travel and subsistence expenses
  - cost of equipment
  - office costs – printing, stationery, postage
  - marketing and advertising costs
  - legal and professional costs, insurance and so on
  - taxes

❝❝If you can't see enough margin in your forecasts, look at this as a positive discovery before it's cost you any money❞❞

If the figures aren't adding up when you're carrying out this process, avoid doing any of the following: panicking, consigning your idea to the dustbin or trying to fix it.

This is likely to be a slow and iterative process, but it's absolutely necessary and it's worth it. If you can't see enough margin in your forecasts, then look at this as a positive discovery before it's actually cost you any money (or your business). Go back to the plan and look at how you can either drive more sales or, more realistically, control costs and overheads.

It might be a case that you delay taking on offices for six months or hiring any staff. If you've factored in a salary for yourself and this is a lifestyle business, then a clear margin won't be as important as if you haven't or you're looking for fast growth.

Never cook the figures, though. What's the point? You're only kidding yourself and it's a serious no-no with investors. Reputations and relationships are based on trust. Understand that there's a big difference between cooking the figures to get what you want and telling the future as you see it. You should never put figures down you know to be untrue and unattainable, but you can perfectly legitimately put figures down you think you can deliver and then not hit them.

If you've done your forecast and the figures aren't adding up, keep working at them and get someone else in to have a look at where you could drive productivity. If after that your sums are still not working, then it's time to face up to reality, move away from the figures and rethink the concept: maybe your market just isn't big enough or your product isn't priced right.

Remember, this is about proving to yourself that you have a viable business which is going to sustain your income and investment or time and money, so it needs to be build on solid foundations. You wouldn't knowingly build a house on anything else, so don't kid yourself into building a business on anything but 100% conviction.

Cashflow The amount of disposable cash in your business at any one time.
Forecast A prediction of future performance based on previous trading figures or the performance of similar companies.

Smarta in Action: Third Year Abroad

Founder: Lizzie Fane
Company: Third Year Abroad
Company profile: Inspires students to study languages at university and make the most of their year abroad.
Founded: 2009

Overview

The beginning of her third year at university studying in Italy proved to be a bit of a nightmare for Lizzie Fane. 'I'd had a few problems with accommodation and registering on my courses,' she explains. Having encountered these difficulties, Fane was surprised when she couldn't find a single resource of information for students like her.

On her return to the UK, she decided to start a website of her own. But first, she needed to work out whether her idea was viable.

How she did it

Fane needed to prove to herself the numbers would add up, so she started looking into the potential market, seeking out similar websites or competitors. When she couldn't find anything similar to her idea, she began to draw up a list of requirements for the website based on friends' experiences.

Market research was crucial. Fane sent a market research questionnaire to members of her target demographic, trying to determine what people thought of the information and resources available to them on their year abroad, even going as far as to find out the number of flights each person took, and whether or not they bought a new mobile phone or opened a foreign bank account.

The next step was to look at the wider market. Fane got in touch with the Higher Education Statistics Agency (HESA) and the National Centre for Languages (CILT), both of which allowed her to search their databases. She also looked at figures collated by Erasmus, the largest exchange programme in Europe.

The numbers added up. 'My research showed me the website could be a viable business opportunity,' says Fane.

Tips

Understanding your target market is essential when you're starting a business. 'It helped me find out what problems my target customers were having so I could work out the best, simplest and most affordable solutions for them,' says Fane.

Smarta in five

1 If you can't prove your idea will be profitable, it's a hobby not a business

2 Make honest financial forecasts to prove viability to yourself

3 Don't cook the figures, you'll only be cheating yourself

4 Ensure your forecasts include what you'll pay yourself

5 If the figures don't work, go back to the drawing board until they do

4.7
Don't assume it, prove it

"Try online on a small scale first on somewhere like eBay or Amazon – they've already got users and infrastructure. Your job then is about selling online. You just have to do things like pricing, product imagery, copywriting, logistics, and so on. You'll realize people want to return stuff, there's fraud, there are all sorts of things which you probably did not think about. Then if it works you can graduate to having something again quite simple."

—Ashley Friedlein, Econsultancy

"Part of my research was trying to set up accounts with suppliers in order to test the model. I sent my prescription out to the laboratory and got a pair of prescription glasses for £6. Then I tried to sell them to friends. A guy came in to deliver a desk and I sold to him. There was no company existing at that point. I was just fiddling around with the idea and getting a sense of whether it worked."

—Jamie Murray Wells, Glasses Direct

> "When you first start off try to find four, five, six companies, even if you're not going to charge them straight away, to get them on board, get them evangelizing your product, get them using it, get their feedback. Over the first six months these people are going to be your best salespeople."
>
> **—Andy McLoughlin, Huddle**

> "I just went around with all the samples of my shoes in the back of my car."
>
> **—Alexandra Finlay, Fin's**

There's no better validation of your business idea than convincing someone to stump up some real money to buy it. There's no more compelling evidence to present to an investor or the bank – and to put your own mind at rest – than hard sales.

Sales remove a lot of doubt and will signal a lowering of risk and a heightening of opportunity to investors. What was a product or service that people 'might' want is suddenly one you've proved they do want and are prepared to pay a certain amount of money for.

It increasingly makes sense to take your product to market as early as possible. We've talked in Chapter 4.5 about the need to test and develop from the outset. In turn, it makes sense to start trying to sell small amounts of product as early as you can or, if you're in the service industry, carry out a number of small projects and pieces of work.

You'll be perfecting your proposition and picking up valuable feedback as you go along, but you'll also be establishing an initial customer base.

WWW
How to set-up an eBay shop: www.smarta.com/ebay

Look for ways to dip your toe in the water before a full launch. If you're selling products then test them on eBay or on market stalls, or ask small independent stores to stock your goods on a discounted trial basis. If they're reluctant, offer them sale-or-return terms or even let them pay once the items have sold.

At this stage and on this scale, you should only be holding small amounts of stock anyway and won't have calculated an immediate return on it, so you can afford to be flexible about how your payment model works without disrupting your cashflow.

If you're in B2B, then offer to help out a potential client by offering to take on a project on a pay-on-results basis – then make sure you get the results!

You can even start this process while you're still in the planning process. It's all useful feedback and takes the pressure off a big launch. With a bit of luck, when you do get to day one proper you'll already have a paying customer or two.

Innocent Drinks and Cobra Beer are two businesses which started selling their product to independent shops and restaurants door to door on a sale-or-return, trial basis from the boots of their respective owners' cars. In the case of Cobra, founder Lord Karan Bilimoria was selling by the boxload from a clapped-out Citroën 2CV saddled with £20,000 worth of student debts.

But for both businesses, what would later be viewed as small and arguably not particularly cost-effective sales were nonetheless an invaluable starting point: establishing a customer base, brand awareness and, crucially, proving a demand they could present to investors.

Make sure the first bit of business you do, even if it's more for testing and research than proving sales, is with genuine potential customers, not friends or family. It's guaranteed friends and family will love your product and promise to buy it – if they don't you've really got problems – but this won't prove anything about the likelihood of broader sales. Investors want to see genuine interest from the market and target audience you've indentified in your business plan, not merely evidence that nepotism is alive and well.

> **" Investors want to see genuine interest from the market and target audience you've indentified in your business plan "**

You also need to ensure that any efforts you put into trying to prove sales have long-term value. Try to collect the name, address, email and mobile telephone number of anyone you interact with and ask them if you can keep them up to date with how the business is going, when you'll be trading properly and so on. Collect any positive feedback you get and use it as testimonials in your marketing, even in your packaging or business plan. Any supporting evidence or real-life interest adds weight to what you're doing.

> **" Collect positive feedback and use it in your marketing "**

The ability to email people who already understand what you do is really valuable – and is also a reason why you should start a blog well ahead of your launch to collect more data and generate interest.

The ultimate confirmation you can secure is a written sales order you can take to the bank or investors. Provided that you've got your overheads and cashflow under control and aren't paying yourself a fortune, you shouldn't struggle to secure funding to fulfil solid sales orders.

> **" The ultimate confirmation you can secure is a written sales order "**

The more you prove you can secure solid revenues, the less risk you're assuming and the quicker your business will make the leap from business plan to real-life going concern.

Smarta in Action: Gatszu.com

Founder: Simon Swan
Company: Gatszu.com
Company profile: A recruitment marketplace that empowers employers, introducing them to a network of fully vetted, independent recruitment agencies and allowing the two parties to trade efficiently under one set of transparent terms and conditions.
Founded: 2009

Overview
The middle of 2009 wasn't a good time to launch a recruitment business. Redundancies were widespread: many companies had frozen recruitment completely. Swan knew he had great plans and a strong concept, but realized he had to prove his model, both for himself and for the bank manager he would need to convince to lend to him further down the line.

How he did it
With just £1,000, Swan developed and built a fully functioning website. Next, he had to prove there was demand for what he was offering. The idea of a recruitment marketplace was a completely new concept, so it was up to him to educate potential customers.

Swan made heavy use of social media to spread the word to employers and employees. He kept the service free, which of course didn't do him any harm. Employers started signing up to the site and using it, even though it was nothing flashy as yet. Swan's model depended on the number of people who were signed up to the service, so getting target customers to do just that was the equivalent of making sales for the business.

With a busy working model, Swan had proved that his idea worked and he started getting good leads from his bank. The bank wasn't yet ready to give him a loan, but they pointed him in the direction of a government-backed funding initiative for technology-based start-ups.

'That we'd got so far down the line with just £1,000 demonstrated our commitment and tenacity. They liked that,' he says.

And what happened when he approached the funding initiative? 'They could see we had worked hard and made sacrifices to get the business to a point where it was trading and attracting serious interest,' says Swan. 'We demonstrated we were very entrepreneurial; we had earned our stripes.'

Tips
A small budget shouldn't stand in the way of testing your model. Do what you can with what you have to get the attention of potential customers – and investors.

Smarta in five

1 Real sales validate your claims and forecasts

2 Get product out as early as possible, but listen to the feedback

3 Offer stockists or potential clients an incentive to take your untried goods

4 Sell to real people or it's not a real sale

5 Collect the data of people you sell to

4.8
Write a business plan

"I wrote a business plan purely because I thought it would be a great exercise. I'd never written a business plan before, I had no idea. Just from starting on page one, it emerged. It turned into a sort of 50-page document. It had to be edited down quite a lot, but it taught me a huge amount in the writing of it."

—Alexandra Finlay, Fin's

"A business plan is a hurdle in many respects which forces you to look through the various elements that make up a good business."

—Alan Gleeson, Palo Alto

There's no escaping writing a business plan, but there absolutely shouldn't be. Writing a business plan shouldn't be a chore you have to do to tick a box for the bank. Business plan, first and foremost, is for you: it's your documentary proof that starting this business makes sense and is a calculated risk, not a blind leap of faith.

> **A business plan is for you**

Your business plan concisely outlines what your business does, who its target customer is and how it will make money. It charts your path to profitability and various targets you've set for its growth. As such, your business plan should act as a live document to benchmark your performance and to run all key decisions past.

WWW

There are more than 500 generic and industry-specific free business plan templates on Smarta: 'www.smarta.com/business-plans

Don't get hung up on the notion that a business plan should be a certain number of pages or words presented in a particular way. Instead, focus on ensuring it contains all the basic essentials, doesn't exclude any key figures and is presented in a format that's simply to consume and not too taxing to read – that way it'll work for you and anyone else.

The activity of writing a business plan has traditionally been overdebated, overanalysed and overcomplicated, when it's actually quite simple. Remember: there are no hard-and-fast rules and all you're really doing is documenting what you know so far about your business and then looking forward to where you want it to be in, say, a year's time.

The plan should have an executive summary (a short description of your business) and then cover market research, an account of your marketing and sales strategy, details of your management team and staffing, some information about how the business operates and, last but not least, financial forecasts.

Your plan should be clear and concise, anchored in fact and evidence. Aim to have plenty of white space rather than endless dense text, and use tables, graphs and pictures of products. A good plan can be skim-read in about 15 minutes. Use bullet points and clear headings to make sure this is possible.

To make your plan consistent with what investors are used to seeing and to ensure you've covered all the main angles, break down your business plan into clearly defined subsections.

Suggested subsections for your business plan

The executive summary

Unsurprisingly, this is a synopsis of your entire business plan. Its role is to highlight the key points that you go into in greater depth later in the document. It's sometimes the only section a potential backer will read, so it has to be enticing while also providing a good understanding of the business. Typically, the executive summary should cover a couple of sheets of A4 paper or 800–1,200 words.

Description of the business

This section should cover the basics of the business in terms of where it stands today, where you plan to take it and where it has come from. Include details of when you plan to start trading or (if you've already started) when trading began. You should also provide details of the company's history and the current legal structure (are you a sole trader, limited company or partnership?).

Describe your product and your unique selling points or USPs; in other words, why people will want to buy what you're selling. Outline how you plan to develop your product or grow the range you have to offer.

Provide details of any patents, trade marks or design rights you own. If intellectual property – whether in the form of clever branding or unique technology – is important to the success of the business, explain how this can be defended.

Remember to avoid jargon. You may be an expert in your industry sector, but the external audience for your business plan won't necessarily have the same degree of technical knowledge. What they want is a clear view of the business's prospects.

Market research and sales strategy

Provide details of your competitors, direct and indirect. Who are they? What is their market share? What niche will your product or service fill in the existing market?

Equally importantly, you should be clear about your customers. If you're selling to individual consumers, you should provide details of the target group in terms of age, gender, income, interests and so on. In the B2B market, you should detail the kind of company you are planning to reach. In both cases, the plan should explain why your target customers will buy from you. Provide some information about the size of the market and the market share you plan to achieve.

Provide information on your marketing and sales strategy, the channels you plan to use, pricing and service offering.

Your management team and employees

Investors and financial backers will want to know if you have the skills in place to deliver on your goals, so provide information not just on your managers but on all members of staff.

Include external advisers such as lawyers and accountants, as this will also provide assurance that you have the necessary skills in place.

Set out how much time and money each person will contribute and what you plan to pay in terms of salaries. This will help both you and external parties assess whether you have the right cost base in terms of personnel. Include any plans for recruitment.

Your operations

Include details of your current or planned location, the costs and why you chose it. Provide details of the facilities you require to produce your product or service. This should include both in-house facilities and any aspects of the business that have been outsourced.

Management information and control systems are also an important element in the operational mix. You should explain what systems you plan to use – for instance stock control, quality control – across the business. Provide details of any weaknesses and how they can be improved. In addition, you should also detail your IT requirements, both now and in the future.

Your financial forecast

This is a crucial section that explains everything you've previously said about the business in key numbers. You need to include forecasts covering sales, profit and loss and cashflow.

Typically, these forecasts will cover three to five years, including where the business is now (and in the short-term future) and where you see it going. How quickly will sales grow and when is the business expected to turn a profit? What is the cashflow outlook?

You should include information on the capital you require, all sources of revenue, any securities (investment assets) that you hold and outstanding loans.

Ensure the projections are realistic. If you have a trading record you have something to go on, but if the business is new then you will be reliant on educated guesswork based on your market research. Don't be overoptimistic. Always include details of the research you've carried out to arrive at your forecasts.

> **"Your business plan should work as a live document"**

Remember, your business plan should work as a live document and be of genuine value to you. If it's not, then it probably won't be of any real value to anyone else. It might be a time-consuming activity, but get a business plan right and it'll be time well spent for a number of reasons.

WWW

Access comprehensive support to nail the ultimate business plan at www.smarta.com/business-planning

Smarta in Action: Balineum

Founder: Sarah Watson
Company: Balineum
Company profile: Balineum designs and sells fabric shower curtains, high quality towels and luxury bath mats – everything to make your bathroom beautiful.
Founded: 2007

Overview

Having launched Balineum to huge acclaim in 2007, Sarah Watson decided she wanted to grow the company. To grow it, though, she would need money, so she needed to make sure her business plan would be watertight.

How she did it

When you're looking for investment, it's important to tailor your business plan to the person you are approaching. To begin with, Watson needed to decide between approaching a venture capital (VC) fund or an angel. She was looking to raise around £400,000 which, she says, is 'too little for a VC fund but too much for a single angel investor'. Instead, she decided to approach several private investors.

To secure investment, Watson knew all the numbers in her business plan would need to add up, so she brought on a financial director who helped her go over the maths and tighten up the numbers and, in her words, 'kicked the crap out of' her business plan and her financials. 'We needed to work out how much money we really need, and what we are going to spend it on,' she explains.

The next task was to create a 'hit-list' of investors and business angels she would target. 'The chances are if you have had any kind of success in homewares or online and are wealthy, you're on my list – and if you haven't heard from me yet, it's probably because I haven't got to you yet,' she laughs.

Tips

A business plan is more than an itinerary, it should be able to demonstrate your idea and prove your model to potential investors. Tailoring it around the investors, like Watson did, will improve your chance of securing investment and demonstrate you are serious about borrowing from them.

Smarta in five

1 Business plans are exciting! They validate your dreams

2 Business plans should be currrent and up-to-date

3 Don't hide anything and use honest figures

4 KISS: Keep It Simple Stupid

5 Imagine you'd read 50 dull business plans, how would yours read next

4.9
Realise you need cash – but you don't need to roll in it

"When I first got going, we had no outside funding and fortunately even to this day we've never had any. You just put the money back in that you're making and let it generate itself."

—Charlie Mullins, Pimlico Plumbers

"Be careful what money you raise early on if you go to investors, because it could hamper you – it could determine how much money you can bring into the business later on. Keep it sensible."

—Sokratis Papafloratos, TrustedPlaces

> "The decision never to take finance came about from not wanting to have to answer to anybody else, be that a bank manager, a venture capitalist or an angel investor. You're the only one working for the company who's not taking your salary, so keeping hold of that equity is all important, because that's the pay day in the future really."
>
> ## —Matt McNeill, Sign-up.to and eTickets.to

You do need money to start a business, let's not pretend you don't. For all the talk about how the barriers to entry have tumbled for start-ups and how technology has made many of the previous obstacles 'nearly free', they're not completely free. Plus, it's not simply the cost of its assets your business needs to sustain, it's also the cost of you.

> **WWW**
>
> For help and advice on raising working or growth capital: www.smarta.com/raising-finance

The truth is that most people can't just quit their job and start a business. You probably don't have the luxury of a nest egg that enables you not to earn a salary for a year and you don't have the disposable income to save what it'll take to survive until your business touches profitability. You're going to have to consider how you'll pay the mortgage and rent, eat and provide for your dependants. If that isn't already in your business plan, it's time to put it in now.

If you're struggling to raise any money whatsoever, you need to be realistic about when the best time to start your business is. We'd usually advocate the sooner the better, but there's no point starting in such a precarious financial situation that your business is never going to get a fair crack at survival. Keep working for as long as you can and resist all the burdensome overheads we identified in Chapter 2.2. Adopt the ultra-lightweight start-up mentality to ensure any revenues coming in are going into maintaining yourself (in the essentials not luxuries) and growing the business.

> **WWW**
>
> Got a burning finance question you need answered right away? Ask one of our finance experts free of charge: www.smarta.com/q+a

Plenty of entrepreneurs also continue working on a part-time or freelance basis during the early days of their business, basically doing whatever it takes to make it happen.

Once you've overcome the challenge of securing the bare minimum to sustain you, we think being forced to bootstrap your business isn't so bad after all. The sobering economic climate we find ourselves in seems to have led to a realization that when you really need to, you can make what little money you have go a long way. There are also several upsides to not being flush with investment money. Here's why.

> ## " When you really need to, you can make a little money go a long way "

You'll break even sooner

If you've got more money than you need, it's hard to be frugal and maximize what you spend. Having money coming out of a tap can make you lazy and affect your decision making. If every penny counts, you'll be more motivated to perfect your business model and reach profitability as soon as you can, because rather than being one of several targets, it'll be mission critical.

> **If every penny counts, you'll reach profitability as soon as you can**

You'll be more creative

The most creative and innovative businesses are very often those with little or no money. Why? Because they have no alternative. When you don't have a marketing budget you have to come up with ideas of how else to grab attention. It's no coincidence that the best guerrilla marketing campaigns come from small companies.

You'll have the freedom to do it your way

With no investors breathing down your neck and no bank loan repayments to reach every month, you're far more likely to stay true to your vision. It's all too easily for your decision making to become clouded by external pressures, but by bootstapping you won't have to deal with this. Provided that you continue not too burn through too much cash, you can focus on perfecting your model and proposition, not continually fighting fires and racing time.

You hold on to your equity

There's nothing wrong with taking finance in exchange for equity, but hold off until you've got a fully formed proposition and an established customer base and you'll have the right to command a far better deal than if you're pitching for start-up capital. Likewise, while you're unlikely to be doing an equity deal with a bank, you could well qualify for superior interest rates and more flexible repayment terms once you're in a better negotiating position.

Your mistakes will cost less

One thing you can guarantee about your first six months of trading (if not two years) is that you'll make plenty of mistakes. Typical start-up mistakes tend to come from spending money badly and so when you're bootstrapping you shouldn't lose too much. With cash at a premium, it's also likely you'll be far more frugal in how you spend it and less likely to bet the farm, because there will be so many other ways to spend the money.

You'll make sure you're getting paid

Sounds simple, but small businesses are really bad at getting paid. Big companies are bad at paying as a result, because they know most start-ups will be too scared of upsetting them to chase for monies owed. When you're bootstrapping you'll soon get over that because you'll have no choice.

Money does make the world go around and it's a myth of modern business to pretend you don't need it at all as a start-up. But what is true is that if you're of the right mindset, it's easier than ever before to make what money you have spread further. There are also plenty of upsides to not having too much too soon.

Even if you do find yourself in the enviable position of having investors queuing up to lump into your business, think carefully about how much you need and, crucially, at what stage. While investors won't appreciate you not accounting for how much you'll actually need and then going back cap in hand (especially if it's to sustain your own living costs), they will respect you for being careful with your money and keeping the business lean.

Equity The term commonly applied to the stock or measure of ownership of a company's shares. If you own all the company's shares you own 100% equity in the business. You may sell a slice of equity to an investor.

Smarta in Action: Corporate Homes

Founder: Kemi Laniyan
Company: Corporate Homes
Company profile: Corporate Homes is a specialist residential letting agency providing apartments for young professionals new to the UK.

Overview
Laniyan had just been forced to finish another business that she'd invested a lot of money and time in when she decided to start Corporate Homes. Despite not having money or a job, she knew she didn't want to go back to work for someone else and still wanted to run a business of her own. That meant she had to find a way to market the new business with no money. 'My challenge was to find a way to create my website, brand and marketing material with a non-existent budget,' she says.

How she did it
Laniyan explains, 'I decided to do everything in-house and make use of the internet. I found a ready-made logo rather than paying a big fee for a graphic designer to create it. I bought one from an American firm which cost me £4.'

From internet research, she found a company that let her build her own professional website easily, guiding her through the steps and offering a range of templates to choose from to simplify the process. 'In total it cost me no more than £3.09 per month hosting my website, and it was free for the first month.'

But her business website needed to be more complex than just an out-of-the-box couple of pages – all her business operations would happen through the site. Luckily, she'd chosen a web-hosting company which suited her needs for that too. 'I was also able to create a database on the site, using a separate online database system. My database for displaying all of the properties cost £9.99 per month.'

With her logo and website created, she needed to get the word out. Rather than turning to an expensive design agency, followed up by even more expensive printers, Laniyan printed up simple leaflets in-house. She recognized they didn't need to be flashy, full-gloss brochures and in fact, 'they got us more business than I ever managed'.

The total cost of launching her business? £17.08.

Tips

'Research anything you want to do for your business online first. Do everything yourself during the early stages of trying your idea out,' says Laniyan.

Smarta in five

1 Starting a business isn't free, so be clear how much money you need to survive

2 If you're short on cash you'll make profit quicker

3 Perfect and prove your model before you seek finance

4 Being lightweight, flexible and free of overheads is to your advantage

5 Start small to prove you can borrow to get big

4.10
Keep your friends and family

"Spending all your time on the business is a prerequisite. Getting all your friends and all your family to invest in it is also a prerequisite."

—Walid Al Saqqaf, TrustedPlaces

"To raise money for a very small business is very, very difficult to do. I always say there are three people you can get if from: F, F, and F – friends, family and fools. There are an awful lot of people with money out there, but you have to seduce people. It's a seduction technique."

—Simon Woodroffe, YO! Sushi and YO! Group

"Once I had my business plan, I drove around with all the samples of my shoes in the back of my car. I saw friends, I saw people who had I met in the fashion industry and professional venture capitalists – but I also spoke to my next-door neighbour and my godmother. Everyone wanted to get involved."

—Alexandra Finlay, Fin's

"It's a big risk: you've got to be absolutely sure not just that you're emotionally completely committed to what you're doing but that actually, rationally there is a way forward in a business sense. I think we get confused, and there's a danger you can confuse your friends or family. It's either 'I'm passionate about this brand or this project or this product' or whatever it is you've started, or the reality is, it's not working out mate."

—Ben Keene, TribeWanted

Ah, the three Fs of raising start-up capital: friends, families, fools. Raising cash from your loved ones will provide probably the most favourable, fast and bureaucracy-free money you'll ever get your hands on. As bank lending has dried up, borrowing from friends and family has increased by six times what it was in 2008.

> **The word 'fool' is there for a reason**

But the fact that the word 'fool' is tagged on the end is for a very good reason and should serve as a massive alarm bell not just for them but for you as well.

Before you borrow money from anyone, step right outside of your dream, for a moment throw off how confident you are that your business is going to prosper and accept the fact that the every single day businesses fail. Over two-thirds of new businesses fail within the first five years – we hate to say it, but there's a good chance you will too. Not only do they fail, but they cost people and institutions thousands of pounds that they once invested with goodwill and confidence.

Loans from loved ones come riddled with potential problems. It might seem like the most natural thing in the world to turn to your inner circle, especially if they're keen and your conscience is satisfied you're offering them an opportunity to share in the rewards of your hard work. But really, think more than twice about this.

WWW

Read our in-depth online guide on borrowing from FFFs: www.smarta.com/friends-family-fools

You might be expecting us to recommend that you take money from friends and family; after all, almost everyone else does. And of course, there's no denying an interest-free loan can't be beaten. That said, we don't agree and we don't recommend it.

It might be the cheapest money you can get in a purely financial sense, but it's also potentially the costliest in every other way. If you can't repay them when you said you would or in the worst-case scenario can't repay them at all, then does it seem so cheap?

Do you really want to lose your cousin, brother, mother or life-long friend's money? Are the longer-term repercussions worth it? Is repaying them a pressure you want to take into the business and into your personal life? Whose money would you rather lose – your friends and family's money or the bank's?

> **"Money from friends and family is the costliest in every way other than purely financial"**

Our advice is that you should never take money from friends or family if you have to persuade them to give it to you. Don't borrow an amount that is meaningful to them or you. If they're particularly wealthy and £1,000 is never going to make a significant difference to them – and it's an amount you could scramble together from elsewhere if need be – then that's different, but never take money that people are likely to need in the extremest of unlikely emergencies and that you couldn't get hold of should the need occur.

The old maxim of not mixing business with pleasure has become an institution for a reason as well. Putting aside the worst-case scenarios, the everyday pressure isn't to be dismissed either. Borrowing can be such a heavy weight on a relationship that even when things are going more or less as well as they could, it can still cause unwanted strain.

> **"Never take money from friends or family if you have to persuade them to give it to you"**

Much as you and the lender know, trust and like each other, when money gets involved, everything changes. No matter how much you try to avoid it, talk of the business will start seeping into your social life with them. For an innocuous 'What have you got planned for the weekend?' read 'I'm due my next dividend or repayment, shouldn't you be working Saturdays?' and 'how exactly did you afford that holiday?'.

Of course, borrowing from friends and family does work for some people. If you do decide to, we recommend you do everything you can to future-proof the agreement against all the big and small pressures involved so that all parties are absolutely clear about what they're entering into.

Do the following.

Write it all down and make it legal

Let a document be the bad cop. When everything's written down, rather than 'Well, I thought you told me in the pub XYZ', the answer is there in black and white. Likewise, no matter how close you are, make the lending legal. This shouldn't be expensive with a small start-up if you can find a friendly law firm and should serve as both a mark of security and a sobering reminder that this is a professional, legally binding agreement. Don't be tempted just to make your own document and both sign it, this almost definitely won't be comprehensive and include all potential outcomes and scenarios, nor will it stand up in court.

Make ground rules

Figure out at this early stage how you'll report progress to your FFFs. Consider when you'll provide updates and what detail they'll give. You also, of course, need to have worked out repayment or dividend terms – remember to factor in any grace periods on payment deadlines – and add an extra 12 months on to when you think you'll be able to repay them, just in case.

Finally, but crucially, talk out what happens in case of an emergency – if the business fails, if it needs a serious cash injection, or any other fateful possibility that you or your solicitor points out.

Smarta in Action: Clippy

Founder: Calypso Rose
Company: Clippy
Company profile: A fashion accessory company appealing to young girls and women. The Clippy range is all about personalizing: the bags come with pockets that can be filled with photographs and mementoes, creating a unique and personal accessory.
Founded: 2004

Overview

When Calypso Rose made a bag to show off her collection of Polaroid photographs on her kitchen table, she was astonished when people stopped her in the street wanting to know where she had bought it. Inspired by the idea of turning it into a business, Rose began to search for manufacturers. For the business to take off, she knew she would need capital, but the idea of borrowing from a bank was too scary.

How she did it

Instead of undergoing a grilling from a bank manager, Rose approached her parents for the £2,500 of start-up capital she needed. Borrowing from her parents meant that if the business didn't work out, she could take her time to pay back the loan without having to worry about interest.

Rose had to spend time convincing her parents to give her the loan; the family talked about it for several months before her parents committed. 'The risk was we could lose the money,' says her mother now. 'In fact, we had committed to the loan, but changed our minds. It was only after a huge amount of cajoling that we finally agreed to it.'

Rose worked out that she only had to sell 250 bags to break even, which meant she could begin paying back the loan. With a stall on Portobello Road market, she managed to sell every bag within a month.

Smarta in five

1 Borrowing from FFFs can save you a fortune, but cost you in many other ways

2 Never borrow from friends or family if you have to convince them to invest

3 Never borrow meaningful money

4 Overestimate the time it'll take you to pay the money back

5 Do everything by the letter of the law and agree ground rules

4.11
Let the bank say 'yes' (they want to)

> "The bank helped out. I've got a basic overdraft from the bank, and the main reason we got the overdraft is because we've proved we can bring in a decent amount of money from the start."
>
> **—Ben Keene, TribeWanted**

> "We love information. Any information you give us will help us work out what you're trying to achieve, and will help us work out whether you're going to be successful or not."
>
> **—Peter Ibbetson, RBS**

> "It's a numbers game – you should almost notch up your rejections. My formula in life is that for the 20 times you ask, you should expect to get no's the first 19 times and only then should you start expecting to get a yes."
>
> **—Sahar Hashemi, Coffee Republic**

Are banks lending sufficient money to small businesses? It's a question that's been debated by politicians, business organizations, the media and entrepreneurs alike since the onset of the banking collapse in 2009 and the subsequent slow recovery of the economy. It's a debate we decidedly can't solve, so we don't see any point contributing to it, other than to make a few simple observations we think are more relevant.

Regardless of whether they're doing enough, UK banks are open for business (and issuing new lending to small businesses at roughly half a billion pounds a month, according to the British Banking Association). Banks don't make money if they're not lending. No bank has ever deliberately passed up the opportunity to make an investment that it believes offers safe, sensible returns.

Now for some harder facts to swallow. Banks don't lend money to businesses that aren't viable. They've probably adjusted what their view of 'viable' is in recent years. They don't always get it right and they turn down businesses that then go on to prove they they're more than viable. Deal with it. Really. That's just how it is and bar some cyclical economic turbulence, that's how it'll always be.

The critical point, though, is that banks are lending. Not everyone is getting bank loans, but plenty of companies are. And provided that you present them with a solid reason to lend you money, there's every chance they will. That said, you have to take this seriously and be realistic about what banks need to see to lend money on their terms – not yours.

Too many businesses rush to the bank ill-prepared and then complain 'banks aren't lending'. They go with a raw idea, a business plan that isn't correctly researched or thought out, no market research, no testing, no testimonials of sales, and they simply don't present themselves as viable and investment worthy, whether they've got the next Google in their back pocket or not.

The hard truth is that it's not the bank's job to see through your overenthusiasm, nerves, naiveté and lack of preparation. It doesn't work like that, so lose the chip off your shoulder and learn to play by their rules.

> **It's not the bank's job to see through your lack of preparation**

Remember also that banks have been dishing out loans to the same types of company for a long time. They might not let us see it, but they have a lot of data on what businesses work and don't work, what a business plan should and shouldn't look like. They might not be right all of the time, but they're not bothered about that either; they're right enough of the time for them to turn a profit.

Your job, then, is to show the bank you're as good, prepared and organized as they expect you to be (and want you to be, remember) and as their data shows you should be. You have to show them that to get them interested – and then show them you've got another 10% to get them excited.

> **Your job is to show the bank you're as good as they expect you to be**

Sahar Hashemi, co-founder of coffee-shop chain Coffee Republic, had 39 rejections for bank finance before she finally heard the magic 'yes' word. She knows people who got around 700 rejections before being accepted.

WWW

Hundreds more articles and videos on banking: www.smarta.com/banking

Rejections for small business bank finance are not unusual for the reasons discussed above. But rejection shouldn't spell defeat. So when you come up against your own personal Dr No, don't lose faith. Learn from your mistakes, keep going, and use the guidelines below to give yourself the best shot at making your next pitch for bank finance that bit closer to being successful. Even if you are still 38 applications away from the answer you desperately want to hear.

The first response to rejection should be to find out why. The best entrepreneurs learn from each rejection they get rather than being defeated by it, using the most specific feedback they can obtain to refine an application and stand a better chance next time. Be positive and ask the bank manager who denied your request for finance for the reasons. Find out exactly what you're missing. Don't be shy – they'll appreciate your determination.

The lending criteria: Show them the money

Remember that banks have spent decade after decade collating and analysing business performance data to figure out what exact requirements a business needs to fulfil to make their investments as low risk as possible. Lending criteria are the result of all that information and calculation.

WWW

Watch our insider video with the head of RBS small business banking, who reveals what you need to do to secure a bank loan: www.smarta.com/insider-bank-advice

The most basic of criteria is the ability to demonstrate how any borrowing will be repaid. You need to show a provision for this within your everyday cashflow forecasts, not simply promise to do it. The bank needs to see that their lending will work, and not just on the basis of your best intentions.

It's true that security remains high on the lending criteria of UK banks. If you don't have security to offer, ask about government backed loan schemes for companies with limited credit, but extensively research what individual criteria you need to qualify and get a result. Ideally, speak to businesses that have obtained EFG-secured lending.

That said, the banks insist that security is a deal breaker. Providing clear evidence that your business will generate enough revenue and clear profit to repay them is the clincher – and the more you can do to prove that the better.

Chris Kane was turned down by five banks when he started Greendale Construction in 1989 at a time when the market wasn't strong, he had no track record and no money of his own. However, once the company had secured two permanent contracts, the bank was satisfied and gave the lending that enabled Chris to grow what's now an £8m-turnover business.

It's your job to present the evidence: put everything on the table and don't try to hide anything. Show the bank all your financial information, bring your current cashflow and profit and future forecasts. Take supplier lists, show your competitor analysis. Use graphs, tables and diagrams to make what you're saying quantifiable, real and easy to understand – but most importantly, ensure that everything you say is underpinned by fierce financial thoroughness. Knowing your numbers like you're about to go on *Dragons' Den* gives the impression that you're professional and in control of your business.

There's no doubt also a degree of finding your Mr or Ms Right. Ideally you want to find a bank manager who understands your sector and who you're able to connect with. It won't make a difference on the pure lending criteria of your financials, but it will increase the likelihood that they'll pay extra attention to your application and be more willing to work with you if small adjustments are needed.

For all the cases where determination eventually pays off, there also comes a stage where you have to give up. We want your business to succeed as much as you do but if bank after bank is telling you that your business simply isn't going to work, it might just be time to listen. Often the fresh eyes of the bank are able to see that, whereas a business owner doesn't necessarily want to admit defeat so easily.

The final piece of advice we've got for securing bank finance comes straight out of the old school: look the part. That means putting on a suit even if you're starting a surfing business. If you speak to some banks they'll tell you this absolutely isn't the case any more, but the reality is you'll be dealing with some individuals for whom it is still very much important. Why take this risk for the sake of an hour's discomfort? It also shows you're mature enough to take a viewpoint outside your own and look at the bigger picture of what your clients' expectations might be, not your own.

WWW

Apply for a business bank account and loan through Smarta's easy-to-use application tools: www.smarta.com/business-banking

If you put all this in place, there's every reason banks will want to lend to you. You just need to meet them on their terms. After all, they're the ones with the money and it's your job to impress them.

Smarta in Action: Green Energy Options

Founder: Patrick Caiger-Smith
Company: Green Energy Options
Company profile: Offers a range of Home Energy Hubs that make energy visible and help you to manage, understand and reduce the amount of carbon dioxide you produce.
Founded: 2006

Overview

Having run his business, Green Energy Options, for two years, Patrick Caiger-Smith was delighted to close a 'decent-sized' contract with one of the UK's largest utility companies. There was one catch, though: the timing of the contract meant the business would have to borrow some extra working capital, fast. 'If we didn't get the financing in place we would have jeopardized the terms of the contract,' says Caiger-Smith.

The timing couldn't have been worse: in the middle of the recession, Caiger-Smith knew banks would be unwilling to lend.

How he did it

Because of the economic climate, Caiger-Smith anticipated a rejection. 'It was touch and go whether or not it would happen,' he says. 'If it hadn't managed to come through, it would have delayed our plans significantly and potentially jeopardized the contract.'

When he approached his bank manager, Caiger-Smith was completely open about the issues he faced: a lack of credit and a short turnaround time. He made it clear that the loan wasn't to give the business additional cashflow or cover losses, it was there to help finance an order book. His bank manager was understanding and recommended a government-backed loan to cover the shortfall.

If Caiger-Smith had attempted to bluff or lie his way into a loan, it almost certainly would not have come off. Instead, his honesty strengthened his relationship with the bank. And he got the money he needed. 'We established regular meetings. We'd invited each other to things to keep up to speed about what was happening with the business. That meant they knew exactly where we were and what the future of the business was looking like,' he explains.

Tips

Although credit is getting back on track, banks are still careful about the amount they will lend. Build up a relationship with your bank manager. Keep them informed, even if it doesn't seem there's a lot of point in doing so. If you can show that the numbers are stacking up, you can prove to them that if the contract is fulfilled, there's a good chance of you paying back the loan.

Smarta in five

1 Banks are lending to viable small firms – you just need to meet their criteria

2 Don't pitch to a bank until you're ready

3 Get your financials in shape and show them everything

4 Find out the reason for any rejections and rework for model and pitch

5 Find a bank and bank manager who understand your space

4.12
Look for a guardian angel (if you're sure that you need one)

"I'm a numbers person. However you want to talk about it, my main criteria is a return on capital."

—Duncan Bannatyne, *Dragons Den* and The Bannatyne Group

"Every investor looks at an investment with the same set of criteria in different measures. I think one of the things they look at is the genetic make-up of the entrepreneur. You have to be a very particular kind of person to survive as an entrepreneur. You have to be extremely focused."

—Richard Moross, Moo

"It's natural to be reluctant to give equity away. But at the end of the day, your business has to grow, and I would be very cautious about restricting it because you're sentimental, or you're protective over the equity."

—Jamie Murray Wells, Glasses Direct

Private investors, more fetchingly dubbed business angels, account for between £800m and £1bn of early-stage investment each year. *Dragons' Den* may have thrown angels into the public spotlight but they remain elusive and, while £1 billion looks like a big figure in isolation, it's only equivalent to six or seven weeks of bank lending. Angels are increasingly active, though, especially while interest rates remain low and other investment vehicles are high risk.

Taking investment from an individual or number of individuals in exchange for an equity stake in your business has obvious appeal. While you're giving away a slice of your pie, you're getting your hands on growth capital you can spend now without having to worry about making monthly repayments. In many cases you're also bringing on board the services of an experienced entrepreneur, their wealth of knowledge and, if you're extra lucky, their contacts book.

Angels aren't philanthropists though. They're in the game of making money, not donating it, and they place a high price on their time. They won't be looking to mentor someone out of the kindness of their heart.

> **Angels are in the game of making money, not donating it, and they place a high price on their time**

Angels will be looking for smart business propositions with fast-growth potential where they expect to realize a return inside typically two to three years, stretching to possibly five. In addition to a pure investment opportunity, they'll typically entertain proposals that are in their area of expertise, that engage something they're passionate about, an idea that captures their imagination or, very occasionally, an individual who exudes enough confidence for them to take a punt on them.

Normally you'll need to tick four out of five of these boxes if not all of them. Angels get dozens if not hundreds of investment opportunities a week and can afford to be picky. They rarely need to do a deal, either, so you've got to be seriously smart to capture their attention.

> **Angels want to find entrepreneurs with serious knowledge and passion**

They'll usually want to see the financial evidence a bank will want to see, bar the ability to make immediate repayments, but they'll normally make a decision far more quickly – possibly within the first 15 minutes of meeting you. Even more so than when you sit down with the bank, you have to be at your dynamic best when pitching to an angel. These are smart entrepreneurial individuals and they want to find people like them or someone with serious knowledge and passion; probably all three.

On the upside, angels understand how entrepreneurship works and will be prepared to take a longer-term view than the banks. That's why they're often suited to technology or science companies with long plays that won't necessarily be generating immediate profit, but offer long-term value and exit potential.

So how do you find the invisible man?

1 Scrutinize other deals

Don't start your search looking for any investor, begin by looking for the perfect angel. Want to know who invests in companies just like yours and has the expertise you're looking for? Look at businesses like yours. Search private equity websites, trade mags, financial papers and competitors' sites to discover where investment in your sector and stage of growth is coming from. Take note of investors you want to explore further and founders/MDs of companies to contact; their insights will be invaluable.

2 Network your ass off

Investors are continually looking for the next big thing, the start-up creating a buzz. Be where they're looking. Get to the events your target angels attend and where you know other investment-ready companies or investor-connected MDs hang out. Ask for attendee lists in advance so you know who to speak with.

A note of caution: that doesn't mean turn into Mr or Mrs Party Animal 2010. No one invests in a drunk. Neither does it mean reeling off your pitch the minute you shake hands. Avoid the hard sell, but do talk passionately about your business and who you're looking to meet. Angels don't back ideas, they back people. Relax and be yourself. Always follow up the next day via email or social media.

3 Angel networks

The British Business Angel Association (BBAA) might sound stuffy, but you'll soon realize that angels don't fly solo. They know each other, they talk and typically they share investments to minimize risk. Angels often make local investments and the BBAA will immediately refer you to your regional chapter. All BBAA associations and investors adhere to a code of conduct. There are 22 registered business angel networks and 20 early-stage venture capital (VC) funds.

Regional networks' fees and ways of operating vary. Usually they'll vet a business plan for a cost and present it to their registered angels. They then take a commission (around 5%) on any completed deals.

Angels' Den is proving an exciting alternative. It's an online pitching and matching service which now boasts in excess of 2,500 registered angels. It charges £499 to get your idea in front of one of its angels and takes 5% of any deal secured. It claims that a fifth of the people using its service have found backers.

Angels' Den was formed out of the frustration of its founder Bill Morrow and his inability to secure funding for a previous idea despite having spent £15,000 joining other networks. See point 5 for advice on matchmakers that can't demonstrate previous success and, more pertinently, guarantees on exactly who and how many people they're pitching you to.

4 Events

Events focused on matching investment seekers with investors are on the increase. While each has its niche, they essentially work around the established OpenCoffee model of paying a fee up front, typically £350–500, to pitch your idea to a crowd of potential investors.

Some are better than others and our advice would be to find out as much as you can about the calibre and background of the attending investors before shelling out. Also look for events focused on your particular sector.

Angels' Den runs SpeedFunding events and charges £249 per person for pitches to between 10 and 20 angels. You'd also pay them 5% of any funds raised. CmyPitch, a site where you upload video pitches, also runs events called CmyPitchLive. They cost £300 plus 5% of completed deals.

5 Avoid middlemen

Networking hard for an investor will guarantee you one thing: at least one person will offer to find investment for you for a bounty. It's usually a slice or a one-off fee, or sometimes both. They're sharks. Be warned: the fee can be 5% for an intro to an angel network, who'll also want 5%, or 10% for completing a deal on their own. Add in legal fees and suddenly the money you get your hands on looks a lot more expensive than when you started out. Make sure you're not paying for contacts you could make yourself with a bit of digging around.

When it comes to pitching to an angel, remember that they'll be looking for exceptional businesses, impressive individuals, evidence that you understand your numbers and, crucially, chemistry. All of this and they'll be short on time, quite often attention and quick to make their minds up.

So you need to be on top of your game and super organized. Expect interrogation of your figures and there's no excuse for not knowing them. While you're likely to avoid the sharp-tongued one-liners and hardened negotiations of *Dragons' Den*, remember that just as the producers pick the most controversial highlights for the sake of dramatic television, successful pitches in the den typically also last for a gruelling two to three hours, not the six or seven minutes that are screened.

Be clear on the growth potential of your business and never try to pull the wool over an angel's eyes. It's highly unlikely to work and will get identified in due diligence, but more than anything it will kill all trust – and without trust you won't have a deal.

If you do chase angel investment, be sure you're doing it for the right reasons and at the right time – and don't take just any deal that's on the table. The deal has to work as much for you as it does the angel and you have to be absolutely certain you can work with them. All parties need to be totally clear on the expectations both in terms of investment, returns and exit, but also participation in the business. Be abundantly clear what level of support an angel will be expected to give, which decisions you will and won't consult them on and how you'll report to them.

Angel investments and relationships vary massively. As much as you'll have to work hard to find one who will be interested in investing in you, it's critical that you find someone who's an equally good fit for you.

WWW

For more advice on finding a business angel:
www.smarta.com/business-angels

Smarta in Action: Wordia

Founder: Ed Baker
Company: Wordia
Company profile: Free online dictionary with video examples from comedians, celebrities, sports stars – and you! Your life, your words, your dictionary.
Founded: 2008

Overview
Ed Baker came up with the idea for Wordia while he was on a quest to improve his own vocabulary. A former television producer, he decided he wanted to engage with language differently, and using video seemed like a great way to do it.

The next step was to find some start-up capital. Having seen Bebo founder Michael Birch speak at a conference, Baker identified him as a potential investor. But with Birch fairly busy after the multimillion-dollar sale of his business, Baker's first challenge was to grab some of his time.

How he did it
Baker discovered that Birch would be speaking at a NESTA conference and decided he would approach him there. After the speech, though, he discovered

that half the other conference delegates wanted to pitch to Birch too. Patiently waiting his turn, Baker noticed Birch's wife, Xochi, in the corner, and got chatting to her. After the scrum was over, she introduced the pair.

'We went for a few beers at a pub nearby and spoke about the idea,' says Baker. 'I was probably a bit overzealous in my pitching to him.' Nevertheless, the ploy worked. Birch was interested in the idea and when he flew back to California, they continued their discussions over email.

The next step was to discuss the valuation of the company. 'It was a strange thing to do because we were talking about the worth of something that hadn't started yet – it wasn't tangible,' says Baker.

They continued to talk and a few months later, Baker flew out to visit Birch in California. 'I had realized you couldn't work out the value of a company remotely via email. It's about the personal conversations and doing business with people.'

Just two days after he arrived in California, after a great deal of number crunching, Baker and Birch shook hands – and Wordia had the start-up capital it needed.

Tips
When he was looking for investment, Baker had a target in mind. Whether it's one investor or several, draw up a targeted list of possible leads and be persistent.

Smarta in five

1 Angels want fast-growth, high-yielding investment opportunities. Is that really you

2 Finding the right angel investor is more important than finding one who'll invest

3 Pay to pitch only if you're sure of the audience

4 Don't pay a middleman to find you an angel you can find for free (or yourself)

5 Be clear why you want an angel, how you'll spend their money and what you expect from them

Part 5
Work smart

5.1
Focus on scary but attainable goals

"Set your expectations in terms of what you can achieve, relatively and modestly, and overshoot them, rather than have expectations that are too high and be disappointed."

—Karen Hanton, Toptable

"I'm a big believer in setting a big scary place that you've got to try and get to and when you're growing very fast you need something that galvanizes the organization and everybody is focused on it. And you know, sales was one thing but there was also the vision of what we're actually trying to create."

—Martha Lane Fox, Lastminute.com

Smart businesses with ambitious growth plans think big and set themselves SBAGs: Scary But Attainable Goals. They don't just plod from quarter to quarter and year to year with no clear idea of what they want to achieve other than 'success'. The secret to all strong leadership is direction and if you fail to give your business direction it has no chance of reaching your destination.

You should always have strategic goals for the company both in the long and short term and be setting both company, departmental and individual targets plotted against hitting your SBAGs.

Targets help you structure growth. Once you know what you want to achieve, you can go about achieving it. If your SBAG for the year is a 50% increase in sales, then you can start setting monthly targets which plot out how you'll hit the figure and looking at what areas of the company the new business will come from.

Targets enable you measure performance across the business and identify areas that are flourishing, working below capacity or perhaps need additional resources. Without agreed targets to benchmark performance, you'll have no indication of what's working from one month to another.

> **"Without agreed targets to benchmark performance, you'll have no indication of what's working from one month to another"**

Provided that it's done well and the Attainable in your SBAGs is really attainable, targets are also an excellent motivational tool for employees and a great way to keep people focused on output on a weekly, monthly and in some instances daily basis. Like all staff incentives, your targets should be geared to rewarding achievement as much as they're in place to highlight underperformance – and they have to be fair.

> **"Your targets should be geared to rewarding achievement – and they have to be fair"**

No part of your business is free from setting targets: establishing and growing revenues, orders and customer numbers; market share; the launch of new products, lines or stores; structural growth; new funding; training and employee engagement; research expenditure versus return; press coverage; brand awareness; customer loyalty – the list goes on. That said, you should be aware not to set targets for the sake of it. Make sure that staff don't feel too pressurized or continually assessed and that there's a purpose to what you're measuring.

There is a danger that if you become too target driven, staff won't stop to come up with creative solutions to problems or spend time on a job if they think they'll miss their targets or be marked down as a result.

Whichever targets you set, make sure they're SMART

S – Specific: use hard numbers and definitive goals rather than fluffy aims, and focus on one part of the business per target. So say, 'I want to see sales increase by 10%' rather than 'I want to see the business grow'.

M – Measurable: make sure you can measure your goal. Use percentages or unit numbers or anything else that is straightforward to measure. This allows you to assess performance and will show you precisely when a target has been hit.

A – Achievable: overambitious goals can be incredibly damaging to morale and plans. Make sure that targets are within reason.

R – Realistic: only create goals that you can achieve with the resources you already have.

T – Time-Specific: set deadlines for each objective.

How to set targets

A good starting point is to start by breaking down your long-term SBAGs year by year. Hone in on specific parts of the business that need attention and look at what needs to be achieved to hit those goals, both in terms of individual targets and resourcing. Think of the way the different cogs in your business push each other into motion. If you want more sales, you'll need to work on marketing and website visits, so you'll need to set targets for both of those to reach one overall aim for business growth.

As a new business, it can feel like you're plucking figures out of the sky when it comes to setting targets. You have no sales history and no real idea of how much you'll be able to achieve. Set yourself targets nonetheless, as it's always better to work towards something and it's imperative that you start measuring. Then get micro with your targets. Instead of monthly or quarterly targets, work on days and weeks.

Make sure you're continually pushing yourself to go that extra mile – that's what SBAGs are for! Smart

> **Smart businesses work hard to smash as many targets as possible – and then set themselves even higher ones**

businesses don't coast along hitting their baseline. They work hard to smash as many targets as possible – and then set themselves even higher ones. And when they're not hitting them they get proactive about why they're not and creative about finding solutions. Having clear target data will give you far more scope to find solutions that keep you on track to achieve big results.

Smarta in Action: Lingo24

Founder: Christian Arno
Company name: Lingo24
Company profile: A translation company based in Aberdeen, founded as an online business. It now has operations in the UK, Panama, Romania, China and New Zealand, not to mention 100 members of staff worldwide and a turnover in excess of £3 million.
Founded: 2001

Overview
Arno wanted to get more out of his sales team and knew that setting targets would be the way to do it. But things didn't go to plan at first. He had to fine-tune his strategy to make it effective.

How they did it
Arno unwittingly made his first set of targets for his sales team hugely overambitious. Staff constantly fell short of what he expected of them – until he realized it was his targets at fault.

So he decided that instead of plucking hoped-for figures out of the sky, it would be better to talk through what would be realistic with each employee.

The sense of ownership this fostered, and the motivation created by the newly attainable goals, has massively raised morale and productivity. 'It's like our employees have got their own little business within our business, and they're trying to hit goals for their business,' Arno says. 'Rewards work in the interest of the business and the individual.'

He's set up a system where staff get bonuses if they meet targets, and the amount they get increases in steps; the pot at the end increases with each completed 25% of the target. This keeps them focused and motivated, Arno explains.

He now swears by creating targets for 'almost every aspect of the business'. 'It clarifies to every individual in the company exactly what is expected of them in hard numbers.'

Tips
Offer employees a prize that is just within reach and tie targets to financial reward. Money is a great incentive, because success alone isn't a draw for staff like it is for you. Be ready to adjust targets to make sure they are actually attainable, while still pushing staff to work hard.

Smarta in five

1 Be ambitious but realistic: set Scary Big Attainable Goals

2 Have clear targets for everything – 'to be successful' isn't enough

3 Set targets that are SMART: Specific, Measurable, Achievable, Realistic, Time-specific

4 Agree all targets with staff and offer incentives and rewards for hitting them

5 Measure what's tangible, don't stunt creativity

5.2
Don't let cashflow kill you

"You don't have the luxury of time. As soon as you think you've got a problem, particularly if it's a cashflow problem, you need to start getting someone in to help you and make the changes you need to right at this moment, even if they're completely ruthless. Because it's far better to do that than think, 'Oh, it will work itself out and a white knight will appear on the horizon'."

—Rachel Elnaugh, Red Letter Days and *Dragons' Den*

"Instead of having a monthly delivery which means that you've got to pay for a month's worth of stock, get a weekly delivery which means that by the time you pay for that weekly stock you'll probably have sold it."

—Deborah Meaden, *Dragons' Den*

> "It doesn't matter if you're making a profit, it's about how much money have you got in the bank. It's really, really dangerous to ignore that. Even if you get someone else to come in and do your finances for you, you need to understand it."
>
> **—Matt McNeill, Sign-up.to and eTickets.to**

Exactly how much cash is in your business right now, at this second? If you don't have a business yet, what's the total sum in your current account, wallet, down the back of the sofa and in your spare coppers pot? If you don't know, we don't care how smart your business idea is, you're not ready for business. Forget all the rest: cash is king. Ensuring that you've always got cash in your business is more important than anything – absolutely anything else. Why? Because if you run out of cash, you're finished. And if you don't know at any one point how much money you've got at your disposal, your business is on its deathbed.

We're not being dramatic, it's that simple. If there's one thing all the entrepreneurs featured in this book agree on, it's that cashflow is the lifeblood of your business – and several of them have learnt that the hard way. It's not up for debate.

Let's take this pretty commonplace situation: you're due to be paid £5,000 by a client and have a new contract lined up worth £10,000. Suddenly what's looking like a good month turns bad, when the £5,000 fails to land and you can't start the new contract on time because the money you have in the bank only covers your fixed overheads and not the materials you need to buy. You end up losing the new contract, and are suddenly without any way of meeting your next month's outgoings and go under, despite having big £25,000 and £100,000 contracts confirmed for later in the year.

This might seem extreme, but it's an everyday example of how otherwise perfectly viable and profitable businesses go under by simply not keeping enough cash in the business. Most start-ups that fall foul of cashflow problems tend to be paying too much attention to day-to-day cashflow and not pre-empting costs or delaying income beyond their control. You need to make detailed cashflow forecasts spanning at least the next few months, ideally the next year. And critically, you always need to allow for a contingency sum: always expect the unexpected.

Even if you're not a figures person, don't avoid this. It's really not as hard as it sounds and is information you simply need to know. A cashflow projection is generally divided into short periods of weeks or months, and is usually done for a year or a quarter in advance. Map out exactly when money is coming in and going out. A spread-

> **❝Always expect the unexpected – your cashflow is information you simply need to know❞**

sheet with dates across the top is one way to do this, or better still get organized properly from day one by using one of the many accounting and bookkeeping software packages that come with ready-made cashflow forecast templates.

www
You can find tools to help with cashflow at
www.smarta.com/tools

Your money coming in will be from contracts you've won and sales you make. If you sell B2B (business-to-business), or your B2C (business-to-consumer) customers don't pay on the spot, you need to allow for late payments, or no payments at all. B2B customers will generally take 60 to 90 days to pay depending on the payment terms you agree, but you have to expect them to be at least a month late after that.

The money going out will be for all the materials and costs involved in any contract you win or product you have to finance, all your suppliers' bills, utilities bills, business rates, rent, cleaners' bills, business expenses and so on. Anything you spend, basically.

Update and adjust your forecast as and when payments come in (or go out). You've only created a forecast, so you need to readjust it with the actual data to make it as accurate as possible when you can. Obviously you won't yet know what contracts and sales you'll achieve in the future, so remember to input these every time something has been signed off and you know you'll be getting money in.

Protecting your cashflow: the 12-step plan

1 Have your back-up plan ready – talk to your bank about credit

Once you've made your forecast, it should be easier to spot the times when you're going to be short on cash, buying you time to sort out the problem. It is absolutely essential that you tell your bank as early as possible if you're going to need an extended credit facility for times like this. Take all your cashflow workings and forecasts and look to secure an overdraft facility to help you out for times when cashflow dries up – but don't dip into it unless it really is a cashflow emergency.

2 Set out a clear payment policy – and be strict about it

Late payments are going to be your number one cashflow issue. As a rule of thumb, businesses will pay bills as late as they possibly have to. It's your responsibility to get the money you're owed in when you need it. Set a payment period you can handle. Issue invoices as soon as an order is placed, then follow up with a gentle payment reminder email a couple of days later. You have to chase and chase again, email and call (without being annoying – you don't want to lose a customer!). Remember to factor in the possibility of late payments into your forecasts, but if someone's missed the deadline, don't be afraid to call them every other day, if not daily. Just do it with a smile and keep explaining you're a start-up and you need the cash!

3 Offer discounts for prompt payment

Not massive ones, mind. But if you can afford it (that is, you still earn profit on the transaction), it's well worth incentivizing customers to pay on time – or even in advance – to save your own skin.

4 Pay your bills as late as you can

Always pay on time when you can, but if your cashflow is getting dangerously low, hold off paying your suppliers and bills for as long as you can. If you're getting pushed for payment by a partner you value, be honest and say you're having a difficult week or month and give them a clear date when they can expect payment. Stick to it and the client will appreciate your honesty. Miss it, though, and they might start to wonder if you've a serious cashflow problem.

5 Negotiate better payment terms with suppliers

Ask your suppliers if you can have more flexibility with your repayment dates – again, play on the fact that you're a start-up. Promise them more lucrative business in the future if they help you out.

6 Check your bank account daily

Obvious stuff, but you've got to be on top of those numbers. Make sure you can access your account and finances wherever you are and from your mobile. There are no excuses not to be able to any more.

7 Sync yourself safe

Wherever possible, make sure that you time big payments (wage payments, large bills, rent) for when you know you've got cash to spare. Your cashflow forecast will show you when these times are.

8 Don't buy what you don't need

Sounds simple, but so many businesses stockpile more product and materials than they need for the job (or sale) at hand. It's a complete waste of cash.

9 If you're not a numbers person, get someone who is

From day one. Don't trick yourself into believing it's something that can wait. That said, you have to understand the basics of money in, money out yourself. There are no excuses. It's simple enough for anyone to pick up and you shouldn't be in business if you can't instantly know the state of your balance sheet.

10 Use accounting software from day one

No, an Excel spreadsheet doesn't cut it. There is a myth that accounting software is hard to use and that it's easier just to keep a spreadsheet. Seriously, that's wrong and nonsensical. It's more complicated to keep accounts on a spreadsheet and much easier to make a mistake – one error in a formula and all your numbers could be wrong. It's harder to read, it's not as safe and it won't integrate with your iPhone. It'll save you money to have software (certainly more than it costs you). The less you know about money, the more you need the software.

11 Get an accountant

Again, stop screaming that you can't afford one and start realizing that bean-counters are your friends: they save you more than they'll cost you and they'll keep you on track. You can afford one from the minute you make sales. It can be a morning a week, but if cashflow is the lifeblood of a business (which it undoubtedly is) and you're not a finance person, you need to get professional help, now.

12 Don't get into the trap where you're not making profit on what you sell

Sounds obvious, but it's easy to keep your prices fixed and lose control of what its costing you to produce what you're selling. Don't confuse turnover with profit.

WWW

Get organised with professional cashflow software: www.smarta.com/business-builder

Cashflow's mortal enemies – and how to combat them

Bad credit controls: run a credit check on first-time customers so you don't get any nasty surprises.

Overtrading: be careful that you only take on as much business as you can manage.

Excessive credit or financing: remember, borrowing money costs, so try to keep it to a minimum.

Holding excessive stock: if you often have more stock than you can sell, think about changing your patterns of ordering.

Poor marketing: falling or slowing sales should act as a warning sign, so take action.

Substandard management accounting: if you keep tidy accounts, you should be able to predict impending cashflow crises.

Lax invoicing and ordering procedures: maintain measured and regular contact with your customers.

No line of credit for emergencies: consider all funding options – factoring, invoice discounting, hire purchase, loans, leasing and mortgages. Use over-drafts for short-term requirements.

Depending too much on one customer: because if they decide to start buying elsewhere, you'll fold. Make sure that you have an even spread of customers and that you'd be able to survive if any one of them stopped buying from you.

Smarta in Action: Antares Supplies

Founder: Ian Walker
Company: Antares Supplies
Company profile: A small industry trader who supplies nuts, bolts, power-tools and the like to workshops and engineering companies.
Founded: 2007

Overview
Walker first learnt about the importance of good cashflow management the hard way. 'I had a big deal that I wanted to land at the beginning of this year but needed £1,500 to secure it. When I approached the bank they would only lend it to me if I put my house on the line.' Not wanting to take that risk, he had to turn to friends and family instead. Now, he takes a range of precautions to safeguard his cashflow.

How he did it
'Cashflow is always going to be a problem for a small business, especially in the early stages of its lifecycle,' Walker explains.

He's got into the habit of being selective about work he takes on. 'I have consciously whittled down my clients to ensure that they are reliable and trustworthy.' This means he doesn't need to offer incentives or discounts encouraging people to pay on time. A simple polite phone call does the trick instead.

That's not to say he takes it easy on those who do slip through the net. 'If clients have taken 90 days or longer to pay an outstanding account, I send them a letter asking them to pay promptly or their account will be limited to cash-only accounts. I always follow up with this.'

He points out you need to understand a business's size and structure and how long they're likely to take to pay. With larger companies, it can apparently take 60 days just for an order invoice to go through their systems.

Smarta in five

1 Poor cashflow kills otherwise perfectly good companies

2 Make a cashflow forecast and stick to it

3 Always have a contingency cashflow buffer

4 Offer customers and clients an incentive to pay in advance

5 If cashflow dries up, don't pay anything until you have to

5.3
Drive profitability and productivity

> "We get over 60% of our business from client referrals so that's always been really at the core of our strategy."
> **—Matt McNeill, Sign-up.to and eTickets.to**

> "A big, big warning: when you go into that growth spurt, keep your eye on the dull stuff – buying or ordering, the systems and processes, the accounts."
> **—Deborah Meaden, *Dragons' Den***

> "We had to make redundancies, and it was really sad and hard. They were in roles that weren't directly making us revenue and we just had to say: 'Gosh, I mean let's just be honest about it. Is paying this person to do something that isn't really generating revenue the right thing to do during a recession?'"
>
> **—Ryan Carson, Carsonified**

Once you start to bring in steady revenues, it's time to stop trying to scramble for sales anywhere you can and get strategic about where the profit points are in your business. That means taking a good hard look at your bottom line and identifying what is making you money – and what isn't. It's time to get real and drop the things that aren't making you enough money (no matter how precious they are to you), and focus on those where the margin and the strongest flow of sales are.

Identify your strongest products and look at how you can drive more sales by focusing on marketing them more effectively to their target audience. Explore how you can get your proven product in front of more people. If you provide a service, start to segment your clients by how much they spend and what you think they'll spend in the future.

If you've undersold to secure clients, then it's time to start moving those clients up to a sensible threshold where you can start to see your margin. Ideally you will have been up front about offering reduced rates, but if not then you'll have to do it slowly – and increase the value of the service you provide. Likewise, if you've broken the market by undercutting competitors' price mark on products, it's time to start building that margin slowly back up and looking at bolstering your other USPs to keep you differentiated; unless, of course, price is your USP.

> **" Is there scope for increasing the price or reducing the costs on a product with little margin? "**

Although it's rare that your bestselling product happens to be your most profitable, analysing the data is just as useful. If a product is shifting units but doesn't have much margin, is there scope for either increasing your prices or reducing the costs associated with that product? Can you source or manufacture it for less to fatten your margin? Is the packaging unnecessarily elaborate? In turn, don't dismiss product out of hand that's not selling. Why isn't it selling? Is there room to negotiate on price?

Assessing the profit points in your business isn't just about direct sales, though it is about assessing performance across the board in anything that contributes to the bottom line in a positive or negative sense – and that includes people. By the very nature of business, productivity translates into profitability.

Look at your team and ascertain where the profit centres are. Who is bringing in the money, who is spending the money and who is contributing to making the money, even if they're not directly doing it themselves? If someone is costing more than they contribute to the business, is their position still valid? Not if you want to run a profitable business.

One of the most telling ways to assess productivity in relation to profit points is to imagine you were recruiting a whole team afresh and allocate the resources where they make optimum sense. Apply day zero thinking. If you do that and have anything rather than a loose mirror it's time to make changes, whether that's changing someone's role or making alterations to the shape of the team.

Make sure that staff are incentivized and motivated and be proactive in keeping morale high. Social events for the team might also come straight off your bottom line, but a happy team is likely to generate multiples of whatever you spend.

Examine all your fixed overheads and see if there's any way you can squeeze them further to keep more money in the business. Are you at capacity in the office? Do you need to be somewhere so big? Could you move somewhere smaller or more cost-effective, like a special deal on a serviced office where overheads such as phone bills, internet and utilities could be included in the cost?

Look at what aspects of the business could be outsourced. If you needed two web developers to build your website, do you still need two to maintain it? Equally, driving profitability isn't only about shaving costs, it's also a case of investing where you'll see an upturn in revenues as a result. If your sales department will be three times as effective with an extra body, then get that person in. Is your marketing manager prevented from carrying out her most effective work by the day-to-day minutiae an assistant or even an intern could help with?

WWW

Free help and advice on pricing: www.smarta
.com/pricing

Examine your processes. Are you missing any easy wins? Are you incentivizing customers to make referrals? Are you collecting and using data to drive return sales and enhance your customer experience? Now you're doing more business, are you able to negotiate better buyer terms with your suppliers?

Also consider getting an accountant to perform an overview of the business and your accounts. It's likely they'd save you more than they cost and will recommend a series of cuts you could make to reduce costs.

Carry out thorough health checks and performance assessments to ensure your business is operating at the peak of productivity and driving maximum profitability. If you're growing quickly your business will be constantly changing, so it's essential to keep your business plan, targets and SBAGs up to date and in line with current and expected performance. Remember, the more control you have over your business, the more calculated the risks are that you're taking.

Smarta in Action: MTD Sales Training

Founder: Sean McPheat
Company name: MTD Sales Training
Company profile: Leading international sales training company with 20 trainers and six admin staff that has trained over 700 companies and over 10,000 staff.
Founded: 2001

Overview

McPheat recognized that some of his staff were working more efficiently than others, and that organization was a problem for many. He wanted to give all staff the ability to work as productively as possible so they could cope with ever-increasing workloads and so bring in more work.

How he did it

He started by organizing a series of workshops and meetings with employees. 'We went back to the basics and stripped out all of the tasks that we were doing to see if they were adding value, and to check the right person was doing them. Everything we did needed to contribute to our company goals. And we needed to be ruthless with this!'

He reviewed employees' skills against what needed to be done, and reallocated tasks where appropriate. 'At the end of the process everyone knew what they needed to start doing, stop doing, do more of and do less of.'

McPheat then also invested in task-planning software across the whole company, as well as training for effective work scheduling, to make sure the good habits stuck.

Tips

McPheat says, 'Take a step back. You can be so wrapped up in fire-fighting and "doing stuff" that you are constantly running at a million miles an hour without any time to catch your breath! Make sure that you periodically take the time to review what you are currently doing, why you are currently doing it and whether it is contributing to your company goals.'

Make full use of software to work smarter. Applications like electronic mind maps and using your scheduler more effectively can really make a difference in your productivity and clarity of thought. Don't see them as an expense, see them as a way to save time and to make you more money.

Smarta in five

1 Identify your profit points and focus on them

2 Find out where you're least productive and why

3 Ditch or slash the products, services and overheads that are losing you money

4 Focus on the easy wins

5 Carry out regular health checks and performance assessments

5.4
Relish the quick win

> "You have to recognize that you need to make certain other people wait, allow certain small priorities to fail, to postpone certain deadlines so you can achieve the big milestones, and complete the larger projects, that will completely change the way that you lead your life or that your business functions."
>
> **—Tim Ferriss, The 4-Hour Work Week**

> "The problem with start-ups is they want too many things to get done. Thus you have to be utterly ruthless at prioritization. You have to be really good at only doing what needs to be done."
>
> **—Doug Richard, School for Startups and *Dragons' Den***

> "It costs five times as much to win a new customer as it does to retain a customer."
>
> **—Chey Garland, Garland Call Centres**

> "By keeping our business within London, we can offer within-the-one-hour service. I think one of the danger points is wanting to be all over the place, but there's enough people in the areas you live in. There's millions of people here, loads of customers, why not just concentrate on here? Why travel two hours away when you don't have to?"
>
> **—Charlie Mullins, Pimlico Plumbers**

Right, we need you to focus now. Just that: focus. Stop chasing any and every mouth-watering opportunity and concentrate on picking the quick wins – the core business that's right in front of you.

Prioritize what you've set out to do and learn to ignore every other distraction. Don't go reaching above your easy sales for more lucrative deals you might not land, in the process knocking back what could have been a nice regular income and ending up empty handed. And definitely don't go chasing deals that will involve the cost of a ladder to get anywhere near them with only a small chance of success.

Enough of playing with the analogy. It's a serial fault of new businesses to over-stretch themselves chasing business they shouldn't have been going after. In their defence it's easy to see how it happens: turning down the chance to chase the big deal goes against the entrepreneur's natural instinct to sniff out an opportunity.

However, your priority as a new business should be to bring in steady revenues and establish your brand among a solid customer base. In almost every circumstance with this goal in mind, the lowest-hanging fruit should be all you're focused on.

Be ruthless, as Doug Richard suggests, in your pursuit of nothing but prioritizing your core business, even when every entrepreneurial bone in your body tells you it'll be okay to make an exception on this one occasion for this one can't-miss-out deal. Don't do it. Keep telling yourself you just don't have the time or the money to focus on anything else. If you have resources you can afford to take away from your core business, then you're not operating at capacity.

> **"Your priority should be to bring in steady revenues and establish your brand"**

Stick to your business plan. You spent weeks, maybe months, writing it, charting your route map to success, and at no point did it mention the distractions that are likely to present such temptation, so resist them and stick to the game plan.

> **"Keep telling yourself you don't have the time or the money to focus on anything else"**

Your sales analytics should also demonstrate that a steady stream of sales is more productive and likely to keep you on track to achieve your targets. Analyse this, though, and check that while you're picking the low-hanging fruit you're not actually picking mouldy fruit that's fallen to the ground and not offering enough value to be bothered with.

Analyse the most profitable services and products, as we discussed in the previous chapter, and focus your attentions here – it's your core revenue. Focusing on a regular, reliable stream of sales also provides a fair better structure to grow the business on. It's better for cashflow and you're spreading your risk, as opposed to being reliant on a handful of high-value clients you couldn't afford to lose. Instead, by bringing in steady sales you've a stream of revenue to secure investment against or to invest into expanding the business.

Having a stable revenue stream from an established customer base will eventually provide the platform from which to expand as well. However, this shouldn't be until you can do so without taking your eye off the core business or resource away from it.

What this means is that you need to get seriously vigilant with your resources. Direct your funds where you see returns – and not anywhere else.

If you're not sure what your low-hanging fruit is, start by dropping or de-prioritizing deals that are proving cumbersome to manage or difficult to close, regardless of how big they promise to be. If you're not seeing revenues and can't perceive any compelling reason that will change any time soon, then cut it free – especially if you're spending money to sustain that aspect of the business.

In short, don't make your life any more complicated than it needs to be. If it's easy, and it's going to earn you money, just do it. Not sure whether it's going to be easy? Take a step back from negotiations and do some careful analysis of how long the work will take you and how much it will cost. If it's too much, go for an easier deal, or find a way of simplifying things for yourself while still keeping the other party sweet.

Remember one of Smarta's favourite acronyms: KISS – keep it simple stupid.

Smarta in Action: Toptable

Founder: Karen Hanton
Company: Toptable
Company profile: A website for booking restaurants, Toptable has grown to list more than 30,000 restaurants in 14 countries.
Founded: 2005

Overview
Once she'd got her website up and running, Hanton realized there was a quick-win way to get customers back on the website by looking at broader trends in her marketplace.

How she did it

'When you see the success of YouTube and all the social networks and so on, you realize people like to be involved,' Hanton explains. She decided to tap into the trend for user-generated content. 'Every time a person books and goes out to eat through Toptable, the next day we send them an opportunity to rate and review the restaurant. People love doing that. Everybody is a direct critic.'

This brings customers quickly back to a site they might otherwise use only once every few weeks or even months. And it requires next to no administrative time from her team. The reviews in turn entice new customers and get people to spend more time on the site reading them. It creates a whole load of new content that Hanton doesn't have to pay an employee to create. And it fosters a sense of trustworthiness and community among site users.

Hanton has also used a loyalty scheme model to keep customers coming back. 'To get people to increase the frequency that they use our service, we get them to collect reward points. It's been very successful. It's not an original idea. It's very like Air Miles, but our headline is book six times and eat for free. We just build that into our marketing budget.'

Again, this has saved on expensive advertising and marketing budgets trying to grab the attention of new customers. She's just maximizing the worth of her existing customer base in the way that has the least impact on the workloads of her team.

Tips

Look to wider trends and other effective models in your marketplace and see how you can implement them. If there are quick wins that require little administrative time for your business, snap them up. User-generated content is a great example of this.

Smarta in five

1 Focus. Focus. Focus. Do nothing you aren't meant to be doing

2 A big deal isn't a big deal unless you win it

3 Prioritize the areas you know you can get regular revenues from

4 Don't get distracted by opportunities outside your business plan

5 Focus on income that you can rely on to build your business

5.5
Negotiate on a paperclip

"You can hire a market research agency or you can go set up with a couple of laptops in a place that has free wifi at a time that is not too busy, and you can walk up to people and say: 'Hi, can I take five minutes of your time and show you something new that I'm working on and get your opinion?'"

—Sokratis Papafloratos, TrustedPlaces

"I had to print 30,000 catalogues and make my new clothes collection, but amazingly even though it was a new business, I did persuade people to give me credit terms for that first order. Had I not had those credit terms, we'd have never launched the company."

—Laura Tenison, JoJo Maman Bébé

"The option of building my own factory would have cost millions of pounds, which I simply did not have. So I had to convince an existing factory to work with me to produce SuperJam on a big scale. I travelled all around the country and obviously most of these huge, publicly listed food companies were a bit sceptical of a 17 year old coming along with no experience, no money and, in fact, little more than just a set of recipes and this big ambition to transform the world of jam. But eventually, I found one factory who had suffered from the decline in jam sales, had a lot of spare capacity in their factory and they thought that maybe SuperJam would be the answer to their problems."

—Fraser Doherty, SuperJam

It doesn't matter whether you've got £3 million in the bank or you're down to your last £100 which you could spend in 100 different ways (and we know which is more likely), you should negotiate on everything. The first price is never the best price. If Theo Paphitis questions the price of everything he buys, then so can you.

As a start-up you should be hustling and haggling for a bargain at every possible juncture. Yup, that includes paperclips. Remember, every pound that goes out of the business is another pound you've got to make before you hit break even. You shouldn't starve your business of the essential resources it needs, but you should be doing everything you can to keep the costs as close to zero as you can get them. Push hard to get any discount you can and remember, where someone's making a profit and wants to sell, there's always scope for negotiation.

Before you spend money on anything, ask yourself if you really need it. We mean really, *really* need it. What would you do if you couldn't have it? Unless the answer is 'I wouldn't be able to run my business', it's a non-essential item. Note: hardly any new 'office-based' businesses actually need an office. If you have somewhere to sit in your house and a computer, you can get away with it. Hold your meetings in the coffee shop.

WWW

Jump online for insider negotiation tips from crack salespeople: www.smarta.com/negotiating

For items that are essentials, never go into a purchase situation looking to pay the full price. How much scope there is for negotiation will depend on the seller's margin (they're unlikely to sell at a loss), but always haggle. This isn't about bullying people into giving you a discount, it's about negotiating to a deal point where both sides get a deal: you get your reduced price and the seller makes the sale with some, albeit not as much, profit.

A deal always needs to be struck on good terms. No one's going to give a freebie to someone they don't like and you shouldn't look to do any deals that leave a bad taste in the mouth and

> **A deal always needs to be struck on good terms**

where you're unlikely to want to work together again. Instead look to broker something mutually beneficial, a 'you scratch my back, and I'll scratch yours' agreement, if you like.

The most obvious way to leverage a discount is to trade something in exchange. Here's a list of ideas:

- Your service or product free or heavily discounted
- Free advertising on your website
- Future business in return for a discount or freebie
- Offer to connect them with a potential client
- Convince one of your journalism contacts to write about them
- Tweet about them (make sure you've got plenty of followers first)
- Trade skills or resources you have that they don't
- Offer to publicize them to your customer base and contacts

The key is to make the seller see the value in doing business with you. One of the best ways to secure a discount is to promise the supplier future business. Tell them about how ambitious you are, how brilliant your business is, sell them your dream and get

> **Sell them your dream and they'll see the benefit of helping you out**

them punch drunk on your enthusiasm. If they buy it, they'll see the benefit of helping you out now and securing you as a lucrative customer for the future.

Equally, you need to think about the long-term implications of the deal you strike as well. Getting a good deal should not come at any expense. You need to be good to your promises and deliver back any value you promise to. Fail to do that or don't stay true to your word and that person probably won't work with you again. They certainly won't offer you a discount. Take the opposite tack and exceed the value you promised so the seller feels vindicated and will cut you a similarly good deal in the future.

Before you make any significant purchases, always consult your contacts and networks and ask people where they got good deals, discounts and who the best person was to negotiate with. The success of sites such as Martin Lewis's money-savingexpert.com is proof that not only

WWW

Check out Smarta's tool sections to find suppliers recommended and rated by Smarta members: www.smarta.com/tools

does it pay to shop around, people are always prepared to pass on information about where they got a good deal from. There is a lot of information out there and a lot of people willing to help, so don't make a significant purchase without checking it out.

Smarta in Action: Dust and Vac

Founder: Lisa Langmead
Company name: Dust and Vac
Company profile: Cleaning company based in Knutsford, Cheshire, with experience in domestic and commercial cleaning.
Founded: 2008

Overview
Lisa Langmead dreamt up the idea for Dust and Vac as she was scrubbing her loo at home. Realizing she actually quite enjoyed it – and needing the extra money – she launched her own cleaning company using her savings. When it came to getting the word out about the company, though, Langmead needed a creative solution.

How she did it
With a budget of just £15 for marketing, Langmead realized she wasn't going to be able to compete against larger cleaning companies in the area. Although she had found a company that let her build a free website, it wasn't going to be enough. She needed a marketing method more targeted to her local area.

Even distributing flyers was out of the question. Having collected quotes from local printing companies, she realized it was going to be too expensive and besides, flyers are often lumped in with junk mail and thrown away before they can be read.

Langmead appreciated she needed to stand out, and it was while she was ordering iron-on nametags for her children's school uniforms that she came up with a more creative solution. Using similar nametags but with her company details on, she ironed them on to supermarket-bought scouring pads and distributed them to houses in her local area.

The reaction was immediate. One man emailed Langmead to say he had recommended Dust and Vac to his daughter, while another client saw a friend using one of the scourers to wash up – the labels are meant to withstand machine washing so they never come off – and was so impressed, she employed her.

Tips
You don't have to have buckets of cash to start your business, just think creatively. If you can't afford to do something the conventional way, find another way to do it. Not only will you catch clients' attention, if you do ever decide to borrow money or get investment, you'll be able to show you can manage your money.

Smarta in five

1 Negotiate everything: the first price is never the best price

2 Make sure you really need something before you buy it

3 Do your homework: where's the best place to buy and who's the best person to speak to?

4 Barter hard: what can you offer in exchange for free?

5 Everyone's a winner in a fair deal

5.6
Embrace weaknesses

"It's very important to think what the competitors will do when you appear on their space. You need to think that through and you need to have an answer to that. You need to have the resources to get you through that."

—Sir Richard Needham, Dyson and Smarta chairman

"The stage from start-up to the target is the most dangerous moment and the engine room can fail. Growth spurts should come with big warnings and you've got to keep your eye on the dull stuff."

—Deborah Meaden, *Dragons' Den*

"Each step is a great leap of faith, but an entrepreneur needs to embrace them rather than fear them."

—Jamie Murray Wells, Glasses Direct

O ne of the most powerful exercises you undertake to strengthen your business or fireproof your business plan is to try to work out how to kill it. We're serious. Put yourself in the shoes of your most calculating competitor and imagine if you were them what you'd do to bring your business crashing down.

Even if you're bringing in decent revenues and all is rosy, don't lull yourself into a false sense of security that it's flawless: it's not. No business is. Instead get proactive about discovering where the holes are, however small, so you can set about covering

> **❝❝Don't lull yourself into a false sense of security – no business is flawless❞❞**

them. If you're just starting up, see this as an opportunity to reinforce your business plan through a process of due diligence.

The trick is to know exactly where the chinks in your armour are, so you can deal with them before your competitors do. And of course, it's not just competitors you need to be aware of. The world of business and consumer trends are changing so quickly that you need to be continually reassessing your model and checking that what you're doing makes total sense. What might be an opportunity in January could be a threat in June if consumer demand has shifted, the economy has changed or one of your competitors has suddenly made up ground.

You need to be assessing your business and identifying your weaknesses at regular intervals – six months is probably as long as you can leave it. This isn't an act of paranoia and we'd always suggest you focus more on your own business than your competitors, but staying proactively ahead of threats is the best way of countering them. When you're identifying weaknesses you'll also spot opportunities – they come hand in hand.

The trusty old SWOT analysis is the best place to start when it comes to identifying weaknesses. SWOT stands for Strengths, Weaknesses, Opportunities and Threats. Strengths and weaknesses are internal: resources, skills and capabilities you and the business already have or don't have. Opportunities and threats are external: they set you against your competitors and market and often look to the future. Opportunities are generally areas for growth and profit, while threats are things happening in the market that could damage your business.

WWW

For a free SWAT analysis template, visit www. smarta.com/SWAT

Examples of the trusty SWOT analysis

Strengths

- Expertise in sales, marketing etc.
- Strong management team
- Good reputation, known for great customer service, strong brand

- Well-located business
- Patents
- Reliable supply chain
- Low overheads
- Quality product or service
- Innovative product or business doing something new
- Low-price product

Weaknesses

- No in-house accounting experience
- Not enough clear routes to market (how you sell)
- Lack of cashflow
- Poor IT infrastructure
- Not having an established reputation
- Relying too much on one customer – they might let you down

Opportunities

- Entering a growing market
- Offering a service competitors don't (e.g. online, 24-hour, new or more niche service)
- Faster delivery times than competitors
- Better quality than competitors
- Strong partnerships with other companies that competitors don't have
- Doing better during seasonal peaks or troughs than competitors
- Selling in a country or location competitors can't reach

Threats

- Your competition
- Stricter taxes or new regulations imposed on your business or product
- Shrinking market demand
- Lots of competition from big-name brands
- Competitor brings out a rival product or service
- Competitor offers a quicker delivery time than you
- Loss of key staff to competitors

The thing is, spotting your own weaknesses and threats isn't always as easy as drafting a load of bullet points. You need to dig deeper to find those minor chinks that can potentially lead to major damage and so make your SWOT analysis more comprehensive.

Take a leaf out of the London Olympic bid team's book. In 2005, they beat off competition from the likes of New York, Moscow, Madrid and the favourite Paris to secure the 2012 Olympics. The secret to their strategy? The team pretended to be their competition – Spain, Russia, the US – and tore their own plans to pieces. That's right, they did exactly what we prescribe at the top of this chapter: they pretended to be their own worst enemies and ripped all their hard work to bits.

Scrutinize your own business. Be ruthless. Rip apart every idea you have: how you'd outcompete, how you'd show your business up and make customers believe it wasn't up to scratch, how you'd wangle better supplier deals – ultimately, how you'd destroy your own business.

Don't keep this process to yourself. Rope in your staff and maybe a trusted outsider. You'll be amazed at the flaws other people spot that you're too close to see.

Don't get too disheartened at the holes you uncover, though. This is a constructive process, remember. Everything you discover makes you stronger. If you need to work harder to differentiate yourself or have a potential cashflow or resource issue on the horizon, it's way better to know that now. Knowing your weaknesses is one of the most powerful strengths you can have. It doesn't just prepare you for battle, it provides you with the foresight to sidestep them and plough ahead with growing your business.

> **" Knowing your weaknesses is one of the most powerful strengths you can have – it provides you with the foresight to sidestep them "**

Smarta in Action: Teeny Beanies

Founder: Kerry Swinton
Company: Teeny Beanies
Company profile: A UK-based company which makes kids' bean bags, soft toys, cushions and keep-sake bags, and fun and colourful accessories.
Founded: 2007

Overview
When the recession hit, Swinton realized her business was at risk: many people no longer had the spare cash to spend on pricey gifts. She needed to find a way to side-step that weakness and safeguard her business's cashflow and future.

How she did it
Swinton didn't want to lower the quality or price of her designs, which are based around a range of characters. But she appreciated she needed to be flexible if she wanted to keep sales coming in.

'So I introduced a range of new products which were smaller and more affordable, as well as new characters which kept my brand growing and my customers intrigued,' she says. She made sure she still kept new products high quality and long-lasting, despite them being cheaper.

Her broader product range actually increased her customer base as well as maintaining sales.

She also made sure she kept a competitive edge over big-name rivals, whose size allowed them to drop prices to survive the recession, which was another potential threat. 'I like to build a one-to-one relationship with customers. I tend to call customers rather than email. I market myself as the face of the brand, and attend retail and craft shows to connect with new customers and create a presence for my brand.'

She also continued to work part-time while running her business – 'just to ensure that I have enough funds to keep my business growing'.

Tips

Many of your business's weaknesses will be a result of things you can't control: a dip in the economy that means consumers are spending less, big-name competition that's not going to go away, a recession that threatens your cashflow. So make sure you're flexible enough to innovate your way to safety. And take every precaution you can against threats to your business, which might well mean part-time work.

Remember to keep doing the things that give small businesses an edge: brilliant customer service and a personal touch.

Smarta in five

1 Think SWOT: Strengths, Weaknesses, Opportunities, Threats

2 Be honest: attack as if you were the opposition

3 Consider internal and external threats

4 Identify which threats and weaknesses you can act on now – and do it

5 Address your strategy to seize opportunities and counter threats

5.7
Partner up to power on

"It's got to make sense for what you're trying to achieve and what you're trying to do and it's got to be mutually beneficial. Lots of partners can bring more than cash to a business."
—Kanya King, MOBO

"We used the internet to hunt down partners, whether they're in formulation or manufacturing or supply chain. There are trade magazines that you can use and resources online where you can go to learn about these types of industries and types of partners for the first time. It was a combination of internet research and just calling people."

—Simon Duffy, Bulldog Natural Grooming

> "We had a great partnership with Levi's when they sponsored our stand at Notting Hill Carnival. We went to them and said: 'Look, we should definitely be working together because here are your qualities, here are ours. We should be doing something together. We'd fit very well.' You've got to make sure you've got the same kind of audiences. Then it's trying to create something together."
>
> ## —Gordon Mac, Kiss FM

If you want to get ahead twice as fast with half the effort and expense (and who doesn't?), then teaming up with like-minded companies is the route to take. Smart small businesses understand the logic of forming strategic partnerships and are building powerful alliances with companies they trust will help them get ahead. You might well loathe the phrase, but this one's a 'no brainer'.

Why wouldn't you want to extend your reach to more customers than you can hit on your own? Equally, why would you turn away the possibility of sharing the cost of reaching those customers with a company that is in no way competitive to you? Like we say, it makes total sense. That said, you need to be completely clear about what you're trying to achieve before entering into any partnership. Any deals you strike should make life easier, not harder, for both of you, so be strategic about your objectives and who you work with.

> **Pool your resources, save some cash and make twice the noise**

Start looking for potential partners who, while not directly competitive, share the same target audience or demographic. If individually you're working hard and spending good money to get in front of the same people, then immediately there's a common ground and it makes sense to pool your resources, save some cash and hopefully make twice the noise.

Draw up a list of target companies it would make strategic sense to work with and arrange an informal meeting to explore what mutual opportunities there might be. Here you should get an instant feel for each other's ethics and company cultures. The first rule of a potential partnership should be that both you and whoever you're partnering with get on, are clear about each other's intentions and trust each other. If that's not there the partnership will be stunted and won't deliver the value you want it to. In fact, you'd be better off not bothering.

Provided that you are happy in principle to work together, start exploring in detail each other's objectives and what you both have to offer. For you to deliver and derive true value, you'll need a thorough understanding of each other's brands, what your current goals are and what in each other's models and minds would signify success from any work you do together.

Strategic partnerships vary massively. It can be as simple as promoting each other's businesses to the other's customer base, a skills or resource trade, agreeing to cover and publicize news on each other's websites and social media sites, or perhaps jointly sponsoring an event.

Try something small first. It tests the water for both of you, shows how committed you both are and allows you both to walk away before any money or reputation gets

WWW

Start networking for potential partners now by searching the Smarta community for businesses in your space: www.smarta.com/network

wasted should you not actually enjoy doing business together or a partnership was badly received by either company's customers. Avoid doing anything that doesn't offer additional value to your customer base or is likely to damage their brand affiliation to you. Remember, a bad reputation takes seconds to gain and years to lose.

If the trial goes well, look at regular joint and mutual marketing opportunities which both parties can track and also think about broader, more permanent alliances you could forge, such as an official joint venture to enter hostile new markets.

Strategic partnerships offer real potential for smart businesses to team up and collectively take money from larger companies for which neither of them could previously have hoped to compete.

On the flipside, be wary that the moment you share your brand with anyone you don't put your reputation at risk beyond your control, so it's essential you pick your partners strategically. For instance, if you're a wedding organizer and you partner with an unreliable florist, no matter how immaculately you take care of all the other arrangements, if the wrong flowers turn up or they don't turn up at all, it'll be your brand that will be tarnished.

Embrace strategic partners by all means, just pick who you choose to work with very carefully.

Smarta in Action: ArenaFlowers.com

Founders: Will Wynne and Steve France
Company: ArenaFlowers.com
Company profile: An international direct-to-consumer online retailer of ethically sourced flowers, plants and gifts – and now the third biggest flower business in the UK.
Founded: 2006

Overview
ArenaFlowers.com has used strategic partnerships with big companies such a PayPal, L'Oréal and Sega. The seal of approval of working with those companies then led to contracts with household-name brands such as Boots and Transport for London.

How they did it
Wynne explains that the team started off searching for small strategic partnerships. 'We spent a lot of time looking around. It can be pretty thankless and you get nothing for a lot of the time, and you question whether it's worthwhile. But getting that first deal is important.'

The team's first big-name partnership came after they spoke at a PayPal conference about online fraud. (Note: putting yourself out there is key to finding partnership opportunities.) PayPal then approached them and a deal was done.

Having one big partnership under their belts helped them secure more. 'Once you have one it gives you credibility, and then bigger ones will consider working with you.'

ArenaFlowers.com went on to do a partnership with L'Oréal around Mother's Day. L'Oréal created a mini-site and ArenaFlowers.com was branded next to it, offering discounted flowers alongside L'Oréal products.

ArenaFlowers.com didn't have to pay for the partnership opportunity. In fact, Wynne says he doesn't understand paying for a partnership opportunity – it should be balanced and mutually beneficial.

He warns that working with bigger companies can entail much more admin – he's had to go through a four-day audit for one contract! – but the kudos it gives you makes that more than worthwhile.

Tips

Contact prospective partners directly. Wynne recommends using LinkedIn to find other businesses, and to check you're approach the right person within them. 'Just be up front and say you want to do a deal. But give consideration to what they're looking for and how it will help them.'

He also recommends asking your partners to provide references to prospective new ones.

Smarta in five

1 Collaboration enables you to achieve more in less time

2 Work with companies with complementary but different propositions

3 Only collaborate with people you trust and respect

4 Test the water with something small first

5 Never put your brand in the hands of a company which could damage it

5.8
Deliver knock-out sales pitches

"When we went into our Sainsbury's pitch, the lady really quizzed us on all of our ingredients and all these technical questions and challenges associated with natural products. Luckily for us we'd done a lot of research, so we could answer all of them. It gave us credibility from the off."

—Simon Duffy, Bulldog Natural Grooming

"We listen a lot. And we don't ever tell a client something just because they want to hear it. Don't be arrogant in a pitch. Don't tell the client their business. Do not be underprepared. Do not go into a pitch not having known who the people in there are or actually what they do as a business."

—Jonathan Simmons, Public Zone

It's said that great products sell themselves, but that's a half truth at best. As we indentified in Chapter 2.1, people talk about exceptional businesses and word of mouth is definitely the most compelling and cost-effective form of marketing which all businesses should aspire to generate. But word of mouth alone is rarely enough.

If that were true you wouldn't see adverts for the iPod – without doubt an exceptional product – but you do. The iPod has sold in excess of 200 million units worldwide, is the ubiquitous mp3 player and trended more effectively than arguably any product in history, yet Apple still spends millions of dollars advertising it. Today you imagine that it might actually be quite easy to walk into a room full of people and sell something as great as the iPod, but back in 2001 when the first one was released it launched to mixed reviews and Apple's cachet wasn't quite what it is now.

It's not just great products that need selling, it's brands too. Gone are the days when brand powerhouses such as Marks & Spencer and John Lewis didn't need to advertise. No matter how sexy or esteemed your proposition or reputation, you've got to be able to sell it.

And quite right too – after all, the art of selling is as old as business itself. If you can't sell your business to the man on the street, then is your business really so special? Your ability to sell at least your concept should be the acid test of so many other functions of your business and the validity of your business itself.

Yet selling continues to instil fear in budding entrepreneurs, petrified at the notion of explaining why what they've got is worth paying for. It's a conundrum. The only logical explanation is that we've forgotten the basic principle of sales. It's really simple and comes in two of the easiest rules you'll ever hear: *Don't* treat sales as persuading someone to give you their money for something you're selling. *Do* treat sales as providing something valuable someone will want to spend their money on. Selling should be a fair trade: if you're selling a quality product or service at a fair price, then you should be looking forward to making fair trades people will want to make, not dreading the prospect of having to talk them into it.

> **Don't treat sales as persuading someone to give you their money for something you're selling. Do treat sales as providing something valuable someone will want to spend their money on**

Smart businesses realize that a hard sell is not a smart sell. Storming in all guns blazing and delivering some cheesy spiel about the magical powers of your product won't get you anywhere. Do that and you immediately put up people's defence mechanisms: if they feel like you need to sweet talk them into a deal, they'll become equally cynical. The natural healthy sales environment of one side looking for a solution and the other offering one is immediately displaced.

Anyone and everyone can sell and in the smartest businesses, everyone does. Selling is critical to understanding both the identity of your business and the needs of your customers. Until you've gone face to face with a customer and heard what they really want from your business and what you sell, you won't truly appreciate what it is you need to offer. Even if it's only for a day during induction, make sure that all your staff in every position experience customer interaction in a sales environment.

> **"A hard sell is not a smart sell"**

For big sales pitches, preparation is everything and you need to tailor every presentation to the individual client and situation. Even then, hedge your bets. Make a short and a long version of your pitch. The short version will last no longer than five minutes, for those who look bored and short on time. The long version can be more like 15 minutes. Decide which to use when you get there and you can sense how interested the person is, and switch from one to the other if need be halfway through.

> **"Make sure that all your staff experience customer interaction in a sales environment"**

The most important thing to remember is: it's all about them. Everything you say in a pitch should show how you can help the person you're talking to with your product or service. It's not about the advantages of your product over your competitors, it's about meeting your prospect's needs in the way that's right for them. Keep that in mind, always.

Open your pitch by asking questions. Find out what your target buyer wants and what they dislike about the product they usually buy or the supplier they usually use. Of course, not everyone will want to badmouth their long-term supplier or facecare product to a complete stranger. Sidestep that by talking about problems in a more generalized way. Say you've researched a certain issue (the one you suspect they're facing) and you've found there's a widespread problem. Then lead into: 'What's your experience been of that?' Use the word 'experience' not 'problem' so it doesn't inadvertently place any blame on them. Find out what they want to improve and then tailor your pitch to giving it to them.

If you're selling B2B, then the more of this information you can find out on the phone before the pitch, the better. Otherwise, come armed with a whole different range of answers to possible problems they may have and how your offering will fix the problem.

Think about creating a story when you're writing your pitch. Give your sell some emotional connection. Make it interesting: explain why you started the business and show your passion for what you're doing. It'll make what you say much more engaging and make the person warm to you. You need to drop in evidence and numbers too, but slot those in where they're needed. Start with the story, then add some facts.

Tailor your pitch to make it win–win. You need to present a case that makes them want to buy from you. That means coming armed with numbers and ideas that show how they will profit and grow by doing business with you, or quickly judging what will appeal to them when they walk into your premises.

Know your numbers. Figure out your ideal and lowest-case scenarios for any product or service you're selling. There's no point doing a deal just for the sake of it. Figure out the lowest price you're willing to sell for that still makes you a worthwhile profit. And never go below it. Also, know how many units you can handle logistically if you're selling B2B.

Practice, practice, then practice again. Write notes on your pitch, then practice out loud, at least 10 times – you need to get to the stage where you don't need notes. Don't try to be word perfect. Just make sure you know the content your presentation covers and be sure you're getting every figure right.

WWW

Watch the sales tips of top entrepreneurs: www.smarta.com/videos

It sounds obvious, but always make sure you're talking to the right person. Many businesses will send someone too junior to make a decision to a sales meeting, just to feel things out. You might not be able to figure this out until you're in your first meeting, but then you can casually ask: 'So

During the pitch: Sneaky tricks

Stay calm. Think about how much effort you've put into the pitch, how well prepared you are, the confidence you have both in the business and your own ability. There's nothing to fear and no need to be nervous.

Use their first name – or don't. Using someone's first name regularly makes them warm to you. That said, you need to judge how they want to be addressed. If they seem pretty old school, addressing them as 'Mr Jones' or 'Ms Kent' might could put you in their good books and then if they invite you to use their first name, you're in.

Keep them engaged. Ask them if they follow what you're saying and if it makes sense throughout your pitch, and go over things again if they sound unsure. You have to keep them on board at all times. Show your passion. You needed to be loaded with enthusiasm. You're selling your vision of the business as much as anything.

As you bring your pitch to an end, thank them for their time and tell them that you're genuinely keen to take their questions and talk through any queries they might have. This will show you're confident on your subject and suggest you've nothing to hide. Explain to them that you can leave them with written copies and that you can also email a version across. If you're extra keen to impress, leave them a copy on a branded USB stick.

Once the pitch is done, it's time to get down to negotiations. To glean how the smartest business people close a deal, refer to Chapter 3.12.

who else is involved in the buying process for contracts like this at your end?' If someone more senior is mentioned, you know who to call next.

Do your homework. Glean everything you can from the obvious sources and ask your contacts if they have any information or experience of dealing with the client. You should tailor every sales pitch you make, so the more you can find out in advance the better it will be.

If your sales pitch doesn't prove a success, don't take it to heart. Instead, look to learn from the experience. Sales is a patience game. You can do 100 pitches and sell nothing, then make 10 sales in a row. Just keep trying.

The key is to measure your success rate. If you're not getting much luck, try different approaches and different pitches. Write down after each attempt what you said and how the prospective buyer reacted. Then refine your pitch to fill it with all the good stuff and drop the things that aren't working.

Smarta in Action: Applied Language Solutions

Founder: Gavin Wheeldon
Company name: Applied Language Solutions
Company profile: A translation company that now has more than 14,000 specialist translators and offices in California, Chicago, New York, the UK, France, Spain, Bulgaria, India and Guatemala.
Founded: 2003

Overview
Wheeldon pitched for and won a £32 million contract when he was just 23. He's been making successful presentations ever since.

How he did it
Wheeldon's learnt the tricks of the trade. He writes notes on his pitch, then practices out loud, five or six times. At least one of those run-throughs is in front of someone else. He says it's OK to take in your notes, but also, 'If you haven't practiced to the point where you don't need notes, you might question whether you've practiced enough.'

Wheeldon says he always begins a pitch by asking the people he's pitching to what *they* want from an investment or contract. 'What they're effectively telling you is how they want to be sold to.' Otherwise, he warns, you could 'talk for 20 minutes and not hit one single point they're looking for'. You then tailor the focuses of the pitch to their wants, emphasizing the strengths they would be specifically interested in.

He's learnt that realistic forecasts are a key part of a pitch (if they're required). If they're overly ambitious, you lose your integrity. If they're too pessimistic, the person you're pitching to loses interest. Wheeldon gets around this by giving the investors or firms he's pitching to three different scenarios: best case, middle of the ground and absolute worst case. 'As long as your worst-case scenario still

looks sensible, then everything else is an upside – and they really appreciated it.'
It also shows you've thought things through properly, and you're aware of the
variables that could affect your forecast, which is always impressive.

Tips
Practice, practice, then practice again. Make sure you can show you have a
realistic view of the future by providing the three-case scenario when forecasting.
Be realistic, not overly optimistic. Use questions to draw out what your target really
wants to hear, then present it to them.

Smarta in five

1 Every business owner has to be able to sell

2 A smart sell is never a hard sell

3 Don't put down the competition, prove your merits

4 Do your homework and tailor every single pitch

5 Don't rush to close: make your buyer feel considered

5.9
Tweet your way to the big-time

"People get the notion of marketing to social media wrong by approaching it as marketing through social media."

—Doug Richard, School for Startups and *Dragons' Den*

"When people say, 'Twitter doesn't work', it's a bit like saying talking to people doesn't work. It's exactly the same."

—Brad Burton, 4Networking

"Twitter has enabled us to create far more personal connections with partners and our peers than traditional media would allow. Not only are we tweeting about business, but we're also tweeting about what's going on in our lives. Obviously it's important to achieve a balance, but it's allowed us to meet people we otherwise might not have met and build a rapport with clients and investors."

—Glenn Shoosmith, BookingBug

Twitter has arrived on the scene and made itself such a powerful business tool (trust us) in such a short period, it actually feels like a gamble gifting it a whole chapter. Will it still be around by the time you get hold of this, let alone in an another year's time? The reason we *have* given it a chapter is that we're convinced Twitter will only get more important to small businesses. It might have arrived in a whirlwind, but we are convinced it is here to stay. We think that in a year's time Twitter won't just still be relevant, but we'll be talking about its significance to business in the same breath as we do Google. The smart businesses already all over Twitter would probably argue it's already more significant. Really.

> *In a year's time we'll be talking about the significance of Twitter to business in the same breath as Google*

Twitter may have started out as a love-in for the tech and media industries, but the same could be said for text messages. And like SMS, Twitter is now being used by just about anyone from any background, industry and age-group going, from Stephen Fry to the BBC to Dell to your cousin's 13-year-old niece – and yes, just about everyone you're likely to do business with. Your customers, your partners, your suppliers, your potential investors and quite possibly the person who might one day buy your business.

Although Twitter has been around since mid-2006, it went mainstream around the end of 2008 and its popularity has been ballooning since then. For the simple reasons listed above, if you're in business and want to interact with your customers, it's no longer a choice whether to be on Twitter or not, it's an undeniable necessity.

For those at the back who remain dubious, let's start with the basics. What exactly is this Twitter everyone's talking about, how does it work and, for those who've tried and didn't get it, why, er, didn't I get it?

Twitter describes itself as 'a real-time information network powered by people all around the world that lets you share and discover what's happening now. Twitter asks "what's happening" and makes the answer spread across the globe to millions, immediately.' Which actually sums things up pretty nicely.

You provide regular updates of up to 140 characters, called 'tweets', of what you're doing or something you find interesting. Your tweets can include links and pictures, and you can address tweets to someone else on Twitter. You have a profile page where other people can see all your most recent tweets and a one-line bio (well, 140 characters) about you, plus hyperlinks to your website.

You 'follow' other people or organizations you're interested in, which means you receive their updates. You then get a chronological list of all those people's updates so you can see what they're all saying. Anyone can follow anyone, you don't need to be approved, which is why many people like Twitter – it's democratic and very open.

You can also search for words or issues you're interested in and see what people all across the world are saying about that thing right this second (in 'real-time'). You can only get such instant results on Twitter, as Google hasn't yet developed the technology to search the internet this quickly.

Used correctly, Twitter enables you to:

- Have a more personal and sustained relationship with customers
- Grow your customer base by getting the attention of people interested in your industry or some aspect of your work
- Publicize your business
- Build your brand
- Track what other people think about your industry, business or products
- Grow your network of contacts by letting you make contact with people you don't know offline
- Cold-contact and market to people without annoying them
- Drive more traffic to your website
- Position yourself as an expert in your field by sharing news and information relevant to your business and by answering questions
- Provide amazing customer service in a really easy way
- Get the latest up-to-date industry news and events
- Position your business as up to date and in touch, for being on Twitter
- Provide customers with details of special offers, new products and other news you have

And the best part is, it's completely free and really, really easy.

The best way to get a feel for how Twitter works is to look at a few people who are using it. Try looking at http://twitter.com/smartaHQ (that's us!) and http://twitter.com/stephenfry to get you started.

Because we know there's some pretty solid resistance out there, let's persist in asking another of those FAQs: Very nice, but can Twitter really benefit my business? Now you know what we're going to say: *yes*. Seriously, we'd challenge any business not to derive some value from it in one form or another.

> **❝❝We'd challenge any business not to derive some value from Twitter❞❞**

If you don't believe us, we'd ask you to do one thing. Go to http://search.twitter.com and perform the following searches:

- Your business name
- The name of your product/service

- Name of your business/product/service and name of your area (e.g. search 'Hairdresser Brighton')
- Search for the names of your competitors (the business owners and the company names, as some businesses tweet as an individual rather than as a company)
- Terms that people might use to talk about your industry, area and other businesses like yours
- Something that you've found frustrating when starting up (business plans or health and safety inspections, for instance)

We've tried this test out at numerous speaking events around the UK to halls of Twitter sceptics and every time the searches have returned Twitter users or conversations relevant to their business. Every search either finds a potential customer, a competitor or at the very least useful information that will help them.

Ask yourself this: how can you not afford to be in a place where both your potential customers (and with more than 160 million users they almost certainly are) and your competitors are? If you're serious about running a smart business, you can't.

Creating an account on Twitter

Choose a name that represents your business, or the fact that you own that business. If your name's Mike and your business name is Tuley's Trousers, you could go for 'TuleysTrousers', 'Tuleys_Trews', 'TrousersMike' and so on. Even something quite light-hearted like 'trousersnake' can go down well, though this will very much depend on the tone of your brand! The name you pick is called your 'handle'. Keep it short and easy to remember.

Use your logo as your picture.

Use the background of your profile page to display your business's logo or, if you have one, a brightly coloured and interesting photo of products, along with your business contact details. You can find out how to do this by searching 'how to create a Twitter background' online.

Fill in your one-line bio with something snappy that explains your business.

Include a link to your website and, if you have one, your blog.

The lingo

You can address other users by starting your tweets with @username (no space between @ and their name), for example '@smartaHQ I'm reading your book right now!'

A direct message (DM) is a private message sent between two people who follow each other. Good for exchanging contact numbers with someone you've been chatting to.

A retweet (RT) is when you forward on someone else's tweet. It's etiquette to put RT @username before the copied tweet. RT useful links other people have tweeted about or events your followers would be interested in – or just particularly entertaining tweets. For example, 'RT @SmartaHQ Our ultimate guide to using Facebook for business http://bit.ly/cPWiqB' or 'RT @StephenFry Oh dear. My hair is simply too long. I look like James May's twin sister'.

'Trending topics' are the most talked about things across the whole of Twitter right now. They will usually be big news stories or shared Twitter jokes, for example when we announced the Smarta 100 Winners Smarta100 was trending. You can see all current trending topics listed on the right-hand column of your home page.

You'll notice many trending topics have a # before them. Twitter users use the hashtag (#) when they're talking about a specific subject, so that other users can search for the hashtag term to see what's happening. For example, when the Mumbai bombings occurred in 2008, people tweeting about them used #Mumbai. If you wanted to find out the latest news, you simply searched #Mumbai and you could see the latest tweets from all across the world that were talking about them. This is a great example of how Twitter is such an effective tool for spreading information very quickly.

What to tweet: Getting started

- Start by following a few people in your industry, competitors, businesses you find interesting, celebrities you like and, of course, @SmartaHQ to get a feel for how people tweet.
- Test the waters by tweeting yourself. Avoid just banging on about your own business or things you've been doing. Try to share interesting news and links.
- No one wants to know if you're having a cup of coffee, but they will want to know if you're a plumber and you tweet a link to a useful website offering tips on how to fix easy plumbing problems in the home.
- Keep it industry relevant: comment on industry news or, occasionally, compliment competitors (this is a much more friendly and collaborative space than traditional business).
- That said, mix in a bit of personal stuff – it gives you personality.
- Tweets with links in them are generally more popular than those without.
- Provide new information, insight or opinion.
- Offer to answer people's questions relating to your industry. The Twitter community responds best to people who are helpful.
- Try to make your tweets no more than 120 characters, so they can be easily retweeted.
- Aim to tweet at least once a day to get started. You should aim to be tweeting about once an hour when you get into it, but don't worry about that yet.

Using Twitter to do better business

Start by downloading Tweetdeck (or Hootsuite, they do the same). These programs let you organize your followers and have ongoing searches running for things relevant to you. You can use them to engage potential customers. Create a column that searches for your business names, and other columns that search for any terms relevant to your business (and also your location, if relevant).

Let's carry on with the plumber example. You're a plumber based in Kingston. You set up columns searching for 'plumber Kingston' and 'problem pipes' and 'plumbing problems'. Someone tweets: 'Anyone know a plumber in the Kingston area?' You can reply offering your services and telling them you can be there in an hour. Someone else tweets: 'Got a massive problem with my bathroom pipes! Eek!' You can @ them saying: 'I'm a plumber – what's the problem? I can advise by DM'. Getting it? You're reaching new customers you might not otherwise have found, you're establishing a reputation as a really helpful and friendly plumber, and you're spreading the word about your business. Pretty good for 30 seconds' work and not a penny spent!

Here are a few other tips to get you going:

- Regularly @ your followers who have the most followers. The more often they retweet you and engage in conversation with you, the greater chance you have of reaching their audience too. You can use http://analytics.ad.ly/ to find out your most influential followers.
- Definitely respond to anyone saying anything about your business or products. Thank them for their feedback and thank them if they say something positive.
- Always respond to any criticism of your business quickly, positively and helpfully. Pick up on it by searching for your company name.
- After you've spent a little while establishing yourself, start subtly, and occasionally, introducing your business or products.
- Tweet about news or deals rather than just existing products so people always feel like they're getting some benefit from following you rather than just being sold to.
- If you are going to talk about a new product, do it in a way that conveys your personal excitement about it rather than in sales speak. This makes it an emotional thing that people can relate to rather than a sell they will turn off to.
- Don't overdo it: mention products and your business only as often as you would to your normal friends. You wouldn't email them every week trying to sell them your wares, so don't do it on Twitter.
- Use Twitter Karma or Friend or Follow (both free) to purge your account of people who aren't following you back – these services show you who's following you back out of the people you follow. As you're limited to following 2,000 people at first, this will allow you to maintain the highest quality of followers (those who follow you back and remain part of your audience).
- Use a service like Tweetie so you can tweet from your smartphone, if you have one, to keep the tweets coming regularly.
- Offer exclusive deals on Twitter and ask people to RT them – this can spread your business name like wildfire. Make sure you track how many people use the discount code when they make a purchase to see if it's been effective.
- Add your Twitter handle to your email signature and any new business cards and stationery to get more followers.
- Encourage customers to @ you if they use Twitter.

There really are hundreds of guides on the internet on how to use Twitter as a business and get more out of it, and there's enough to say about it to fill 100 books, let alone this chapter!

So now we've given you a taste for what Twitter can do, the best thing for you to do is get on Smarta.com and take a look at our Twitter resources, including our downloadable free e-book. Check out Mashable.com too. It's probably the most comprehensive and up-to-date website out there for advice on using social media, Twitter very much included. You can also start Googling advice. There are a huge number of blogs and sites out there that give in-depth advice on using Twitter as a business. We really have only just scratched the surface here.

Finally, and most importantly, always measure the results you're getting on Twitter. You need to make sure it's worth your while carrying on, and you need to get a feel for which tweets are most successful. Track how many RTs you get and how quickly you are gaining followers (be patient though: it takes months, not days, to build up a following). Fine-tune your strategy. If you're really not getting any love on Twitter, spend that time working on another strategy instead, and come back to it at a later date when you might get a better uptake.

And feel free to chat to us @SmartaHQ if there's ever anything we can help with!

Smarta in Action: Findababysitter.com

Founders: Tom Harrow and Ben Ferrier
Company: Findababysitter.com
Company profile: Findababysitter.com lets UK parents search for all types of childcare in their area, and helps childcare workers to find work, sidestepping the need for expensive agencies.
Founded: 2006

Overview
Harrow and Ferrier have racked up just under 1,000 followers – impressive for a niche business. They use Twitter to find customers, share news, for marketing and to find potential partners.

How they did it
The Findababysitter.com team started out on Twitter by following people in the childcare industry. 'We haven't used any of the cheats you can use to grow your following more quickly, it's all been organic – quality is important, not quantity.' To increase their reach, they include their Twitter handle (@childcareuk) on outbound emails, in website articles and newsletters. As a result, their following is relevant to their business.

They use it to keep an eye on competitors and they're in touch with peers on Twitter. They've forged partnerships through it by meeting followers offline.

'We use it to search for people talking about us and engage them,' Ferrier explains. 'We have searches set up for people looking for babysitters. We say hello and offer them a free trial, just to surprise people!' The free trials have often led to people signing up for their paid service. Customers don't typically use Twitter as a customer service channel, but rather to chat and find out parenting news.

Findababysitter.com runs promotional offers and competitions through Twitter too, often tying them in with its Facebook activity. 'We recently ran a Mother's Day competition to find the funniest things kids had said to their mum, with a daily winner and one overall winner. We created a hashtag for it.' It drove good traffic and was cannily self-propagating, as they could retweet every funny quote and generate more interest.

'We're building a bridgehead out there,' says Ferrier. 'It's been invaluable.'

Tips
Build a following who have a genuine interest in your business. Then use Twitter as a slow-burning brand builder with a personal touch, rather than a sales weapon.

Smarta in five

1 Believe the hype: Twitter offers value for all businesses

2 Listen first: use Twitter as a research tool before doing anything else

3 Keep it real: be yourself and write your own tweets

4 Offer value and don't sell

5 Once you've made the commitment to tweet, tweet!

5.10
Don't buy advertising

"The two most effective ways I found of promoting the products are just letting people taste the products (we do that in big events in stores), and we print quite a lot of money-off coupons. We also did a give-away with *The Sun* – that was the biggest promotion I've done."

—Fraser Doherty, SuperJam

"We didn't have much of a marketing budget, but we did have Sophie Rhys-Jones, who later became Sophie Wessex, involved. So we did an exercise on the London Underground where men got dressed up as kings. They'd come to you and proclaim themselves 'King of Shaves' and say they were going to save you from 'your stubble trouble'. We did a leak to the *Evening Standard* and, because they thought Rhys-Jones' back story is in it, it ran that 'Sophie launches King of Shaves on the London Underground'. It got huge press coverage."

—Will King, King of Shaves

Has social media really killed the advertising star? Search the web and you'll find plenty of articles revelling in the death of traditional advertising at the hands of Twitter, Facebook, YouTube et al. Why would you waste your time spending big money on print, television or radio advertising when you can open a dialogue to both mainstream and niche audiences for little more resource than your time?

It seems you wouldn't. Overall advertising industry spend has fallen for three consecutive years now, with even online spend tumbling from 40% annual growth in 2008 to just 2.3% in 2009.

With industry in decline, the economy floundering and traditional advertising facing a second-generation web challenge to its traditional formats, conversely costs might have fallen sufficiently to appeal to small businesses previously unlikely to consider such spend. It's true there's certainly more room for negotiation across television, print, outdoor and radio rate cards, but whether prices have fallen sufficiently to make them either accessible or cost-effective is questionable.

When Smarta phoned *The Guardian* it was quoted £34,000 for a colour full-page ad to a readership of 340,000, with the *Bristol Evening Post* coming in at £4,147 to get in front of 143,000 people. We were told a television advert would cost between £35,000 and £50,000 to produce, with 15 30-second slots on ITV2 after 5 p.m. coming in at £55,000. Local papers, trade mags and radio quoted less, as you'd expect, but it was hardly what you'd call loose change or, tellingly, typical small business spend.

Advertising's not dead then, but nor has it fallen down market enough to be a viable option for most small businesses – and if it had, could it really compete with the opportunity-laden world of social media? Other than targeted pay-per-click advertising (and that's not cheap), in our opinion, no.

> **" Advertising is not a viable option for most small businesses "**

So, other than social media, it's business as usual for small businesses, who have long had to rely on working creatively to publicize their businesses as an alternative to ad spend. While social media has opened up endless possibilities, smart companies can still court attention offline by thinking that little bit smarter than everyone else.

Look for collaborative opportunities. If you run an ice-cream parlour, how about offering to operate a free or profit-share booth in the evenings at your local cinema or theatre, or simply to give away tubs in exchange for the exposure it'll give you. Teaming up with complementary companies to market to each other's data lists is another favourite.

Work hard to carve out PR opportunities, develop your personal brand (see Chapter 6.8) and do whatever it takes to get your message out there without parting with your hard-earned or non-existent cash. Think about any publicity stunts you could pull to grab some attention. As Jamie Murray Wells found with Glasses Direct, conducting a high-profile dispute with a high-street giant can do wonders for gaining exposure that would otherwise have cost millions – although we'd advise that you pick your fights carefully.

If you have a product, find ways for people to try it or interact with it. Marketers call this 'experiential marketing' and can charge you a small fortune to carry out street promotion campaigns, but we recommend you take to the streets yourself and save a load of money.

The key is to be creative and do something different which both fits in with your brand and your target audience will understand. Jamie's stunt worked so well not just because of the publicity it courted, but because he knew that by positioning Glasses Direct as the David to Specsavers' Goliath, he'd resonate with customers who appreciated the savings a small independent company could deliver in contrast to a large multinational. The same approach wouldn't have worked if Vision Express had tried it, for instance.

If you can't afford to advertise, do whatever it takes to get seen, tried and talked about. Be bold, hustle and make some noise!

Guerrilla marketing

As inspiration for how you can get creative as an alternative to traditional advertising, here are five guerrilla marketing campaigns, albeit by bigger companies, that show the power of thinking differently.

1 IKEA, New York

From clear-walled 'rooms' suspended from cranes to a 30-foot parody of an Absolut Vodka ad with an apartment's worth of furniture glued to a billboard, IKEA has a history of great marketing stunts. During Design Week 2006, New Yorkers were treated to five days of comfort, IKEA style. The company teamed up with marketing agency Deutsch to make life that little bit more comfortable with 650 different 'experiences' all over the city, including padded park benches in Union Square, bus shelters designed for 'comfort and flair', thousands of picnic blankets laid out in Central Park and even oven mitts on the number six train, all with a card bearing the slogan 'good design can make the everyday a little better'.

Sadly, the spirit of generosity didn't catch on: most of the furniture was stolen within days.

2 Half.com, Oregon

Back in 1999 when the internet was crowded with dot-com start-ups, Half.com founder Joshua Kopelman quite literally put his business on the map by convincing Oregon town Halfway to become the world's first 'dot-com city' and rename itself Half.com for a year. In return, Kopelman offered the city a $100,000 package of benefits, including subsidized internet access, stock in the company, free giveaways and, crucially, a promise that the change would boost local tourism.

The plan worked a treat. Within weeks, Kopelman and residents of the town had appeared on various news shows, the *Today Show* and in the *Wall Street Journal*, and Kopelman's gamble had seen a very rapid return. Just three weeks after the town renamed itself, eBay bought Half.com (the company, not the town) for more than $300 million – a 3,000% return on the initial investment.

3 T-Mobile, London

In one of the most well-publicized guerilla ad moments of the last few years, T-Mobile transformed the concourse of London's Liverpool Street Station into an enormous disco, with hundreds of seemingly innocuous commuters slowly joining in on an enormous dance routine, which was then aired during a high-profile advert break on Channel 4. The ad received a huge amount of press coverage, bringing T-Mobile's tagline, 'Life is for sharing', to the forefront of the public imagination. So much so, in fact, that the ad's success had unwanted consequences. A few days after it was aired, 12,000 teenagers descended on Liverpool Street in an effort to recreate the ad, forcing staff to close the station due to overcrowding.

4 Carlsberg, London

Carlsberg has been running the same 'best in the world' campaign for years now, but in April 2007, Londoners suddenly began to see its genius when the company left 5,000 £10 and £20 notes all over the city, bearing the sticker 'Carlsberg doesn't do litter, but if it did, it would probably be the best litter in the world'. Even though it was handing out cold, hard cash, the campaign cost Carlsberg just £50,000, a snip if you compare it to the average cost of creating a television ad campaign.

5 Médécins du Monde, Paris

Drawing attention to the plight of people living on the streets is a difficult task in any city, but when French humanitarian organization Médécins du Monde distributed 300 identical tents emblazoned with the charity's logo to homeless people in Paris, the sheer number of tents set up along the city's canals drew attention to just how many people were sleeping rough. The effect was immediate: Parisians voiced their outrage and the French government was forced to pledge 7 million (£5.75 million) to create 1,270 hostel beds in the city, making it one of the most effective guerrilla marketing campaigns ever undertaken.

Smarta in Action: Trading4U

Founder: Bradley McLoughlin
Company: Trading4U
Company profile: A trading firm that acts on behalf of consumers wanting to get rid of unwanted items worth £75 or more. It sells them on online marketplaces such as eBay.
Founded: 2007

Overview
McLoughlin's website now turns over a huge amount, but back in the day he had to manage a tight advertising budget ultra carefully to get bang for his buck. That didn't mean he got it right first time, though.

How he did it
McLoughlin started by experimenting with a press advertising campaign. 'We spent a great deal of money on a full-page ad in a top gadget magazine,' he explains. 'But it didn't even generate one phone call. It simply didn't see any results.'

Not wanting to give up just yet, he ploughed on – crucially, by trying out different formats to test the design, not just the medium. 'We tried four adverts. I looked at the first two and thought there must be something missing. We went for very different approaches on each one but it just didn't work for us.'

Since then, McLoughlin has shifted his focus to online advertising. He's carried on experimenting with different types of advert and amounts of coverage, but always with an amount he can afford to play around with without costing the business an excessive amount.

As a result, he's found his business's advertising sweet spot with pay-per-click (PPC) advertising. 'We started spending about £1 a day but now we're on a £40-a-day budget,' he says. 'But you've got to make sure you keep track.'

That's what it's all about: micro-managing and analysing advertising results continually to make sure you're spending wisely, and reallocating budget swiftly when needed to maximize the impact of your spend.

Top tips
'With PPC, as long as you keep it optimized, you'll see results. Otherwise, the campaign might not be as efficient.'

Smarta in five

1 Traditional advertising isn't dead, it's just expensive

2 Social media does offer better value and more opportunities for small businesses

3 Look for collaborative opportunities to get your brand into new places

4 Develop your personal brand

5 Get creative, think guerrilla

5.11
Work your website harder

"The only way to build a website if you are a non-technology person is to have as detailed a plan as possible and a roadmap. Often you'll hear people saying their project took three times longer than expected. But projects slip at their beginning. So try not to change the spec as you're going along. Do quite a granular project plan and meet frequently."

—Karen Hanton, Toptable

"SEO is by far the most cost-effective way to get a presence on the search engines. You can throw all kinds of money at pay-per-click marketing, but you do need to have money to make it work. The only real way to build a sustainable SEO strategy is by just putting really great content on your website, relevant things that people will comment on and talk about. Really, that's all there is to it."

—Matt McNeill, Sign-up.to and eTickets.to

"I did employ a PPC company. But I've learnt Google AdWords myself. I've been educating myself for the past year now. I've actually achieved higher results than the company I employed."

—Bradley McLoughlin, Trading4U

"To get web traffic, we put our content on partner websites, we do direct marketing, paid search, natural search, email activity, affiliate activity, and we have done some brand activity. It's about having a combination."

—John Paleomylites, BeatThatQuote.com

We're not going to waste our time making a case for why you need a website, we're going to trust that you're not stuck in 1996 and realize that in 2010s every single business should have a web presence. So instead we'll assume that you've either already got a website or are in the process of getting one, and focus on the two web issues that still baffle even the smartest businesses owners: ending up with the website you asked for without being ripped off and then, once you've got it, getting it to appear anywhere near the first page of Google for anything your customers are likely to search for.

> **Every single business should have a web presence**

To help you keep a tab on what you should be paying for varying degrees of functionality, we've done a quick audit of trustworthy designers, developers and providers and come up with the following price guide.

What a good website will cost

Too many business owners are getting ripped off by slow, bad or plain unscrupulous design companies and developers. It has to stop! Here's the info you need to keep your contracts in check, the different elements needed to build a website, what they cost and who should handle them.

Registering your domain

This should be quick and easy – do it yourself. Use services such as GoDaddy, 1&1internet or 123-reg. **Ballpark figure:** £10–£20

Hosting services

Most internet registrars include hosting packages giving you around 10Gb, as well as a couple of email addresses. **Ballpark figure:** £2.50 per month for 10Gb

Building your website

There are plenty of off-the-shelf products which let you build your own website for next to nothing, and these really are the way forward unless you need something fancy or you want a complex online shop. Try Google Sites, Mr Site, Moonfruit, Template Monster and others like them. You normally only need dedicated designers and developers if you're pulling out all the stops, or if you're doing a flashy redesign.

Design

For complicated websites, some businesses choose to pay a separate graphic designer to create a brand and determine how it will look before they hand it to a development team to be coded. This takes longer – think days and weeks. **Ballpark figure:** £250 a day. Save money by tweaking pre-made templates from websites like OneDollarTemplates or Template Monster instead of having them designed from scratch.

Development

This is the coding process which turns images created by a graphic designer into HTML code (which is what makes your website – HTML is all the stuff that goes on behind the scenes of a site). If you're having a complex, content-driven website designed, there's a good chance you'll need this done separately to the design. **Ballpark figure:** £300–£400 a day. If it's a simple brochure site, converting the designs into code should be a relatively straightforward process, whereas if your requirements are more complicated, the development and testing process could take months.

> **WWW**
>
> See the Smarta Business Builder at www.smarta.com/tools/SmartaBusinessBuilder

Copywriting

You can probably do this yourself, it's just the wording for your website. If you choose to employ a copywriter, you're looking at £200–£300 a day.

Photography/images

Never underestimate the importance, or the cost, of images. There are dozens of image libraries, charging between £2 and £200 for images. Istock.com is a good option at the cheapest end of the spectrum. Flickr.com also has some free images – just make sure you use those licensed under the Creative Commons and attribute the photographer.

Blog

If you want a blog custom-designed for your website, include it in the brief for your designer. They can usually create templates for free plugins such as Wordpress, Movable Type or Blogger. **Ballpark figure:** free, although you will have to factor the design cost in.

More ways to avoid paying too much

- Spend time looking online for websites you like, then contact their owners to find out which company they used and how much they paid. This will give you a better bargaining tool when it comes to agreeing a price.

- Get quotes – lots of them. The more quotes you get, the better idea you will have about how much you should be paying. If you're in doubt, find out how much other businesses in your industry with similar websites paid.
- At the beginning of the design process, set a project plan and agree on delivery dates with your design and development teams. This will allow you keep track of their progress throughout the design process and be kept abreast of problems as they arise.
- If you want to use your website to keep your clients up to date with news but don't want to pay to have a content-led site designed, ask for a basic brochure site and include a blog which is free to install and simple to update on a regular basis.
- If all you want is a basic site, printing companies with in-house designers can sometimes get the job done for less than £200.
- Try PeoplePerHour to get quotes from freelancers.

SEO: Making sure people can find your website

Such is Google's shrouding of its algorithms, there's no way we're going to pretend to know how to rifle you up the search engines. Then again, neither should a lot of the search engine optimization companies and 'experts' charging a small fortune for doing the basics that you could easily do for yourself.

Your page ranking depends on a number of factors, none of which you can, or should want to, fake, so it's a case of knowing what Google likes and doing the best you can. We've outlined the most important factors in the sections below and the basic principles for ticking Google's favourite boxes.

Ensure you've got keyword-rich content

When you optimize your site for search, you need to focus on certain terms people will type into Google to find business like yours. These are your keywords. For example, if you sell garden furniture, your keywords might be 'buy garden furniture online', 'garden furniture', 'garden chairs' and so on.

Use Google's Keywords tool to find the most searched-for keywords in your space and so the ones you want to target. That said, avoid the very top-performing terms if they're getting tens of thousands of searches a month, as you'll struggle to compete for these words. Targeting niche terms can pay, for example 'pine garden furniture under £100' and 'garden furniture shop in Cheam'.

> **❝ You can do the basics of SEO yourself ❞**

Once you know your prime keywords, make sure you use them prominently (but not excessively, as Google won't like this) in any content you've got on the site and in relevant titles and menus. Google loves rich content, so if you only have products on your website, think about getting a blog to offer up regularly refreshed content and remember to sprinkle it with keywords.

Meta data

These are the page titles and descriptions which appear on search engine listings, but not on the actual page of your website. It's continually debated among SEO wonks whether 'meta matters' or not. Seeing as they and so you assume that Google changes its mind with the weather, it's better to play safe and get your meta data keyworded up.

You should be able to access your meta tag and meta description code easily from the back end of your website, whether you used a web designer and developer or an off-the-shelf website package. Ask your hosting provider or developer how if it's not obvious.

Use your keywords to fill your meta data. Your page titles are the bits that appear as linked titles when you see something listed in Google's search results, and meta descriptions are the bits underneath that describe what the page is about. Make sure that both would make sense to someone who read them in a Google listing, as hopefully they will be read. Keep page titles to 66 characters, and keep meta descriptions to 180. If you can fill in meta tags too, just write a list of five to ten keywords, separated by commas. Meta tags don't appear on search engine listings but are 'sometimes' used by search engines anyway, apparently, so it's best just to play the game.

HTML

SEO uses HTML, the 'language' of code that actually builds your website, and other programming languages derived from it. At the moment, Google and other search engines cannot read complicated coding such as Flash or Javascript, although this may be set to change in the future. Make sure you have a HTML version of your site whether or not you use Flash. Talk to your developer about this.

Keep updating your homepage

Search engines like websites that keep putting new content on their websites. So if you don't regularly update your homepage and other pages with new products or news, start a blog that shows a few sentences on your homepage, and update it regularly.

Linkbacks

Linkbacks are links from other websites to yours, and they're one of the most important factors in determining how high up the search listings your website should be. The more linkbacks you have, the higher up you'll be, although the emphasis is more on quality than quantity. A link from the BBC is worth two from some obscure link directory.

Develop a link strategy to help you decide which websites you want to target. Use businesses which are in the same field as you but not competitors, then write to them and suggest a link exchange, where they link to you in return for you providing a link on your site to them. Remember to be clear on which keywords you would like them to use in the link text.

You can also use online directories to boost your linkbacks. Try the DMOZ Open Directory Project (which is free) or the Yahoo! directory, Yell, Thomson Local and Daltons Business (which you'll have to pay for).

You can also try writing articles for article submission websites, which gather free content for their publications. Write articles on your area of expertise, remembering to focus on your keywords and provide several links to your website, and submit them to the article submission site. If publishers pick them up, they will link to your website. Set up a Google Alert to notify you if your piece has been picked up.

Social networking websites such as Facebook, YouTube, Flickr and Twitter are all great ways of generating links too.

Link to other websites

Search engines also like websites that are useful to users, such as ones that link to other relevant sites.

Pay per click

The alternative to all of this, of course, is to stop worrying about your organic search results (the ones which appear through the middle and which Google controls) and instead to pay to appear in the little sponsored boxes to the right and top of the page.

This is called pay-per-click advertising and is controlled by Google Adwords. It's very simple and essentially works on you paying an agreed amount (set by the popularity of the search term) each time someone clicks through from your ad. You set a daily limit so are always in control of your spend.

It's a straightforward, measurable marketing tool, but its cost is increasingly prohibitive to small businesses. If this is the route you intend to pursue, then you must ensure you factor the cost into your model.

A sensible strategy applied by most smart businesses is to use pay-per-click initially while they're establishing an organic search presence, then to reduce it and instead use it to supplement organic search or for specific campaigns.

Smarta in Action: Oxford Learning Lab

Founder: Giorgio Burlini
Company: Oxford Learning Lab
Company profile: Oxford Learning Lab produces, distributes and monetizes high-quality educational videos created in collaboration with sought-after teachers and professors.
Founded: 2008

Overview

Burlini had to find a way to improve his business's visibility online, but the keywords he needed to use to be found on Google were very common. He had to find an innovative way for people to search for commonly used keywords and find his site, without breaking the bank.

How he did it

Burlini needed to use keywords 'marketing', 'marketing planning', 'internet marketing', 'marketing communications', 'SEO' and 'PPC' – all very heavily used keywords. And marketing-oriented websites number in the hundreds of thousands, which makes SEO fiercely competitive. But Burlini needed potential customers to find his site using those keywords.

A pay-per-click campaign would have required heavy investment, blowing his budget.

So Burlini thought outside the box. He explains, 'The second search engine after Google is YouTube, not Bing or Yahoo!. With more than one billion clips watched a day, and 300 million uniques a month, getting YouTube working for you means great exposure. So I decided to create our own YouTube channel, with about 33% of our videos free of charge but carrying our logos and call to action. I did the same on about ten other major videos channels, such as 5min.com.'

He had to work hard to make sure the title, description, meta tags and initial image were right for YouTube's search, but it paid off. Thousands of people now watch his clips, and one in ten viewers goes on to visit his main site.

Tips

Burlini says, 'Always look at all your weapons and not just at the usual SEO tips. Video clips are now featured in natural Google search, and after three months one of our clips is on the first page of Google! Use a website called www.tubemogul.com to help you to upload all your clips in different videos sites. A real time saver!'

Smarta in five

1 No arguments, you need a website

2 Know what you want and what the going rate is

3 Set firm deadlines and clear payment terms

4 Do your basic SEO work yourself

5 Limit your pay-per-click spend

Part 6
Be smart

6.1
Only do what you do best

"I recognized years ago that no one man can be good at everything. There are loads of different departments that need expert people in there, and for lots of those departments my knowledge would be a waste of time. It's very important that you recognize your strong points and your weaknesses."

—Charlie Mullins, Pimlico Plumbers

"I brought on somebody as my ops director who was very driven and very ambitious. He wanted to be the managing director, and said, 'I think I would do this job really well and I think it's time you moved over.' He said it in such a way that it was almost a relief, and I thought to myself, actually I feel like I could go off and do my thing. There was some ego involved, but it was the exactly the right decision to make."

—Simon Woodroffe, YO! Sushi and YO! Group

> "Everybody likes to benchmark themselves against a group of people. I had this renaissance woman concept – I should try to be good at everything. But I realized if I continued to try to do the stuff I'm not good at, I'd continue to be mediocre at it for the rest of my life."
>
> **—Julie Meyer, Ariadne Capital**

> "You've got to be thinking about it all the time. You have to know what you're good at – then you can bring on a team to do the rest."
>
> **—Duncan Bannatyne, *Dragons' Den* and Bannatyne Group**

> "Accounting is not my strong point, so I brought in a finance director to help me really kick the crap out of my business plan and my financials and say, 'Well, how much money do we really need and what are we going to spend it on?'"
>
> **—Sarah Watson, Balineum**

OK, so now it's time to focus on you. Remember, you're worth it. That said, what exactly is it you do? We're deadly serious. So you run this show, you're the centre of all the activity and you call the shots, but that aside, what's your actual role, what are you most effective at and what in reality do you spend your time doing? Are they same thing? When you take a step back and look at it, on a day-to-day basis are you happy with how you work? Furthermore, is what you're doing the best use of your skill set? Is your business deriving full value from you?

One thing you can guarantee about smart companies is that they maximize their assets. Time not to be modest now, because if you take a quick look in the mirror, without a doubt, whatever your industry, size or turnover, one of the greatest assets your business has is *you*. As the founder, you are the driving force, the lifeblood, the very nucleus of the business. Getting the most out of you, maximizing your time, your skills and your performance, is critical to its ultimate success.

You can't start too early with this one and the best place to begin is by asking yourself some honest questions about your strengths and, of course, your weaknesses. Let's be clear: nobody, absolutely nobody, can be (or is expected to be) good at everything.

> **"Absolutely nobody is good at everything"**

One of the mistakes that small businesses owners make time and time again is to believe that they have to do everything themselves and then attempt to do so. In fairness, when you're starting out the probability is that you will have to be managing director, marketing director, accountant, secretary and cleaner all in one, but you should look to move on from that all-encompassing chaos as soon as possible, because it's a recipe for disaster and will stunt any growth plans you've got for the business.

Running a business requires a disparate mix of skills which no one person is likely to possess. By the time you're looking to expand, you should also be looking to share the burden of responsibility. The key is to play to your strengths and find great people to help you in your weaker areas, freeing you to take an aerial view of the business and do what you do best.

You probably already know what your strengths are – for most business people it's instinctive. They're either managers or they're entrepreneurs who lead from the front making decisions at top level and leaving the detail to someone else. If it's not as cut and dried for you, examine your skill set. Are you a natural sales person, more of a strategist or a creative ideas person with an aptitude for marketing?

This is a happy coincidence: the things that you enjoy doing you're more likely to want to spend time perfecting. Similarly, if there's an aspect of running your business that you hate, it's likely to show on your list of weaknesses.

Now do the same for your weaknesses. This may seem a little painful at first but remember, it isn't about criticism, it's about figuring out where you should be focusing your energy. No one from Branson to Trump is fabulous at everything and the smart business owner knows that and doesn't take it personally.

Once you've mapped your strengths and weaknesses, you need to find a way of working that allows you to focus on your strong areas and compensates for the weaker ones. Indeed, this is probably more relevant as, regardless of what you 'want' to be doing, what you can't do is a sure indication of a skills gap you need to fill swiftly, whether by recruiting or outsourcing.

WWW

Hone your personal skills online here: www.smarta.com/entrepreneur-skills

It might seem strange that having spent most of the book urging you to show caution when expanding and taking on any sort of overhead, we're now encouraging you to do the opposite. Indeed, the very reason you've been juggling duties is likely to have been to conserve cash and resist burdening the business with bodies for as long as conceivably possible.

However, there obviously also comes a point where it's damaging not to commit resource to the business in order for it to expand. After all, as the maxim goes, before you can grow you've got to stop working in the business and work on it. You simply won't do that while you're making every decision, signing every invoice and speaking to every customer.

Besides, continuing that way will only damage the business. For you to grow you need to be able to take a step back and focus on developing the most profitable points in the business; as well as chasing the big deals which will bring in money to expand.

For some, the process of self-analysis reveals a rather frightening outcome: whether you like it or not, your business could actually be better off without you. This company you've slaved over creating and built in your vision just might be better run by someone else.

This can be a bitter pill to swallow, but one many natural entrepreneurs have had to come terms with. Some people are far more adept at creating businesses than they are at managing or running them. Some massively successful, established entrepreneurs widely admit they're atrocious people managers or simply lack the focus, patience or attention span to deal with the finer details of day-to-day trading.

> **"Your business could actually be better off without you"**

The smarter business owners accept what they are and work around it. They come up with the ideas, do the start-up phase, but then recruit an MD to come in and run the business. They either withdraw completely and set about working on their next project, or sculpt a role where they're able to contribute to the 'bigger picture' strategy where they can make a meaningful contribution.

If you think that's you, better to act now and start preparing the business for someone else to be able to slot in than to struggle through trying to be something you're not. Not only will it not work, it won't make you happy either.

If you do look to bring in a manager, MD or COO (chief operating officer, as they're often called) to help run the business, take your time and make sure you recruit someone who completely shares your vision. Ensure they're a good culture fit for the business as well, do several rounds of interviews and make at least one of them with employees who'll report in to this person. Then when they start, have clear ground-rules about how involved you'll be and how they'll report to you – and stick to them.

It's most likely, though, that focusing on what you do best will be more about embracing the art of delegation, and that involves learning to let go of not just the minutiae but some of the stuff you believe *only you* can do. Entrepreneurs wouldn't start businesses if a part of their personality didn't believe they could do certain things better than anyone else.

> **"Delegation involves learning to let go of some of the stuff you believe only you can do"**

You have to get over this, though. Other people have to be able to manage the accounts, have a say on branding and cash up. If you want get the most from your employees, you have to give them autonomy. Insist on signing off anything important if you must, but don't fall into the trap of delegating then micromanaging – or you may as well not bother delegating.

The more you understand yourself and how you work best, the more you can understand how to grow and develop your business. Getting the most out of you ultimately means that your business works better – and as an added bonus, you get to focus on more of the stuff you love and less on the things you hate or simply don't do justice to while you could be delivering value elsewhere.

Smarta in Action: Skip-Hop

Founder: Scott Robert-Shaw
Company: Skip-Hop
Company profile: Skip-Hop develops innovative workshops and products related to skip-hop, a fusion of street dance and sport skipping.

Overview
Robert-Shaw and his business partner had been showcasing skip-hop in schools for 10 years and loved it. But in order to grow the business, they had to rethink their business model and focus on building a structure that maximized their strengths.

How he did it
Though he loved doing demonstrations in schools, Robert-Shaw knew his strengths also lay in brand building and strategy. With plans to take the company international and into adult markets, he knew that's what he had to start focusing on.

He decided to step back from delivering his product face to face and hand over that responsibility to two new employees. 'That was the hardest thing: going from you delivering it, which is such a passion. Training other people to come in and do it is so hard, but you have to.' It took a year to find the right two people for the job, but now it's freed up Robert-Shaw to fully focus on strategy and new markets, which he's done to great success, as the brand is now in Canada, Ireland and Brazil as well as the UK.

He also recognized that his weakness was administration. He made sure the people he brought in to the business could take a good heap of that off his hands. He invested in Salesforce customer service software, to streamline processes. 'We realized we had to create a business model that that can run without our constant input.'

It hasn't necessarily been as fun as it used to be – Robert-Shaw says being behind a desk all day can feel 'very frustrating'. But it has let him work on a new website, go international, develop a new skipping rope, and enter new markets.

Tips
Getting the most out of you isn't always the most fun or easiest route, but it is vital for growth. That said, Robert-Shaw says you must still enjoy what you do.

Smarta in five

1 Move on as soon as you can from the start-up mentality of 'doing everything'

2 Make space and time to work on the business, not in it

3 Understand your strengths and weaknesses

4 Learn to delegate and trust others

5 Work where and when you're most effective

6.2
Don't be a rock

"When I started my business off, I thought: how difficult can it be? Anyway, fast forward three months and I'm minus £25,000 in the bank with no income. It was at that point I wondered whether I was managing director or managing depression. It was tough. Nobody prepares you for any of this. I thought it was all private number plates, fish tanks and spinning chairs. The reality is you've got too much month at the end of the cash."

—Brad Burton, 4Networking

"Starting a business is very, very lonely. You're on your own. The whole world is against you. So if you can have an ally that's there with you on the journey, it just makes it more fun. You can stick with it longer, I think, if you've got someone with you."

—Sahar Hashemi, Coffee Republic

"It's really important for any entrepreneurs, especially women entrepreneurs, to have their peer group, their circle of women on the same level. We need to connect with other women and share. It's crucially healthy for women to do that on a regular basis. It's a physical, chemical and spiritual need."

—Lynne Franks, B.Hive

"People often say never give up. I think what's more appropriate is to say know when to give up. Too often entrepreneurs become very sentimental and emotionally attached to their business or to their ideas even when they've realized that there is no end game or it's become a futile exercise. Because they are sentimental or emotional, they can't walk away from it."

—Imran Hakim, iTeddy

There's no point beating around the bush: it's statistically proven that unfortunately, half the people starting businesses this year will fail. Even fewer will see their businesses fly from day one, and even if that does happen, sooner or later there will come a time when they hit a low ebb. It happens to the best of entrepreneurs and, we guarantee, it will happen to you.

For all the upsides, starting a business is tough: late nights, endless frustrations, hundreds of tasks you've never had to face before and have no idea how to tackle, and for many, day after day spent alone. We don't want to put you off, because it is also one of the most rewarding and enjoyable experiences you'll ever have. And most of the time it won't feel anywhere near like the hard work it is because your passion and enjoyment will power you through. But you'll need to prepare yourself to take the crunchy with the smooth.

First things first: it is not your friends' or partner's or family's fault if they don't 'get it'. Unless they've started a business themselves, they will never be able to comprehend quite how emotionally involving and draining it can be. Expect them to say things like: 'Can't you just take a weekend off?' or 'Does it really matter that much?' or 'I can't believe you didn't make it to my birthday!' That's right – they're going to be getting frustrated too, because they'll be seeing a whole lot less of you.

And while you might (hopefully only occasionally) feel like screaming at them for their lack of sensitivity, you also need to remember they are making sacrifices to support you. Talk through your plans and try to help them understand what it's going to be like when you get fully stuck into your business, before the worst happens, so they can be prepared too.

While it's important to have a solid support net in your private life, it's imperative you also start building relationships with business people who will understand and who you can turn to when you hit a wall and need some support. All smart business people surround themselves with not just a team of employees, but a circle of contacts they can call on when times are tough.

WWW

Feeling isolated and like nobody understands, change that now: www.smarta.com/network

The Smarta community is your first port of call if this is resonating with you this very second – go online now and start connecting with thousands of other small business owners just like you who understand first hand the pressures of running your own business. Likewise, start building up a Twitter following and also get out to physical networking events. There will be lots in your area, but we'd recommend Brad Burton's 4Networking as an ideal place to start. Alternatively, Meetup.com is an invaluable website for finding entrepreneur support groups, Female business owners should check out Lynne Franks' B.Hive. both online and offline, while the Open Coffee group runs excellent email support groups. Female business owners should check out Lynne Frarks' B.Hive.

When the sales aren't coming in as you'd expected and the phone isn't ringing or you've just lost a big order, the key thing is to react. People say you shouldn't panic in business and

> ❝❝*Don't panic, but action is preferable to inaction*❞❞

while we wouldn't support knee-jerk reactions, action is definitely preferable to inaction. The worst thing you can do when things aren't working out is to bury your head in the sand. If your business is struggling, do something about it.

Throughout this book we've talked about the need to be flexible. The smartest businesses accept that the business climate is beyond their control and see changing consumer trends as an opportunity to react first, not an obstacle to stability.

Never be wedded to a particular path. Expect to have to make changes at times to your proposition, your model and your team and even your own way of working. When the chips are down there's no time for sentimentality and you have to do what's best for the business. Resist making impulsive decisions and take in the

> ❝❝*Expect to have to make changes to your proposition, your model, your team and your own way of working*❞❞

advice of others, but don't be scared to make the changes that will save your business.

If you're at the stage where the business is haemorrhaging money, look to cut every fixed cost you possibly can. Offices, people, marketing, advertising – cut it back. It's unpleasant, it's upsetting, but you have to remove emotion and do whatever it take to protect the business. Plenty of very successful businesses undergo a natural or forced pruning period after launch, yet go on to to regrow more healthily and later blossom. You just have to take a step back and view these things objectively.

The truth is, the quicker you react to a major problem and the sooner you do something about it, the more likely you are to stop it becoming business critical. As such, it pays to be continually assessing the state of your business and taking a risk-averse approach to both cashflow and overheads. In turn, avoiding this very situation is the reason you need to be proactive in bringing money into the business.

Smart business people never rest: if they're not working on the business itself, they're out building relationships and chasing deals because they know nobody else is going to do it for them. You simply don't start a business and then sit back and wait for it to grow. You've got to be up and at 'em and hustling every day.

All of this said, there is also a unfortunate point where a business can't and shouldn't be saved. Most businesses won't go on for ever and some run their natural course, while others simply get to the point where debt strangulates any hope of survival. It's at this point where you have to get real about letting go.

We won't dwell too long on a scenario we sincerely hope you won't find yourself in, but pointedly, a situation several of the entrepreneurs in this book have experienced and come back from. The key is to understand that the failure of one business does not need to spell the end of your entrepreneurial career or be any mark against you in the future.

For whatever reasons, if it didn't work, it didn't work. Stop, regroup and focus on the future. That may also include making a decision to shut up shop for the sake of damage limitation and to give you a better fighting chance in the future. Indeed, lenders will look more favourably on someone who accepted a business was no longer viable and acted quickly on that before it got too far out of hand, than someone who ploughed on in denial, racking up more and more debt and burdening more and more creditors.

Business isn't easy and if there's one guarantee it's that 'shit will happen'. It's simply unavoidable, but it's how you react that matters and what you'll be remembered for. Be pre-emptive, proactive and react with boldness and speed with a solid support network behind you, and the chances are you'll come out the other side of any crisis in better shape than you entered it.

Smarta in Action: The Rainmakers

Founder: Ben Way
Company name: The Rainmakers
Company profile: The Rainmakers – Way's current company – is one of the world's leading innovation and incubation companies. It creates ground-breaking technologies and has worked with the US government, Microsoft, British Telecom and the UK Ministry of Defence.
Founded: 2002

Overview
Way lost £25 million on his second company at the tender age of 19. He was an internet and technology wunderkind, but that in no way prepared him for such a huge loss. He had to figure out how to bounce back from the dark times.

How he did it
Losing a tenner can be a hard blow when you're a teenager. Losing £25 million is, for most people, unimaginable. How did he find the inner strength after such a tough ride?

'Naturally, you kind of ask yourself some seriously harsh questions,' he says. 'You wonder whether it was a fluke or whether it was your fault.' Way found solace by approaching his experience from a business mindset and seeing it as a lesson. 'It was a hard, hard time, but I actually learned more from that time than any other.'

It took him about six months to pick himself up and dust himself off. 'When you go through something like that, some very hard event, time is a great healer.'

He says he has learnt to be more philosophical about things going wrong in business. 'You just need to collect your thoughts and evaluate what went wrong. It's hardly a failure, it's an experience.'

Tips
Understand that the fate of your business is often out of your hands, and it's natural for things to go wrong. 'There's only so much control you can have for that,' Way says. See mistakes for the vital learning process they are; don't judge yourself for them. One failed business is not the end of your entrepreneurial career. You could, like Way, go on to do bigger and better things now you've learnt not to take failure personally.

Smarta in five

1 React – never bury your head in the sand

2 Speak to people: don't bottle it in

3 Put emotion on hold and do what's best for the business

4 If your business can't be saved, cut your losses

5 Always be hustling and never rest on your laurels

6.3
Build an A-team

"In 1986 I went to the company accountant and said that I wanted the entire company to have the full profit and loss sheet of the company every month. He said that we will get an immediate turnover increase of some 30%. Because once people can see where the mutual interest actually lies, they will in very, very minute ways use their time better and focus better and direct themselves better."

—John Mortimer, Angela Mortimer

"James Dyson doesn't just go to a head hunter and find an obvious candidate. For example, the man he got to run his Japanese business was a former diplomat. So he thinks outside the box and he gets people into the business who have different skills."

—Richard Needham, Dyson and chairman of Smarta

"I've had people who have really got behind what I'm doing and who have gone so far out of the way to help me. I really think if someone has been successful in what they do and they can help someone else do the same, they really do. I've been so amazed by the lengths people go to – it's been absolutely phenomenal. So the advice I would give is please don't be afraid to give the scariest person in the world a call! They've been there once, and if they can do anything to help and they have the time to, I'm sure they'd be inclined to."

—Alexandra Finlay, Fin's

"I think when you're working in a business you sometimes want to be able to talk to like-minded people and share experiences. Sometimes it's just great to share it with a group and if you have specific problems, they will always be problems that somebody else encountered – and it's great for them to give you their point of view as opposed to always someone within your organization."

—Kanya King, MOBO

There are some amazing individuals featured in this book, but all of them will admit they wouldn't be where they are without their A-team: the supersmart bunch of people they've got to call on. The rocks that are there when times are tough; the confidants they can turn to for the brutal truth; the invaluable contacts and introducers; the superfans and, of course, the über smart team working away in the background.

As we've already said, you can't and shouldn't want to do everything on your own. You need to give yourself the space to do what you do best and you need to ensure you've got a solid support network to turn to outside the business. The final piece of the jigsaw is assembling your A-team, the handful of talented individuals who are going to help you drive your business forward and take it from being just another business to being an exceptional business. These people will form the pillars of the business, become brand evangelists and commit to doing whatever it takes to make your succeed.

Let's make an important distinction: when we say A-team we're not just talking about employees; indeed, to start with they almost certainly won't be. More likely they'll be someone outside of the company who, because they have something vital to contribute, you nonetheless make sure is in your band of committed supporters.

These are the people you can call on when you've had a bad day or hit a brick wall. They can provide a sounding board to bounce around an idea or help you work through a solution to a problem. Smart businesses tend to

"The A-team are the people you can call on when you've had a bad day or hit a brick wall"

surround themselves with smart people: positive, action-oriented types who will act as mentors, advisers and guides along the way.

You may not need to have to look very far to find your A-team. It's likely you'll already have spoken to people about the business who you respect and would like to be involved. During your research process you'll no doubt also have identified people with real knowledge in the space who could be valuable assets. Seek out people who are enthusiastic about what you are doing and have a perspective that could be useful, whether that's because of their personal or professional experience.

Take them for a coffee or a beer, talk to them about what you're doing, listen to their advice. You're basically trying to get them to become a friend to your business.

> **" This isn't about asking for anything, it's about building up your base of knowledge and support "**

Ask them if they know anyone else who may be valuable and interesting for you to meet. Remember, this isn't about asking for money, services or anything else – it's just about building up your base of knowledge and support.

Of course, as your business grows you'll need to find help beyond your A-team of supporters and actually have an extra pair of hands on deck. Don't view this as simply recruiting an employee and filling a resource gap. Whatever the position, go and find the first fully fledged, full-time member of your A-team.

Taking on your first member of staff is a huge landmark – and one of the most difficult and important things you can do as a small business. The first hire is also absolutely crucial to get right and is never something you should rush. It's also something that needs deep personal consideration, which is why we've included it this section of the book and not Part 5. The first people you bring into the business don't just need to fulfil a job spec, they need to be the perfect fit for you. They need to understand what you're trying to achieve, what your vision is, and they need to become engrained in the start-up process so deeply that they become an integral part of the story.

The oldest recruitment rule in the book is especially relevant: hire real slow, fire fast.

It is totally counter-productive to hire people too quickly and yet it is one of the most common mistakes that small businesses make. A typical scenario that crops up time and time again is that of the persistent one-man band, plugging away trying to win new business, when all of a sudden six jobs come along at once. The one-man band rushes to find someone to cope with the new increased demand and hires the first person they can find. This all too often leads to disaster.

> **" Whatever the position, go and find the first fully fledged, full-time member of you're a-team "**

First, you need to establish a consistent requirement for an extra hire, otherwise you could recruit someone to find that three months down the line the work has dried up while you are stuck with the fixed cost. Secondly – and this is actually far more damaging in the long term; like marriage, if you hire in haste you will nine times out of ten repent at leisure – the less time you spend finding the right person, the less likely they are to be right for you.

Your first employee sets the tone for your future hires. Take the time to find someone who is as enthusiastic about growing your business as you are. They too will become an ambassador for your business, so hiring someone who is just looking for a 'job' is not the smartest move. In a small business each person covers a range of roles, so flexibility and a genuine desire to make it work are as important as skills and experience (perhaps even more so).

Bear in mind that if there are just two of you, you are likely to be spending an inordinate amount of time together, so make sure that you have a good personality fit. You need to like them and get on with them. It's also a good idea to revisit the list of your own weaknesses you compiled earlier. Ideally your first employee will be able to fill some of the gaps for you. If you have no grasp of detail look for someone who is very thorough, or if you find networking a chore look for someone more gregarious. Above all, take your time.

If you suddenly find yourself with more work than you can manage and need to fill the gap quickly, the best solution is to use freelancers or contractors. The flexibility this gives you to shop around while still getting the job done is worth every penny while you are establishing your business. Do not make the same mistake as those who have gone before you. No matter how urgently you need the skills, do not hire in haste and always take practical steps to avoid the wrong person. Always take verbal references rather than relying on a letter of recommendation, however glowing it is. Far better to make a couple of calls: five minutes on the phone with a previous employer or colleague will give you a more realistic picture of what the person is really like to work with.

Wherever possible, try to get potential employees to come and spend two days working with you. Pay them for their time and try to give them as many actual on-the-job tasks as you can. Not only will you then be far more confident about their competencies and personality fit, but they can also be sure that the role is right for them.

If you do find after taking someone on that you have made a mistake, act quickly to redress it. It's your business and if you are carrying an employee who isn't working out it will cost you – not just financially but also in terms of wasted time and energy. It's useful to have a probationary period (three months is good) stipulated in the employment contract, during which time you can release the employee at a week's notice. This gives you a good safety net to try someone out. Small businesses need to have all of their resources (human and otherwise) working at full capacity in the right direction. As hard as it sounds, if you've made a mistake in recruiting then acknowledge that sooner rather than later and let the person go.

WWW

Access hundreds of free guides and video on finding your A-Team: www.smarta.com/recruitment

As time passes and the company expands, you'll find that while you keep your outside group of supporters, natural leaders and pillars of the business will evolve and your true A-team will be formed. Look after them and treat them as assets you can't afford to lose. Remember that the only way to replace a member of your A-team quickly, efficiently and reliably and with the minimum of disruption to the business is not to lose them in the first place.

Smarta in Action: The Extreme Sports Company

Founder: Al Gosling
Company: The Extreme Sports Company
Company profile: An innovative youth extreme sports brand that spans TV channels, drinks, shops, mobile phones, theme parks and clothing, and is turning over upwards of £25 million.
Founded: 1995

Overview

Having built nothing short of an empire from the basis of his original start-up, Gosling has had his fair share of bad hires. The lessons he's learnt along the way have been invaluable – but that's not to say he always gets it right.

How he did it

Gosling swears by 'hard interviewing, hard referencing, then more interviewing, then more interviewing' when recruiting new members to the team. His business may be big, but he still needs staff to share the same passion they would have needed to show when he was recruiting in his early days. It's one of the ways he keeps the brand consistent and strong.

'But I still get it wrong,' he admits. 'We just brought a key member into one of our retail teams – not a managing director, but a key member – and we got it wrong.' Having had years of experience of managing teams, Gosling knew what he had to do. 'You've got to make that hard decision and not mess around in any way, shape or form.'

He's been careful to make sure his legal team know that he needs to act quickly when it comes to redundancy, to preserve the health of his business. And he makes sure his team understand that too. 'You need to have the right people around you so that if you get it wrong, you can move very quickly, rather than letting it sit.'

He's also got into the habit of identifying very quickly whether someone is a right fit once they've joined. And if they're not, he doesn't mess about.

Tips

Learn to spot early on when someone's not right. Watch new team members carefully and get regular feedback on their progress, from them and from other staff. Act quickly if you realize they're wrong. Make sure your team understands this mentality.

Smarta in five

1 Behind every great entrepreneur is an even better team

2 Start building your A-team before you've got employees

3 Surround yourself with passion and knowledge

4 Hire really slow, fire really quick

5 Make verbal reference checks in person

6.4
Share the vision, share the wealth

"I picked eight of the key people, my DJs, and I got them to give me £200 for 5% of the company. Then, boy, did they work hard for the station from then on. And that was the key to Kiss's success. All of a sudden it wasn't just a junta with one person running it. I owned 60% and they owned 40%."

—Gordon Mac, Kiss FM

"It's all about a profit share in the business. People need incentives in today's day and age."

—Darryn Lyons, Big Pictures

All successful leaders, whether they're entrepreneurs, politicians or sports coaches, achieve their objectives by convincing other people to buy into their vision. They create a bond built on trust and that shared vision.

If you've ever felt part of creating something really special, be it a single project, a sports team fighting for a trophy or a start-up company battling to establish itself, you'll know just how powerful the spirit of a tight-knit team can be. If you truly believe in the people standing by your side, you believe you can take on the world.

You can't buy team spirit and you can't pay someone to buy into your vision. Sure, you can give someone shares (and we'll come to that), but a financial incentive alone won't be enough to ensure your team is truly onside. You also can't assume that anyone you recruit and guarantee a salary to – no matter how big a commitment that is to you – will automatically share your vision. After all, it's your baby, not theirs.

If you want buy-in to your vision, you have to share it. You have to give before you receive. But it's worth it. Having a crystallized vision everyone understands, believes in and works towards can transform an average business into a terrific one.

Too often a business's vision is a one line platitude inserted into the executive summary of a business plan and then filed away and forgotten about. The true vision for your business should be a living, breathing mantra that everyone in the business tries to embody on a daily basis – and first and foremost it needs to come from *you*. It's *your* vision before it's your company's and so you need to take responsibility for communicating it.

Your vision should be the sum of what you do, why you do it and where you're going with it. It doesn't need to be complicated, in fact the simpler the better. The crucial thing is that everyone buys into it.

To get people to buy in you can't be too dictatorial, however. It might be your vision, but for people to feel like it's theirs as well you need to let them contribute.

Perhaps the greatest ethos that you can cultivate within your team is that everyone's opinion is important. You can do this is by listening and taking everyone's views into consideration – and that means *everyone*, whatever their position. Create a culture where no idea is too stupid and apply this across all business areas and decisions. You never know, sometimes the best ideas come from the most unexpected places. Even if you ultimately disagree and choose a different direction, the fact that their opinion was heard and valued will empower and encourage your staff.

> **Create a culture where no idea is too stupid – the best ideas can come from the most unexpected places**

People are far more likely to be enthused about and committed to a vision they have had a hand in creating. When people truly buy in to the vision for a business their intrinsic satisfaction is exponentially greater, fostering a harder-working, more passionate team. This can only be good news.

Having created a shared vision for your business, you should also look to share the wealth. Incentivizing your employees is an essential part of making them feel valued and, as a result, getting the best out of them.

This can be as simple as creating a bonus scheme. Set a mixture of targets related to the individual role and the performance of the business to encourage people not just to focus on their own area but to support the business as a whole.

A profit share scheme may also work well, as it incentivizes everyone to keep an eye on costs and maximize revenue, whatever their role. You should also consider a shared equity scheme, giving all of your staff a small share of the business in the form of shares or share options.

The John Lewis Partnership does this incredibly well. All of its employees (around 70,000 at last count) are partners, meaning that they all own a stake of the business and share in its success. With a share of the profits all employees have a greater incentive to make the business work, as well as a voice in how things are run.

Employee-owned businesses take a variety of forms and operate in almost every sector of the economy. Some research states that companies owned by their employees are more resilient than conventionally structured companies, outperforming the market during the downturn and demonstrating a lower risk of business failure. The smartest business people make their employees feel that they are truly part of the business, rewarding them financially and giving them a voice in shaping and achieving the vision.

Smarta in Action: Mind Candy

Founder: Michael Smith
Company: Mind Candy
Company profile: One of the world's leading developers of social multiplayer games, helping kids (and big kids!) around the world play and connect.
Founded: 2004

Overview
Mind Candy uses shares to incentivize employees, but has had to readjust its system due to big growth since launch.

How he did it
Mind Candy has offered share options to employees since its very earliest days. 'It helps offset lower salaries at the beginning, when everything's a bit risky,' Smith says. 'It also creates a sense of ownership – it makes the team really want the business to do well.'

Employees got more share options in the early days, because more was at stake for them. Now the business has 'kind of gone over a crest' from start-up to very successful company, risk is much lower, so new recruits get fewer share options.

Smith now uses a three-tiered system for shares: a lower level for junior positions, a middle level, and a senior level for those at the top. 'But people can move between the bands, and we encourage them to. People here are quite young, and we want them to feel their career will be fostered here, so there's always a chance of promotion. And you earn more options by being promoted. It's quite a nice incentive.'

When Smith was first allocating shares he used a percentage-based system. But as the company's grown, he's switched to a share split system. He recognizes the importance of using a system that can adapt according to growth, and has thought out the options already. 'If we're a big multinational in the future we could do a share split, or create an option pool, which would dilute the board's holding but work to attract great new talent.'

It's key to Mind Candy to keep that start-up feel regardless of how big the company gets, and Smith says shares are 'an inherent part of that'.

Tips
Smith says, 'Be quite careful at the beginning how you work out your share system, as you can never tell how big the business is going to get.'

Smarta in five

1 Give people a reason to care about the company and they will

2 Have a clear vision of where the company is going and how it will get there. Communicate it

3 Get people's buy-in by asking them to help sculpt the vision and plan

4 Create an environment where anyone can contribute ideas and be listened to

5 Incentivize people with shares, profit share schemes or bonuses

6.5
Lead from the front

> "I'm very, very focused on giving people opportunity to be good at the job. I tell them that if they don't make any mistakes, then they're covering something up. When you make a mistake, you come and tell me your mistake and then we'll forget it and we'll move on."
>
> **—Duncan Bannatyne, *Dragons' Den* and Bannatyne Group**

> "Offering development and training and growing your people feeds your success."
>
> **—Salma Shah, Beyond**

> "As you get bigger, you don't necessarily know what's going on at the other end of the office. So we tried to keep everything very open. We'd have our weekly lunch meeting where I would stand up and talk about everything that was going on and anyone could ask any question to find out what's going on."
> **—Michael Birch, Bebo**

> "Leaders need to give a vision as a sort of mandate for innovation, so that employees at least know what they can do when they're innovating. Be willing to listen – there's a degree of openness that needs to exist to have ideas come through."
> **—Mark Turrell, Imaginatik**

In every smart business there is (at least) one smart leader. Often this is the founder, but there is no set rule save that somebody has to continually be driving the business forward. Many business owners get caught up with the daily grind of getting everything done and take their eye off the longer-term direction.

Without a clear lead, even businesses with great products or unique services can get lost, or side-tracked along the way. Like the horses in the Grand National that dismount their jockeys, businesses without clear leadership may be able to keep running but they won't win any prizes and may not finish at all.

Leadership means knowing where the business needs to go and how to keep it on course to get there. Even a business with no employees needs leadership. A good leader walks their talk and carries people with them, whether that is employees, clients or suppliers. Leadership is about inspiring others with your vision – if you don't believe in your business and where it is going, then you can guarantee that nobody else will.

If you don't believe in your business, nobody else will

If you do have employees, leadership becomes even more critical. A good leader leads by example. The army officers' rule of never giving an order you aren't prepared to carry out yourself is a good one to remember. Practice what you preach: if you want your team to put in extra hours, make sure you are doing it too. If an authority figure has one set of rules for themselves and another for subordinates, it's not only hypocritical, it's unfair. Leaders with double standards are bound to foster resentment. And if employees are bitter, productivity suffers.

This extends to what's expected of different people within the business. A less-than-average manager will tend to delegate the least appetizing jobs, whether that's writing a particularly sticky pitch or emptying the bins. Showing workers that you're prepared to muck in and do exactly what you occasionally ask others to means that everyone feels more comfortable and less wary of hierarchy.

Not leading by example also runs the risk of personal sloppiness when it comes to presentation, politeness and punctuality, which will seep into employees' attitudes. As a leader, you need to set the standard, so if you want your team to be up to scratch, you need to be too. Same goes for work ethic: an unmotivated leader is hardly an inspiration, so put in the hours and keep up the good mood while you're at it. Employees learn a lot implicitly by observation, and acting as you want them to act teaches them how to improve.

One common mistake made by rookie leaders is telling people what to do without explaining why. It's much easier and more satisfying to complete a task when you understand the rationale behind it. Don't expect people to be mind readers: be clear about your logic and you'll find people much more willing to go the extra mile. Avoid the 'my way or the high way' approach, it doesn't win people over and can be very alienating. It's fine to stick to your guns, but make sure you give alternative approaches a fair hearing.

The best leaders are also prepared to be proved wrong and admit it when they have made a mistake. While a good leader should follow their instinct (see Chapter 6.9) and not give in when they know that what they are doing is right, they equally need to acknowledge when they have made a mistake or when someone else has a better idea. They also give full credit when it's due and never take all the glory for themselves.

> **"Smart leaders are consistent and fair"**

Smart leaders are consistent and fair. Staff will make mistakes, you'll have bad days. Make sure you're consistent in the way you handle situations even when you're not at your best or a silly mistake has wider repercussions. If you take out an argument you had with your partner the night before or the pressure of not knowing how you'll meet the next payroll by unfairly criticizing an innocent employee, you'll instantly undermine any respect they had for you.

Once you've cultivated leadership skills yourself, try to instil them in your team. Leadership is demonstrated every time someone puts in the extra effort to do a superb, as opposed to an adequate, job. Robin Scharma says that 'Leadership – and success – begins on the extra mile'.

WWW
Learn from some of the most esteemed leaders in business: www.smarta.com/videos

Leadership is shown when you stay late rehearsing a pitch for the following day, or when a member of staff calls round every possible supplier to track down a special stock request for a customer. As Scharma puts it, 'Real leadership is not about prestige, power or status. It is about responsibility.' Smart leaders foster and promote this attitude among all their staff – starting with themselves.

Smarta in Action: Ariadne Capital

Founder: Julie Meyer
Company: Ariadne Capital
Company profile: A venture capital firm that pioneered the entrepreneurs-backing-entrepreneurs model. It has created a reputation for working with game-changers in the technology and media start-up world.
Founded: 2000

Overview
Meyer's business may handle big sums of money, but it's made up of a small team of 12. That means she needs to make sure they are self-motivating at the same time as leading her pioneering business in new directions.

How she does it
Meyer thinks the key to leadership is ensuring that your employees trust you, and trust that you're taking the company in the right direction. She says it's important to 'kind of inspire them to work abnormal lives' through that trust. They're going to be working long hard hours and putting a lot more into your start-up than they probably would working for a big company. You have to show them you know what you're doing, set a clear direction and then make sure they're on board – and that they have faith in you.

You also have to trust them. 'The best definition of leadership I ever heard was by Colin Powell who said, "Leaders are those people who create the conditions of trust so that great things can happen",' she adds. 'I just believe you've got to find the self-motivated people. I don't really want to manage anyone.' She says finding self-motivated people is more important than bringing on people with MBAs or similar qualifications.

Tips
Create trust. Have regular one-to-ones with employees so you know you're on the same page. Keep them updated with what's going on in the company, and check they agree with it. Ask them what their fears and doubts are, then explain your rationale and get them on board.

Meyer summarizes it thus: 'We set where we're going, create the conditions of trust, and self-motivated people will follow.'

Smarta in five

1 Even a business without employees needs clear leadership

2 Lead by example – never delegate anything you wouldn't do yourself

3 Explain your decisions

4 Be firm but fair – acknowledge when you're wrong

5 Give credit where it's due

6.6
DO sweat the small stuff

"It's about delivering value and delivering value as effectively and as efficiently as you can."

—John Paleomylites, BeatThatQuote.com

"Brand values don't just happen, you have to think about what sort of company you want to be. Customer service is key. Make sure you really welcome people when they turn up and then when they leave you, you thank them."

—Tristram Mayhew, Go Ape

For most business owners, it's the big things that occupy their thoughts. Winning a new client, negotiating a contract, managing the cashflow – these are crucial to any business and it's completely natural and right that they will take a significant proportion of your time and energy. As critical as these things are, however, very often it's paying attention to the little things that will set you apart from the rest. If you want your business to step up a gear, it's worth becoming a little obsessive over the details and doing the things that everyone else is too busy to think about – particularly when it comes to looking after customers and clients.

This is something you need to work hard to instil in the ethos of your company, and work even harder to maintain. You need to lead from the front in making sure that staff are customer focused at all times. There's no better brand evangelist than you and your staff will follow your example. If you sweat the small stuff, they will too. Most employees don't remember, so the incentive is on you to make sure your company is different and has superior standards.

> **Be an evangelist in making sure everyone is customer focused**

Most businesses push the boat out when it comes to new business. It's a little like the beginning of a new relationship. At first we make more effort to dress up and be on sparkling form for dates, cooking four-course meals in order to impress. As time goes by and we grow more relaxed, generally we let standards slip and start treating our (not so new) partner like part of the furniture.

The same goes for clients. Most people pull out all the stops when they are focused on wooing the client initially, but then go off the boil. To differentiate yourself you need to master the personal touches, and this is where remembering the detail becomes really important.

To keep up the momentum with existing clients, you need to start doing the extra things that other people forget. Most people manage to send a few Christmas cards, but you shouldn't restrict being nice to your clients to once a year when everybody else is making an effort too. Remembering birthdays is an easy one, but it's not the obvious stuff that makes the biggest difference, it's the small but personal stuff that really matters: remembering that your client's child is going to have their first day at school, or that they are moving home. Anything that is meaningful to them.

If you see articles on anything you think may be interesting to a client, cut them out and put them in the post, or email them across with a note. This absolutely does not have to be business related: it could be a restaurant recommendation or something about their next holiday destination. It's the personal stuff that people remember most.

If you have a great meeting with an existing client, remember to thank them as much as you would a potential one. Don't just thank the manager or CEO, you need to show that you value the whole team. Cupcakes are a great idea as they can be shared among everyone rather than just being for the boss.

Paying attention to detail also means understanding differences in people's personalities. For example, some clients may have short attention spans and get bored by presentations. For them focus on the visual and use screenshots, product samples and photographs in meetings to keep them engaged.

Some may be far more detail oriented, preferring reports and statistics. Don't use a one-size-fits-all approach, notice people's idiosyncrasies and learn to talk in their language – with them, rather than at them. Are they the type of people who prefer formal meetings or informal chats over coffee? Once you know the answer, tailor your meetings accordingly.

Sweating the small stuff also applies to keeping on track of your own performance. Be proactive. If you think you have done a not so great job on something, don't let your client be the one to pull you up on it. Call them and accept that this wasn't your finest effort and redo the work. Keeping a client is always easier than getting a new one.

This approach shouldn't just apply to clients, of course, it should be a holistic attitude you take to how you deal with everyone you work with, be it clients or suppliers, employees, partners, investors or connections. To get the most from all of these relationships you've got to give the very most you can as well, and going that extra step to remember the small things others don't makes a huge difference.

Smarta in Action: Ambition Communications

Founder: Rebecca McKinlay
Company: Ambition Communications
Company profile: A marketing communications agency, staffed and run by experienced marketers, the majority of whom have worked in both client-side and agency environments.
Founded: 2006

Overview
Despite having only 10 employees, Ambition Communications counts BlackBerry, O2, The FeelGood Drinks Company, Beating Bowel Cancer, Diageo, The Isle of Wight Festival and Vonage UK as clients. And the attention and care it gives to clients plays a big role in why it can beat much bigger competitors to contracts like those.

How she does it
Almost all Ambition's business comes through the two directors' personal networks, so they make sure to treat clients with the care and attention you would a friend. Ambition Communications always sends flowers to clients on their anniversaries and birthdays, but McKinlay says this is a pleasure, not a chore.

As an example of how far their 'friendship as well as trust' mentality stretches, they're being invited to a client's wedding. Not only that, one of the co-directors is doing the flowers! 'It's thinking: "If I can do something that makes your life easier, I'll do it."' The company also designed and printed the wedding invites.

Paying attention to the little stuff applies internally as much as externally. When a graduate joined for a week's work experience recently, they made sure to pay him – unlike the big-name agency who had used him for free for five months. After McKinlay had offered him a job, she gave him his birthday off – 'without the need for a holiday form'.

It's also making sure they pay attention to what's happening in other companies, the small shifts that can have a big impact on them. When the lead of a client company left recently, for example, they made sure to keep in close touch with other members of the team so they wouldn't get forgotten next time a contract was up for grabs, and introduced themselves to the new person in that role early on.

Tips
Go out of your way to make clients and staff feel valued.

Smarta in five

1 Get obsessive about the small details nobody else bothers with

2 Make the effort to know clients better than your competitors do

3 Give existing clients the new client treatment

4 Say thank-you more often and when people aren't expecting it

5 Build lasting relationships

6.7
Network your ass off

"When you're a start-up you have to spend a lot of time networking, meeting potential partners, getting market information and also meeting potential investors."

—Walid Al-Saqqaf, TrustedPlaces

"Reputation is extremely important, so if you have connections with investors that trust you, that goes a long way."

—Michael Smith, Firebox and Mind Candy

> "People get themselves into a bullshit arms race where they're just continually talking about how important they are and how successful they are and so forth. It's everything that's wrong in networking. We've a mantra at 4Networking: Meet, Like, Know, Trust. Meet people. Get to know them. When people trust you, that's when people buy."
> **—Brad Burton, 4Networking**

> "We're interested in the people behind things. I don't really want to see the business plan, I want to see the individual coming through a room and sit down and talk to me."
> **—Simon Woodroffe, YO! Sushi and YO! Group**

Networking is like Marmite: you either love it or hate it. Fortunately, Marmite, as far as we know, isn't a compulsory requirement for running a supersmart, successful business. Like it or not, networking is. Moreover, it's becoming more and more an integral part of how we do all aspects of business. Traditionally a way of connecting with other entrepreneurs, potential partners, suppliers, clients and investors, the emergence of social networking means that networking has now become the window through which many people first see and form their opinions of you and your business.

In the past, if you didn't network you simply deprived yourself of valuable contacts. Now it's hard to imagine you can even be in business without networking in some form or another. As we've mentioned so much in this book, social media has amplified everything you do – good and bad. So it's more important than ever that you ensure not only that you're embracing networking to tell the world about all the good things you're up to, but also actively managing any negative feedback as well. Quite simply, you can no longer avoid networking, so the challenge is to make it a positive part of your business day.

Google might have tricked us into forgetting this for a decade or so, but networking has been and still is the best way to find the right services, investors, suppliers, partners, PR advisers, and everyone and everything else you need for your business. When you know the people you're dealing with or they've come personally recommended, it makes an enormous difference. For a start, it saves you days of searching through *Yellow Pages* and Google for what you need and it is a much better guarantee of quality than the ability to work your way up the search engines. And, of course, the more people you know, the more business opportunities you'll discover – people do business with people they like. If you're looking for investors or partners, there's absolutely no substitute for personal contact or recommendation.

If meeting new people is something you enjoy and find easy, then you've got a head start. If the thought of it fills you with dread, fear not, you're not alone, but it is something you're going to have to work at conquering. If you want your business to fly, building a wide-reaching, strong network is essential, so the sooner you get the hang of it the better.

The cardinal sin of networking is going into it focusing only on what you can get out of it. Networking is about building relationships, so if you set out with an attitude of taking you'll won't get very far. Concentrate instead on what you can offer and the whole thing becomes a lot more comfortable – and you'll reap far greater benefits down the road.

Everywhere you go there is an opportunity to network. Of course, you can build relationships at events specifically designed for this purpose, from local coffee mornings to large-scale business networking gatherings. However, the best opportunities often come from unexpected places: at the school gates, a friend's dinner party. Networking opportunities present themselves at every turn if you are open to receiving them. For the uninitiated, online forums and networking sites can be a valuable resource, but remember that the best relationships exist both on- and offline. So if you make an acquaintance virtually, cement the relationship with a call or a coffee as soon as it is reasonably practical to do so. Similarly, if you meet someone at an event, keep the momentum going by connecting with them online afterwards – it's a great way to build rapport.

It might seem daunting to approach someone you don't know at first, so if the thought of a networking event fills you with dread, dip your toe in the water online to start with. Online networking is huge and the perfect place for the uninitiated to start. Use LinkedIn to reconnect with former colleagues and classmates – you never know where these people are or what they are doing now. People will always prefer to refer a personal contact than someone they don't know. Register a profile on Smarta and get to know people through the Q&A and the forum – you can easily find someone local who could come along to an event with you.

Twitter is a great way to reach people you can't access through your immediate circle. Follow people in your sector and related industries. Create Twitter lists of people you respect and admire and would potentially like to do business with in the future; it's more likely they will follow you in return. Remember that the only objective is to build rapport: if you approach networking with a view to getting a sale or a contract, you're setting yourself up for a fall. Focus on what you can learn and what you have to offer and the rest will take care of itself.

If you're already in business, the reality is that you probably have a network even if you don't think of it in those terms. If you're just starting out and building from scratch, talk to all the people you know. Ask for their ideas

> **"Networking opportunities present themselves as every turn if you are open to receiving them"**

and input and crucially their suggestions for anyone they think it would be worthwhile for you to meet – a personal introduction is always far more valuable than a call out of the blue. Place absolutely no expectations in the early stages of getting anything from anyone – a successful network is made of a long-term, mutual, sustainable relationships. If you're asking for something right off the bat these are far less likely to develop.

At events, resist the temptation to see a networking event as a business card-collecting competition. It's far better to have one meaningful conversation than 20 that are so superficial it's impossible to have any significant follow-up. Listen to what other people have to say and offer help at every given opportunity. Recommend people you have found useful, introduce them and follow up to see if the conversation was fruitful. Networking is a two-way street: you start by helping other people and sooner rather than later they will be in a position to help you. This is the point at which a network becomes a self-fulfilling prophecy and the opportunities grow exponentially.

Smarta in Action: Broad Grin

Founder: Seán Brickell
Company names: Broad Grin Communications and the Sean Brickell consultancy
Company profile: Broad Grin is a specialist business video communications agency, while Sean also works around the world coaching CEOs, managers and staff on professional confidence and communications skills.
Founded: 2009; 2007

Overview
Brickell says that 98% of his business comes from networking and word of mouth. He once won £50,000 worth of business just from attending one event. In short, he is a supernetworker.

How he does it
Brickell says networking opportunities come all the time. He doesn't segregate his work and social life when it comes to meeting new contacts: 'It can be at the bus stop, a party, just meeting somebody on the train.' He advises anyone new to networking to know what's going on in the world, so you have something to talk about. 'And be able to sum up your business in a colourful way.' That means peppering what you say with interesting anecdotes and talking with passion. You also need to be yourself: 'Being natural is one of the most attractive traits about people – and one of the most underused.'

But what's really key is taking the time to get to know someone, finding out what makes them tick. 'The more you get on to the personal stuff, away from business, the more they will enjoy it and the more you'll get out of it.' It's about discovering the other person's best bits, rather than just banging on about your own. 'Every single person has something about them that is interesting – and they have a skill.' And that's the bit that comes in handy.

Brickell only tends to keep in touch with people he likes. He says it's more valuable to leave a networking event with one or two cards from people you really hit it off with, than 20 who will forget you. He helps out the people in his network where he can, referring them to each other. But he says not to expect anything in return. 'It puts pressure on people. If they like you, they'll help you back.'

Tips
'The secret of communication is in bringing the best out of the other person.'

Smarta in five

1 Networking isn't like Marmite, you *do* have to like it

2 People increasingly form their first impressions on the way you network

3 Personal recommendation trumps search

4 Always think how you can help someone, not how they can help you

5 The more you put in, the more you get back

6.8
Brand yourself

"People always remember personalities. People find it more difficult to remember company names, so once they remember the personality, then they associate it with the brand and the brand takes off by itself."

—Sahar Hashemi, Coffee Republic

"The world is such a busy place that if you're not memorable then people won't remember you or listen to you. I try to be outspoken and use these visual cues – I wear a hat. Things like that help people to remember you."

—Ryan Carson, Carsonified

As a small business owner you *are* your business. More often than not, you are also what differentiates your business from others doing more or less the same. As consumers we tend to go to (and buy from) those we know and can identify with, or feel we know through their brand. In small businesses the founder and the brand go hand in hand, so creating an identity and personality for yourself – your 'personal brand' – is something that all smart business owners do. Consequently, it's also something you can look to leverage maximum value from.

Personal branding starts with who you are – it can't be anything else. You have to be true to yourself and authentic in everything you portray, as otherwise it simply won't wash. That said, you need to be clear what the real you is, what you and subsequently your personal brand stand for. Define your brand.

> " **You have to be true to yourself and authentic in everything** "

What do you do and what do you want people to think first and foremost when they see or hear you? Look at what you're passionate and knowledgeable about – for almost everyone that's closely aligned to their business – and pick no more than three words that describe it.

Think about Starbucks. Famously, it purports not to sell coffee, but to sell the experience. Ask yourself what you sell. David Beckham is a footballer, of course, but he's developed an iconic personal brand with great success by personifying style, leadership and the perfect role model. When the now celebrated and highly successful celebrity chef Jamie Oliver first broke onto our television screens he was strongly differentiated from the conservatism of Delia Smith and precision of Gary Rhodes. Young, raw, vibrant and colloquial, the working-class Jamie who grew up in a pub stood for unpretentious, natural, great tasting food; recipes anyone could cook; youthfulness and fun. He instantly carved out his niche and appealed to a whole demographic of consumers (and corporates).

Once you've established what you stand for, the job in hand is then to start communicating 'you' to the rest of the world. That means living your personal brand publically every day. Again, the more authentic you are, the easier this will be. Create a simple marketing plan about how you intend to do this. No business would just launch into a marketing campaign without planning it first. Do some market research: What are your competitors like? What could your market reach be like? How do you plan to get your word out there? Set yourself goals: x number of new Twitter followers each month, for example.

The obvious place to start is a personal blog which you can set up in minutes. View it as the original source of content that you will use to feed all the other various outlets open to your personal brand. Offer to write columns or guest blogs for any relevant publication: your local paper, a trade magazine in your sector, a business website. Find every platform available to you to get your name out there, but resist the temptation to use this as a sales pitch. This isn't about selling your products or services, but rather about establishing you as an expert in your field. Emphasize sharing your knowledge and your business will expand. Doug Richard calls this becoming a 'super-editor', becoming known for being knowledgeable and engaging on a particular subject.

> **Establish yourself as an expert in your field**

View social media as a permanent marketing campaign. What attracts consumers to marketing campaigns? Value – so start delivering. Stop using Twitter to tell people what colour socks you are wearing, and instead use it to tweet links to blogs, news stories and websites you know your followers will find interesting. That said, don't be dull – keep things personal. The odd sock comment or amusing Twitpic will make your followers feel closer to you. Remember, it's easier to trust individuals than faceless companies. And make sure you really are living your brand. Most of it is obvious: if you're selling organic baby food, it's probably best not to swear profusely on Twitter, and tell about your love of McDonalds.

Don't just rely on a blog and social media, take your personal brand to the masses. Public speaking can be nerve-wracking, but cracking it is all about confidence and practice. Speaking is a terrific way to get your name out there and there are always events crying out for guest speakers. Take every opportunity you can to speak at events big or small. Offer your services for free to start with. Why do this when others are getting paid? Because if people hear you speak and like what you've got to say, they'll want to book you to speak at their event as well. Most event organizers send cards of thanks to speakers after the event. Be the only one who sends them a thank-you card and you can guarantee you'll be the first person they ask back.

Online podcasts and webchats are also great opportunities to be positioned as an authority and engage with a large number of people at once. You should also always be on the look-out for people to collaborate with: offer them a guest spot on your blog in return for a spot on theirs. Remember, this is not about selling anything, you are trying to help people, to educate and ultimately be recognized as someone to listen to – and to trust.

ROI (Return on investment) The revenues you bring into your business as a result of the resource (time and money) spent on a certain activity.

Don't just think about what you're saying (although content remains king), but also what you look and sound like. Make yourself memorable. We all think popstars give their children silly names, but at least Apple, Peaches and Trixibelle will be memorable to their peers. Lamentably, not everyone is blessed with a jazzy name, so find something else to set yourself apart. Carsonified founder Ryan Carson has made himself instantly recognizable in the tech scene by always wearing a trilby – and where would Barbie be without her pink accessories? Whether it's a pair of glasses or a beard, find some way for people to recognize you.

Start measuring your return on investment (ROI). Your major investment in developing your personal brand will be time and in order for you to know what's working and what's not and which audiences are most receptive, you'll need to come up with some metrics to chart it all by.

Make yourself memorable

Smarta in Action: 4Networking

Founder: Brad Burton
Company: 4Networking
Company profile: The largest joined-up national business breakfast network in the UK.
Founded: 2006

Overview
4Networking boats more than 25,000 members and doubles its revenues year on year, mainly down to the fact Burton has put his face to the brand then put himself out just about everywhere.

How he did it
Burton hasn't contrived a personal brand, he's just his loud, enthusiastic self all the time. He's always been at the front of his brand, driving the business forward. The 4Networking website is plastered with his face and he has a personal blog on it that spans incredibly personal issues as well as business insights. As a result, his community feel close to him, and so want to get more involved with the business. This is helped by more than 3,000 followers on Twitter (he tweets prolifically), who he addresses regularly and helps out all the time. He makes himself very accessible online and elsewhere, unabashedly handing out his contact numbers and priding himself on being contactable by 'anyone, anytime'.

Burton also gives regular motivational talks all across the country for all number of different organizations. He always shares his amazing business story: the fact he started 4Networking when he was £25,000 in debt and working as a pizza delivery boy. In fact, he regularly uses snapshots of himself posing as a pizza boy in promotional material.

Building his reputation yet further, Burton has written a book to market his cause and encourage others to start up, called *Get Off Your Arse*, a title very much in keeping with his cheeky chappy personality. It covers his personal story as well as business advice, again cleverly capitalizing on his personal brand and making sure he's known as much for his personality as his business advice. That in turn leads to more public speaking gigs.

Tips
If you have an interesting personal story, use it. Do something to make yourself stand out from the crowd. It will engage your audience. Don't always adhere to the normal way of doing things.

Smarta in five

1 If people buy people first, then people need to buy *you*

2 Understand and make clear what your personal brand stands for

3 Keep it real: the more authentic you are, the easier and more compelling it is to know you

4 Live your brand and communicate it through traditional and social media

5 Speak: take your networking out of social media and into the real world

6.9
Trust your instinct

"I'm a huge believer in gut instinct, and also a believer that business is not an exact science. You can take advice from other people who've been in business, you can read books, you can go to websites, but you've got to really look at it yourself and think for yourself."

—Duncan Bannatyne, *Dragons' Den* and Bannatyne Group

"You have to have that gut feeling. The difference between making a good living and becoming really successful really comes from inside. It's not about the university degree you've got, or about how many A-levels you got at school."

—Barry Hearn, Matchroom Sport

> "I've got my gut instincts, but I've surrounded myself with a team of other guys who are slightly more processed."
>
> **—Brad Burton, 4Networking**

All the advice and opinions in this book are aimed at allowing you to make better-informed decisions. Instead of rushing into decisions you later regret, we hope the book has widened your perspective so you can step back and consider the right moves for your business.

We've talked about the need to plan, map out your vision and effectively forecast how you'll grow. We hope this clarifies your thinking, highlights potential issues and gives you a roadmap to keep you on track.

Yet it would be remiss of us to pretend that however much planning you do, the unexpected won't occur and unforeseeable events won't threaten to throw you off course. Some of the most critical decisions you take will be as a result of the unplanned and it's in these circumstances that you need to summon all of your personal and business instinct to make a call. In short, you need to listen to your gut.

Put this book down for a minute and just think about all of the times when you've had a tough call to make. How often have you gone with your gut instinct? And how often has that instinct been right? On the other hand, how often have you gone against your instinct and with what result? You'll probably find that whether it was in your personal or professional life, all the times when you've listened to your gut and gone with your instinct you've been right. The truth is that instincts are correct – most of the time.

> **In your personal and professional life, your instincts are usually right**

Of course, when you're faced with the tough decisions, particularly the business-critical ones, self-doubt creeps in and the temptation to go against your instinct increases. Resist it: nine times out of ten your first reaction is the right one. This isn't to say that you should make rash decisions when there is a lot at stake – gather all the information available and get advice from people you trust – but ultimately you need to make the decision. As the business owner the buck stops with you and after all the research and discussion are done you must listen to yourself above all others.

Listening to your instinct also mitigates the risk of falling into the all-too-common trap for small (and indeed larger) business owners of 'analysis paralysis', where fear of making the wrong decision actually prevents you from making any decision at all. In virtually every conceivable situation, it is better to make a decision and move forward on that basis than it is to lose valuable time and momentum stuck in an endless circular discussion. Indecision is the worst decision of all.

It's also worth remembering that even if you make a call which you later regret, very few decisions will ultimately be fatal for your business. The important thing is to recognize a bad call early on and take steps to address it immediately. Never be tempted to stick with a wrong decision – it's like continuing to bet on a bad poker hand. The smartest businesses don't necessarily make better decisions than other people, but they make them more quickly and they act fast to change direction if they turn out to be on the wrong path. This means that a potential disaster never becomes more than a minor detour.

As your business experience grows your instinct will fine-tune itself; the longer you do it the better you'll get. There is no guarantee that every decision you make will be the right one – but making no decision at all will almost certainly be wrong.

Smarta in Action: Cyclescheme

Founder: Richard Grigsby
Company name: Cyclescheme
Company profile: The UK's number one provider of tax-free bikes for the government's Cycle to Work initiative.
Founded: 2005

Overview
When Grigsby and his business partner were just starting up, their accountant drew up a load of numbers and forecasts and told them the business looked like a total no-go. Grigsby's business partner just said, 'It bloody well will work.' So they ditched the accountant and got on with it. Now, in their sixth year, they're set to turn over £8 million.

How he did it
Why did they think they knew better than an accountant? 'We already knew there was a gap in the market, we just couldn't get at it. We knew it was going to be a numbers game, but it was just this gut feeling.' It might sound vague, but Grigsby and his partner had previously been running a bicycle shop. So while it may have felt like 'gut feeling' to them, it was actually an in-depth knowledge of the market they were operating in that at least in part informed their decision.

Grigsby says the whole time he'd been running his bicycle shop he'd been doing it on gut feeling, but working in that environment day in, day out must have given him insights that no outsider (accountants very much included) could have understood. Plus, they really wanted the business to work – and determination can count for a huge amount when it comes to success.

It's a slightly different story now he's taking the business in new directions and structuring it around growth. 'Now we have spreadsheets coming out of our ears – and we do have to listen to them.'

Tips
If you know your market, your gut feeling is probably the kind of instinctive insight that an outsider just wouldn't be able to see. But don't rely entirely on gut feeling. Look at the figures too, so you can make an informed decision from there – particularly if you're wading into new waters.

Smarta in five

1 Planning and process support decision making; it's you who makes decisions

2 Gut feel is quite often right, so don't be scared to follow it

3 Avoid 'analysis paralysis' – indecision is the worst decision of all

4 Remember, companies don't die from one bad decision

5 Never stand by a bad decision, especially if your gut's telling you to change it

About Smarta.com

Smarta.com is the ultimate online destination for anyone starting or running their own business. At Smarta, we know that the best business advice comes from those who have actually been there and done it. We also know that getting your hands on that advice isn't always easy.

That's why we created Smarta.com. It's a place where you can access the advice, knowledge and experience of established entrepreneurs, market-leading experts and small business owners just like you. And we provide practical business tools and other useful resources to make life that little bit easier.

Founded by entrepreneur Sháá Wasmund and backed by *Dragons' Den*'s Theo Paphitis and Deborah Meaden, Smarta provides advice *by* business people *for* business people. We understand exactly what it takes to make a business work and what help you need most along the way.

That's why Smarta is crammed with:

Free advice

- Hundreds of inspirational videos featuring some of the biggest names in business (many of whom are also in this book) as well as some you may not have heard of but will definitely learn something from
- Thousands of bite-size practical guides on all aspects of running a business
- In-depth features, reports and downloadable e-books on the subjects that really matter
- Hundreds of real-life case studies as well as "day in the life" videos

Essential business tools

- Register your company, business names and trademarks all in one simple application
- Apply for a business bank account with our fast online application and get a response in 48 hours from our partner NatWest
- Find over a thousand grants and funds available to new businesses from our data-base – it's updated daily and free to search
- Take care of your finances – built for businesses that need the basics our free QuickBooks software allows you to manage invoices, sales and expenses for up to 20 customers and suppliers

Tools directory

As well as the essential business tools above, Smarta also has a directory of tools and resources for start-ups and small businesses. Whether you need to get a logo designed, find a franchise or expand internationally our directory covers all areas of business and is growing every day.

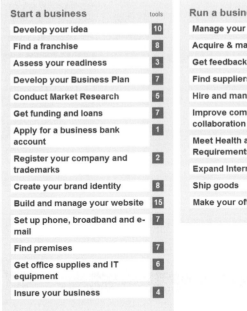

Start a business	tools
Develop your idea	10
Find a franchise	8
Assess your readiness	3
Develop your Business Plan	7
Conduct Market Research	5
Get funding and loans	7
Apply for a business bank account	1
Register your company and trademarks	2
Create your brand identity	8
Build and manage your website	15
Set up phone, broadband and e-mail	7
Find premises	7
Get office supplies and IT equipment	6
Insure your business	4

Run a business	tools
Manage your finances	16
Acquire & manage customers	10
Get feedback from customers	7
Find suppliers	7
Hire and manage employees	14
Improve communication and collaboration	13
Meet Health and Safety Requirements	3
Expand Internationally	5
Ship goods	4
Make your office greener	7

Network

The Smarta network gives you real-time access to thousands of business owners from seasoned entrepreneurs to people starting their first business as well as those on the verge of taking the plunge. Join (it's free!) and start mixing with thousands of like-minded businesses. You can also consult the community when you need advice from someone who's been there.

Expert Q&A

We understand that there is no one right answer when it comes to business advice. That's why we have a panel of experts on hand to help with the really tricky questions. Our panel are all experienced professionals including lawyers and accountants. If you can't find the answer you need in our advice section or you want to dig a bit deeper just log on to the network and ask a Smarta Expert.

Accounting & tax

Intuit UK is a leading provider of business and financial management solutions for small organisations and their advisors including accountants and bookkeepers. Intuit's solutions are based on the simple principle of ease-of-use, backed by the highest levels of service and support.

Our experts   —

Diana Flier

Diana is a payroll and compliance expert with over 20 years' experience in payroll systems and processes. In...

Legal

Mishcon de Reya

Mishcon de Reya is a law firm offering a wide range of legal services to companies and individuals. The team aims to cut through the complexity to provide simple, commercially focused legal advice on a full range of needs.

Our experts   —

Laura Ford

Laura is a solicitor in the Firm's Employment Department. She advises employers and employees on both...

Shika Thakrar

Shika is experienced in advising businesses on company matters, corporate finance, mergers and acquisitions...

Smarta Sponsors

A t Smarta we're very big on collaboration. That's why we're proud to say we work with market leaders in this sector. Smarta partners are among the biggest and best service providers for entrepreneurs and small businesses:

NatWest

NatWest is part of one of the world's largest financial services groups. They are a leading provider of business banking and offer two year's free banking as well as a host of start-up tools and support including free courses and business planning software. Find out more at www.natwest.com/business.

> "At NatWest, we understand how difficult it is to start up and run your own business. We're partnering with Smarta to help make practical tools and support available to everyone. We'd like to wish you the best of luck with your new business venture and hope this book helps to make your dreams a reality."
>
> *Peter Ibbetson Chairman,*
> *Small Business Banking, NatWest*

Intuit **INTUIT**

Founded in 1983, today Intuit is one of the leading suppliers of small business software and has more than four million customers worldwide. They are committed to developing the simplest, most effective business software available. For more information go to www.intuit.co.uk.

> "At Intuit, we know what it's like to run a small business. Our philosophy is simple: easy is better. That's why we've developed our easy-to-use Quickbooks software to help you take care of the basics. Whether you need to track invoices or manage your entire business, our software helps remove the everyday stresses and strains of running your business. We are pleased to be working with Smarta to provide the most effective advice and tools you need to make your business thrive".
>
> *Pernille Bruun-Jensen, MD, Intuit UK*

Mishcon de Reya   Mishcon de Reya

Mishcon de Reya is a London law firm with an entrepreneurial spirit offering a wide range of legal services to companies and individuals including dispute resolution, real estate, corporate, employment and private client. They are committed to achieving their clients' objectives in a practical and cost-effective way that provides a clear return on investment. For further information visit www.mishcon.com.

"At Mishcon de Reya, we provide first-class legal advice to our clients, and we believe that Smarta provides first-class support to entrepreneurs and small businesses. We understand the challenges involved in starting and growing a business and our partnership with Smarta is part of our ongoing commitment to entrepreneurs. Small businesses are the future of our economy and we wish you all the best in your new venture."

Kevin Gold, Managing Partner, Mishcon de Reya

Viking Direct

Viking Direct is part of Office Depot, one of the largest suppliers of office stationery in the world and employs over 1,300 people in the UK. No one in the UK sells more office products to more customers than Viking Direct and their customer service is regarded the best in the industry. To find out more go to www.viking-direct.co.uk.

"The team at Viking Direct are committed to supporting all small businesses and start-ups throughout the UK. That is why we are partnering with Smarta. We believe that this book provides the essential advice and insight that small businesses need. We would like to take this opportunity to congratulate you on taking the first step to starting and running a truly successful business."

John Moore, VP UK & Ireland

Acknowledgements

This book simply wouldn't exist without all the entrepreneurs and business owners who have contributed their time, efforts and, crucially, their experiences and business insights, all free of charge. We and everyone who benefits from this book owe you a massive debt of gratitude.

We'd also like to thank all of our seriously smart partners: RBS, NatWest, Intuit, Mishcon de Reya and Viking Direct. Without your support, Smarta wouldn't exist. We're privileged to work with partners with the vision, dynamism and genuine understanding of what small businesses need to help us deliver solutions that really make a difference.

Likewise, how could we not thank the amazing Smarta board? Starting with chairman Sir Richard Needham through to our champions Theo Paphitis and Deborah Meaden and those that prefer to stay out of the limelight but nonetheless play a vital role.

The assembling of the Smarta book has been a real team effort, and special thanks must go to Hayley Conick, Sophie Hobson and Emma Haslett for their sterling editorial contributions, Rebecca Burn-Callander who was the queen of last minute proofing, as well as Ian Cooper who helped in the early stages.

Thanks also to Meriem Aissaoui, Kevin Burke, Lisa Goodchild and Daniel Meade for their contributions and Jo Pinkney for sourcing all the excellent exclusive offers. It would be remiss of us to forget to thank Mo for keeping Smarta online while we focused on the offline for a change, Ben for making our awesome videos and, of course, the lovely Debs for keeping everything else ticking over smoothly.

Smarta's circle of friends stretches far and wide and we'd like to take this opportunity to try and say thank-you to you all. We sincerely hope you know who you are.

Finally, Matt would like to thank Alex for keeping him sane during all the late-night writing missions and weekends indoors, and Shaa dedicates this book to her beautiful son Jett who, at five, is the youngest and probably smartest member of our team, and The Tosh, who has been our greatest ally.

The Smarta Entrepreneurs

Matt Kingdon	*?WhatIf!*
Brad Burton	*4Networking*
Glenn Watson	*5M Coffee Company*
Rebecca McKinlay	*Ambition Communications*
Will de Lucy	*Amplify Trading*
John Mortimer	*Angela Mortimer*
Ian Walker	*Antares Supplies*
Gavin Wheeldon	*Applied Language Solutions*
Steve France and Will Wynne	*ArenaFlowers.com*
Julie Meyer	*Ariadne Capital*
Lynne Franks	*B. Hive*
Sarah Watson	*Balineum*
Trevor Baylis	*Baylis Brands*
John Paleomylites	*BeatThatQuote.com*
Michael Birch	*Bebo*
Salma Shah	*Beyond*
Darryn Lyons	*Big Pictures*
Alexia Leachman	*Blossoming Brands*
Eileen Gittens	*Blurb*
Glenn Shoosmith and Gregory Bockenstette	*Booking Bug*
Tim Campbell	*Bright Ideas Trust*
Seán Brickell	*Broad Grin*
Sara Murray	*Buddi*
Simon Duffy and Rhodri Ferrier	*Bulldog Natural Grooming*
Caprice	*By Caprice*
Mark Soanes	*Call of the Wild*
Ryan Carson	*Carsonified*
Nick Wheeler	*Charles Tyrwhitt*
Claire Novis	*Claire Dances*
Sahar Hashemi	*Coffee Republic*
Kemi Laniyan	*Corporate Homes*
Richard Grigsby	*Cyclescheme*
Lindsay Drabwell	*DaisychainBaby*
Deborah Meaden	*Dragons' Den*
Duncan Bannatyne	*Dragons' Den and Bannatyne Group*
Theo Paphitis	*Dragons' Den and Ryman*
Mike Clare	*Dreams*
Lisa Langmead	*Dust and Vac*
Richard Needham	*Dyson*
Ashley Friedlein	*Econsultancy*
Antony Chesworth	*ekmPowershop.com*
Dave Wallwork	*Feel Good Drinks*
Alexandra Finlay	*Fin's*
Chey Garland	*Garland Call Centres*
Simon Swan	*Gatszu.com*
Jamie Murray Wells	*Glasses Direct*
Tristram Mayhew	*Go Ape*
Patrick Caiger-Smith	*Green Energy Options*
Naomi Andersson	*Green Hands*
Heather Jenkinson	*Heather Jenkinson Design*
Tremayne Carew Pole	*Hg2*
Alistair Mitchell and Andy McLoughlin	*Huddle*
Mark Turrell	*Imaginatik*
Imran Hakim	*iTeddy*
Laura Tenison	*JoJo Maman Bébé*
Will King	*King of Shaves*
Gordon Mac	*Kiss FM*
Martha Lane Fox	*Lastminute.com*
Christian Arno	*Lingo24*
Sam Conniff	*Livity*
Neil and Laura Westwood	*Magic Whiteboard*
Barry Hearn	*Matchroom Sport*
Divinia Knowles and Michael Smith	*Mind Candy*
Nikhil Shah, Nico Perez and Mat Clayton	*Mixcloud*
Kanya King	*MOBO Organisation*
Simon Nixon	*MoneySupermarket*
Alastair Lukies	*Monitise*
Richard Moross	*Moo*
James Lohan	*Mr & Mrs Smith*
Sean McPheat	*MTD Sales Training*
Sarah Beeny	*MySingleFriend.com*
Sophie Cornish	*Not On The High Street*
Giorgio Burlini	*Oxford Learning Lab*
Alan Gleeson	*Palo Alto*
Charlie Mullins	*Pimlico Plumbers*
Daniel Sheridan	*PlayMade Engergy*
Jonathan Simmons	*Public Zone*
Peter Ibbetson	*RBS and NatWest*
Rachel Elnaugh	*Dragons' Den*
Gavin Dein	*Reward*
Millie Kendall	*Ruby & Millie*
Doug Richard	*School for Startups*
Matt McNeill	*Sign-up.to and eTickets.to*
Scott Robert-Shaw	*Skip-Hop*
Cara Sayer	*SnoozeShade*
Graham Lucas	*Spectrum Office Solutions*
Emma-Jayne Parkes and Vivianne Jaeger	*SquidLondon*
Fraser Doherty	*SuperJam*
Rosie Wolfenden and Harriet Vine	*Tatty Devine*
Kerry Swinton	*Teeny Beanies*
Alex Cheatle	*Ten UK*
Tim Ferriss	*The 4-Hour Workweek*
Al Gosling	*The Extreme Sports Company*
Jack Lenox	*The Founder*
Peter Jones	*The National Enterprise Academy and Dargons' Den*
Jennifer Irvine	*The Pure Package*
Karen Hanton	*TopTable*
Bradley McLoughlin	*Trading4U*
Ben Keene	*TribeWanted*
Sokratis Papafloratos and Walid Al Saqqaf	*TrustedPlaces*
Jim and Geoff Riley	*Tutor2U.net*
Errol Damelin	*Wonga*
Ed Baker	*Wordia*
Simon Woodroffe	*YO! Sushi*

Index

Smarta Business Builder

I n Spring 2011[1], Smarta is launching the ultimate software solution for small businesses. The Smarta Business Builder combines the best of business technologies to give you easy access to all the tools you need to start and run your business.

You'll be able to build a website, create a business plan, set up email, manage your finances and draft hundreds of legal documents – all from as little as £20 a month.

The Smarta Business Builder requires no specialist technical, accounting or legal skills or knowledge. You'll be able to access it anywhere, anytime, from any PC with an internet connection. Simply log in to view your personalised dashboard containing all your key business information.

A single monthly subscription (with no long term commitment) enables you to:

- Manage your accounts and keep track of your money with QuickBooks easy to use software
- Build your own website and set up your business email and hosting with absolutely no technical skills required
- Create an entire business plan from scratch with Business Plan Pro simple business planning software

[1]At the time of going to print the Smarta Business Builder was scheduled to be released in April 2011. For the latest information please visit www.smarta.com/businessbuilder.

- Access hundreds of legal documents and templates — all of which are easily customisable using our document creation wizard
- View all your critical business information in your personalised Smarta Business Builder dashboard

Why your business needs the Smarta Business Builder

Save money

Smarta Business Builder subscriptions start from just £20 per month (compared with a combined cost of over £800 to purchase the tools individually) so you avoid heavy upfront investment. In addition, the Business Builder will help you make significant savings on accountants, web designers and legal fees by giving you the tools you need to do all the basics for yourself.

Save time

We know that when you're starting a business, time is your most precious resource. That's why we've spent months researching and finding the best tools for small businesses so you don't have to. Because the Smarta Business Builder is designed for everyone to be able to use, you don't need to read up on HTML or book-keeping in order to get going. And because your personalised dashboard will give you an instant snapshot of how you're doing you don't need to spend time running and reading reports.

Be flexible

The Smarta Business Builder is designed to be scalable. As you build your business you can add additional tools such as e-commerce, email marketing, CRM and HR management. You can also easily add new users and more advanced functionality. In other words, you can 'Pay As You Grow'.

Take your business anywhere

Running a business is a round the clock activity — you need to be in control wherever you are. With Smarta Business Builder you can access your information from any location with an internet connection — and everything is automatically backed up which gives you one less thing to worry about.

For more information go to www.smarta.com/businessbuilder.